Antonia D. Stephens

D0886451

The Diaries of
EDMUND MONTAGUE MORRIS
Western Journeys 1907–1910

Edmund Montague Morris (1871–1913).

The Diaries of
EDMUND MONTAGUE MORRIS
Western Journeys 1907–1910

Transcribed by Mary Fitz-Gibbon

♛
ROM
Royal Ontario Museum

This book has been published with the help of a grant from the Social Science Federation of Canada, using funds provided by the Social Sciences and Humanities Research Council of Canada.

Mary Fitz-Gibbon joined the Royal Ontario Museum staff in 1950 after taking a B.A. degree in art and archaeology at the University of Toronto. She worked as a teacher in the Education Department, and was responsible for preparing numerous travelling exhibits. In 1973 she entered the Department of Ethnology as research assistant. As well as participating in the development of ethnology galleries, she spent five years working on the transcription of Edmund Morris's diary.

Canadian Cataloguing in Publication Data
Morris, Edmund, 1871–1913.
  The diaries of Edmund Montague Morris:
  Western journeys 1907–1910
Bibliography: p.
Includes index.
ISBN 0-88854-259-3
1. Morris, Edmund, 1871–1913. 2. Painters - Canada - Biography. 3. Indians of North America - Prairie Provinces. 4. Prairie Provinces - Description and travel - 1906–1950.* I. Fitz-Gibbon, Mary, 1915– II. Royal Ontario Museum. III. Title.
ND249.M67A2 1985   759.11   C85-098526-9

Route maps drawn by James B. Loates.
Book design by Virginia Morin.

ISBN 0-88854-259-3
© The Royal Ontario Museum 1985
100 Queen's Park, Toronto, Canada M5S 2C6
Printed and bound in Canada at GENERAL PRINTERS

Contents

Illustrations

Plates

Maps

Colour Plates

Foreword

During Edmund Morris's four trips to the West, in the summers of 1907 to 1910, he kept a diary. At the same time, he recorded in colour the faces of many Plains Indians. The diary, a document rich in ethnographic information, has been in the possession of the Department of Ethnology, Royal Ontario Museum, for more than sixty-five years.

Until now, however, the observations Morris recorded have remained hidden from all but a few dedicated researchers, not because the manuscript was kept locked up but because it was virtually impossible to read. Morris wrote in an outlandish fashion, little more than chicken scratches. In the past, attempts have been made to understand what Morris had written, but never was the diary transcribed in full. Now at long last the task of transcription has been accomplished. Through diligent endeavours over eight years, Miss Mary Fitz-Gibbon has almost single-handedly deciphered the content of Morris's journal. We are indeed fortunate that, year after year, Miss Fitz-Gibbon had the determination and zeal to painstakingly work through the manuscript, time and time again, each time gaining new insights into the meaning of Morris's "hieroglyphics". When she succeeded in decoding most of his entries, it was thought appropriate that the journal be published to release the historical information it contains. This task was undertaken by staff of Publication Services at the ROM, who have laboured to make this a fine publication. The transcript does not alter Morris's wording—spelling errors, except those in proper names, have been corrected and punctuation inserted where necessary for comprehension—and can, therefore, be relied upon as an authentic rendition of Morris's work.

The journal kept by Morris during the four summers that he spent listening to Indians of the Plains and catching in colour their likenesses—among the Blackfoot Confederacy, including the Sarcee, and then among the Cree, Saulteaux, Assiniboine, and Stoney—is a rich source of information about these peoples at the beginning of the 20th century. The Royal Ontario Museum is most fortunate to have many of the pastels that Morris executed and some of the artifacts he acquired during his western journeys. The governments of Ontario, Saskatchewan, and Alberta showed foresight in giving Morris commissions that assisted him on these journeys.

Information in the diary greatly enhances the scientific value of the objects Morris collected, since he often states from whom and when he acquired the artifact, giving additional background details. Such material is so often not available for ethnology collections.

For all those who are interested in the history of the Canadian West, especially in the lives of Plains Indians, we owe a deep debt of gratitude to Miss Mary Fitz-Gibbon for making this diary by Morris available in published form.

E. S. Rogers, Department of Ethnology
Royal Ontario Museum

Acknowledgements

I should like to take this opportunity to express my gratitude to the many people who gave their time and expertise in helping me to produce this publication.

I am indebted to the staff of the Glenbow Museum, Calgary, for their cooperation, especially to Dr Hugh Dempsey, who not only read the transcript of the diary, giving me advice and encouragement, but also checked many details in the diary. Mrs Jean Goldie of the Saskatchewan Archives Board located historical maps and supplied valuable information; Ms Elizabeth Blight and other staff of the Provincial Archives of Manitoba provided information and prints of photographs in their collection; the staff of Queen's University Archives gave me access to correspondence of the Morris family.

Miss Fern Bayer of the Government of Ontario Art Collection and Miss Kathleen Wladyka and Miss Margaret Machell (former archivist) of the Art Gallery of Ontario provided information about Edmund Morris and prints of photographs and paintings by him. Mr Kenneth McCarthy of the Provincial Museum of Alberta, Mr Michael Parke-Taylor of the Norman Mackenzie Gallery, Regina, and Mr Ray Christensen of the Saskatchewan Legislative Art Collection sent information on portraits from their collections and gave permission to reproduce those portraits. The staff of many other art galleries and museums, the administration of Morris, Manitoba, the staff of the Manitoba Club, and Mr C. R. Osler sent prints of paintings in their collections.

I appreciate the help of the many persons who gave me archival information for the notes, including the staff archivists of the Hudson's Bay Company Archives, the Public Archives of Canada, the Royal Canadian Mounted Police, and the Alberta Provincial Archives; Sister Josephine Ouellet of the Roman Catholic Diocese of Prince Albert, Alberta; and Father René Peeters of the Roman Catholic Diocese of Saint-Boniface, Manitoba. Mr J. D. M. Morris prepared the genealogy of the Morris family. I appreciate the cooperation of Miss Jean McGill, who was also doing research on Edmund Morris at the time.

I am grateful to all the staff of the Department of Ethnology at the Royal Ontario Museum: Dr E. S. Rogers gave me permission to undertake this study and assisted with the introduction; Prof. Kenneth E. Kidd (former curator) shared his knowledge of the diaries; Mr Kenneth Lister and Mrs Valerie Grant helped in researching notes; Mr Aaron Brownstone provided details for the illustrations; Mrs Pat Urquhart (former assistant) and Mrs Helen Kilgour assisted in preparing the manuscript and gathering illustrations. Mrs Christine Lockett (former editor) and Mrs Jill Hawken of Publication Services prepared the manuscript for publication.

Notes and Conventions

Edmund Morris recorded in a notebook his four western journeys of the summers of 1907 through 1910. This transcript is divided into four sections, representing the four journeys.

The content of the diary has been transcribed word for word, even many crossed-out passages, which appear within square brackets in the transcript; where a word could not be deciphered, a rule appears in the transcript. Capitals lacking at the beginnings of sentences and punctuation necessary for comprehension have been added. Morris was not consistent in recording the date for a diary entry; all recorded dates have been transcribed and appear here. The page numbers stamped on the original notebook appear in the margins of the transcript, enclosed in parentheses.

Where Morris ran out of space on a page he often wrote around the margins before continuing to the following one; he also added afterthoughts and extra notes in the margins, sometimes marking them with an asterisk and sometimes not. Such notes appear in the outside margins of the transcript, placed as close as possible to the relevant text.

Spelling errors in the diary are corrected in the transcript, except those that occur in the proper names of people or places; the first occurrences of these names are annotated whenever the correct spellings are known. There are often alternative spellings for the Indian names, and Morris was inconsistent in his usage.

The diary transcript is annotated; the notes for each journey are placed at the end of that journey. On the second, third, and fourth journeys Morris revisited many of the same reserves and the same people; usually only the first mention of a person or other detail is annotated. The brief index written by Edmund Morris at the end of the original diary has been expanded and provides references to other mentions of people and topics.

Introduction

The purpose of this publication is to make the transcript of Edmund Montague Morris's western diary and reproductions of some of his portraits readily available not only to scholars but also to general readers. During the summers of 1907 through 1910, artist Edmund Morris visited reserves, drawing faces of the Indian peoples of Canada's Plains in superb pastel portraits and recording facts concerning their lives in a diary.

Edmund Morris, the youngest son of the Honourable Alexander Morris, was born in 1871 at Perth, Ontario, where his father had a law practice. Edmund drowned in the St Lawrence River near Portneuf, Quebec, in 1913, at forty-two years of age and was buried in the family plot in Mount Pleasant Cemetery in Toronto.

Edmund's father was appointed chief justice of Manitoba in July 1872 and immediately moved his family west to live in Winnipeg, then Upper Fort Garry. Later that year he resigned from his post on being made lieutenant governor of Manitoba and the North West Territories. During his tenure of office, he served as the Queen's representative in treaty negotiations with the Plains Indians, and showed a great understanding and sympathy for the plight of the Indians. For this he gained the respect of all who had contact with him. It was partly through the vision of Alexander Morris that the government of Sir John A. Macdonald was persuaded to establish the North West Mounted Police force in 1873 to bring law and order to the West and to end tribal warfare—thereby preventing the wholesale slaughter that occurred in the United States.

Certainly Alexander Morris's interest in Indians must have influenced his children and perhaps inspired his son Edmund to record the faces of the last generation of Plains Indian leaders to participate in the life of bison hunting. Soon it would have been too late.

As it was, by the time Morris began to record with pastel and pen, many changes had taken place in the way of life of the Indians of the Plains. The bison on which they had depended for centuries had all but disappeared. Now the mighty hunters of the Plains had been reduced to subsisting on the rations of beef that were provided on occasion by the federal government. No longer were they free to roam the Plains; they had ceded their lands to the federal government through a series of five treaties (the so-called numbered treaties), signed between 1871 and 1877. By the terms of the treaties, the Plains Indians were to be confined to small parcels of land, or reserves, where it was hoped that they would be transformed into farmers and ranchers—a hope that was doomed to failure.

In 1876, an Indian Act was compiled from various pieces of existing legislation affecting Indians. Among the subsequent additions to the Act was one that struck at the heart of the Plains Indians' religion: an enactment that banned self-torture, an essential part of the Sun Dance (more correctly known as the Medicine Dance, since this religious performance had nothing to do with any worship of the sun). Yet in spite of the drastic changes resulting from the intrusion of the European onto the Plains, the Indians visited by Edmund Morris could still recall with clarity the days when they were rulers of their domain. That was a time when each spring the scattered bands of a tribe reassembled to engage in the communal bison hunt. Camps were set up consisting of large circles of bison-hide-covered tipis and containing hundreds of individuals. These encampments were governed by a number of chiefs and leading men and were policed by the Dog Society. The latter was responsible for seeing that no hunter went after the bison alone and that the hunt was a joint endeavour. If it were not, the bison would probably scatter before many of them could be killed. Sometimes the bison were driven over a cliff or into a large enclosure where they could easily be killed. Generally, however, they were hunted on horseback. Horses had been introduced onto the Plains by other Indians to the south, who had in turn secured them from the Spaniards of the southwestern United States.

Summer was also the time to hold the Sun Dance, to raid one's neighbours in search of horses, and to gain war honours through acts of outstanding bravery. With the approach of fall, the large summer gathering broke up into small groups or bands, each under the guidance of a chief or headman. Slowly the groups made their way into river bottoms or foothill valleys where they could find protection from the fierce winter storms. The fall and winter encampments were selected not only for protection from the elements but also as places where wood and water were easily available, where grass for the horses was in good supply, and where game animals, if not abundant, might at least be found in sufficient numbers to feed the people throughout the winter. With the approach of spring, the dispersed bands began to move out of their secluded winter quarters and travel towards the gathering place agreed upon the previous fall, where another yearly cycle of activities would commence.

These were the colourful days of which Edmund Morris's diaries contain a first-hand record gathered from the elders whose portraits he has left us. And it has been these Plains Indians, the mounted warriors in feather headdresses and elaborately beaded shirts and leggings, with similarly decorated trappings for their horses, who have typified the North American Indian.

❧❀❧

Edmund Morris was well equipped to launch himself as an artist not only by his family connections in government circles, but also by training. At the age of eighteen, on the advice of his father, who was a member of the Ontario provincial legislature at the time, he worked in the architectural offices of Darling and Curry in Toronto with the intention of attending Cornell University or the Boston School of Technology to become an architect. After six months, he found his dislike for mathematics so great that he decided to study art instead. His talent for sketching, which he had developed as a hobby, brought him immediate acceptance into a course in the studio of William Cruikshank of Toronto. He continued with the course until February

1891; he also sketched in the evenings at the Art Students' League. In the fall of 1892, he moved to New York, where he spent a year at the Art Students' League and at the Lisgar School of Art, studying with Kenyon Cox and other artists. He spent the summer of 1893 sketching around Toronto—at Weston, the Humber River, the Toronto Islands, and Old Fort York.

In October of 1893 Morris sailed for France to attend the Julien Academy and the École des Beaux Arts in Paris; he remained there for three years and met many other young artists, including some he had known in New York. While abroad he was able to view galleries and works of art, not only in France but also in Belgium, Holland, England, and Scotland. From the particular artists and works he mentions in his memoranda, which are stored at the Queen's University Archives, one notices a growing interest in portraiture, no doubt originally whetted by his old teacher William Cruikshank. After returning to Canada, he established himself in Toronto; he also joined the artists' colony in a small village on the St Lawrence River, five kilometres above Ste-Anne-de-Beaupré, in Montmorency, Quebec, where he painted landscapes and portraits. His ability in landscape painting was soon recognized by several awards at various exhibitions and by his appointment to the Royal Academy of Artists in 1897. His success in portraiture was to follow.

Morris's first record of the sale of an Indian portrait is dated 1896. He recorded further sales during the following years in his carefully itemized notebook, which is housed in the Department of Ethnology of the Royal Ontario Museum along with other items of his bequest to the museum. In 1906, he was fortunate enough to gain a commission from the Ontario government to accompany the second summer expedition of federal and provincial commissioners who were arranging Treaty Nine among the Indians of the southwestern James Bay area, and to portray the Indian leaders involved in the transactions. His success in this assignment gained him another commission from the Ontario government in the following year to portray major figures in the tribes living farther west.

Morris spent two summers completing these portraits and the results of these western journeys are outlined in the diaries transcribed here. The portraits he produced became a part of the Government of Ontario Art Collection and were later turned over to the Royal Ontario Museum, where they still remain. By showing some of these works to representatives of the then newly formed provinces of Alberta and Saskatchewan, Morris received from those governments further commissions, which occupied him during the summers of 1909 and 1910 and the results of which are also described in the diaries. Five of the portraits made during these two summers hang in the Provincial Museum of Alberta in Edmonton and fifteen in the Saskatchewan Legislature in Regina.

All except two of Morris's Indian portraits are busts; the faces are sensitively portrayed and, along with those parts of costume that show, are accurately depicted. We know the costumes to be accurate because the Royal Ontario Museum was the beneficiary of Morris's fine collection of Indian artifacts, and it is sometimes possible to compare the items of dress that Morris has recorded as acquired from his portrait subjects with those depicted in their portraits. The accuracy of the faces is evident when the portraits are compared with contemporary photographs, many of which were taken by Morris. Morris's sensitivity to the human qualities behind each face is not only observable from the portraits themselves, but is confirmed by his diary descriptions. To what extent Morris changed, touched up, or redrafted his portraits after he returned home we do not know. No quick sketches of his Indian subjects have come to light, and there is only one mention of portrait sketches in his diary, with no reference as to how complete they were. On some occasions, Morris describes the long hours he worked while his subjects posed, and at least one of his photographs shows a completed portrait still on the easel with the subject standing in front of it, a circumstance that suggests that most of the work was completed or almost completed in the field.

Although Morris sold and exhibited portraits such as those of Crowfoot, Big Bear, and Blackfoot Brave, at least two of these subjects as well as two others, Poundmaker and Old Sun, were dead by 1890, and therefore their portraits must have been produced from photographs. These photographs would not have been Morris's own, although the artist did take more than seven hundred photographs, which are now in the Provincial Archives of Manitoba in Winnipeg. It is not within the scope of this volume to describe these photographs in detail—a large number are of scenery and bear little or no relation to his portraits, while the photographs of individuals who were his subjects seldom show the head in the same position as in their portraits, and so would appear to have been of little use in the production of the pastels.

When Morris made a copy of a portrait, as he did on occasion, he was careful to record it as a replica in his notebook of exhibitions and sales, now stored in the Department of Ethnology at the Royal Ontario Museum. We do know that he sometimes made two portraits of an individual while in the field. On one occasion when he was unable to refuse the sale of a portrait to a police officer, he states that he retraced his steps many miles to find his subject for a second sitting. The Royal Ontario Museum's portrait of Carry the Kettle, for example, was made in 1908 and the Saskatchewan Government's portrait of the same man in 1910; even quick observation shows the aging of the two years. Sometimes an individual was portrayed a second time in totally different attire or in a different position from the first. The approach is therefore always fresh.

There is always a question as to the extent to which an artist is influenced by other artists. While Morris doubtless learned much from portrait artists whose works he saw in Europe and elsewhere, there is a uniqueness to his Indian portraits. Among his contemporaries in Canada, George Théodore Berthon (1806–92), William Brymner (1855–1925), his old teacher William Cruikshank (1849–1922), John Colin Forbes (1846–1925), and J. Henry Sandham (1841–1910) were portraitists, but they were involved in recording the non-Indian figures of the day. In North America and in Europe there were artists painting scenes of Indian life, but the scenes were often contrived, imagined, romanticized, or highly dramatized, and the faces were too small for their characteristics to be distinguished. Among Indian portraitists, George Catlin (1796–1872) painted faces on a larger scale, but they resembled faces of Europeans rather than of Indians; De Cort Smith (?–1890) painted heads so small they cannot compare with Morris's portraits; only Frank Humphries (1822–1909), Charles Bird King (1785–1862), George Cooke (1793–1849), and Paul Kane (1810–1871) painted Indian heads that seem to be good likenesses of the subjects. Of these, only Kane, who died the year Morris was born, made sketches of North American Indians in the field, and Morris, by his own admission, did not hold Kane's work in high esteem. Other artists posed their subjects in unnatural settings, such as their Washington studios. Morris seems to stand alone in his generation in portraying North American Indian subjects in their own environment and in whatever clothes they were wearing when they came to him.

Contemporary attitudes towards Indians, whether as "noble savages" or as devils to be annihilated, seem to have crept into most other artists' portrayals of Indians. The natural stoicism of the Indian, without which he could scarcely have survived, was repeatedly stressed to such a degree, by artists steeped in admiration for the British "stiff upper lip" or the American love of Greek Stoics, that the faces became cold and austere and showed little humanity and warmth. Because of the respect that the Indians and Morris held for each other, as witnessed repeatedly in Morris's diary writings, and because of the natural environment that he chose to depict, Morris seems to have been able to retain the stoicism but also to reflect in each face the life and personality of the sitter caught in a moment of reality. While many artists found the natives averse to being portrayed, because of a superstitious fear of having their likeness reproduced and taken away, Morris mentions only occasionally hesitation on the part of an Indian he wished to record, and this he soon overcame, either by quiet conversation with the Indian or with help from one of the local priests. On occasion he mentions paying the sitter, and frequently he exchanged gifts when the portrait was finished.

While as a respected friend Morris had no difficulty persuading an Indian to sit for a portrait, his fine portraits of Indian faces required more than the cooperation of the sitter. Morris was a talented artist and obviously had intense feeling and an excellent sense of balance, colour, and texture, all of which he was able to express beautifully with the pastels he used for his portraits. While some of his oils—such as *Indian Encampment on the Prairie,* now in the Art Gallery of Ontario collection—appear unfinished and blurred and lack lustre, his pastels show none of these deficiencies. Steady improvement is evident in his work. Around the turn of the century it was common to use pencil-like spools of tightly wound paper to rub a surface after applying pastels, and early works, such as the portrait of Crowfoot bearing his monogram 𐤥 , appear to have been finished in this way, with consequent loss of liveliness. In later portraits, such as the Royal Ontario Museum picture of Crow Shoe, produced in 1907, the artist abandoned this technique; in its place he has used techniques common in oil-painting but quite extraordinary in pastels, layering one colour upon another smoothly and clearly, without loss of brilliance or line. While buttons, jewellery, medals, and clothing are rendered in an impressionistic style, the detail in the face has produced a meticulous likeness. The contrast of the realism with the impressionism focuses the attention of the observer on the face, which is dramatically rendered by the sparing use of highlights and broken lines, in such a way as to produce an effect of constant movement and bring a glow of life to the whole face. The expression in the eyes is proud, brooding, and sure; and a hint of a smile marks the lines of the mouth. In contrast, the earlier Crowfoot portrait lacks this glow of life and appears smooth, stolid, and academic.

Morris's wide range of fine colours suggests that his work was simplified by the use of some of the best pastels of his day, possibly purchased in Paris (for Morris was not an impoverished student); however, his paper, comparatively smooth despite its hairy surface, would have been more difficult to use with pastels than the modern rougher varieties, especially with Morris's technique. The very heaviness of the paper must have made the portraits easier to transport. Morris appears to have used no fixative; the portraits would have been kept apart with high stick pins at the edges, in the custom of the day, only the strength of the paper preventing the layers from touching. It is small wonder that Morris mentions leaving them with friends when the opportunity arose.

Morris's portraits of Indian faces of the first decade of the 20th century in western Canada form an historic record, perhaps comparable in their way to that made by C. W. Jefferys (1869–1951). However, Morris does not show the Indian in relation to Europeans; rather, he depicts the strong faces behind which were the strong minds that guided the Indian peoples through the difficult early years of European contact. Certainly they should be to all Canadians, as they were to Morris, as important as the portraits of prime ministers, lieutenant governors, and generals among early French and English Canadians.

It is in his diaries that Morris records the way of life and the history of his subjects and their peoples. He does this through careful, first-hand recording of oral accounts received from the Indians themselves, as well as from church representatives, police officers, government officials, and others. By recording in his diary the versions of incidents, legends, and beliefs told to him by Indians and Europeans he met and, where possible, by comparing these versions with information already published, Morris often tried to verify his findings. The scholarly side of Morris (who we know was an avid collector and reader) becomes apparent both in the content of letters housed in the Queen's University Archives and in his fine collection of books, which was inherited by the Royal Ontario Museum. It is unfortunate that his abominable handwriting, so often decried by his friends, has prevented the publishing of the wealth of historical and ethnological information contained in his diaries until this time. Suffice it to repeat the words of the poet Duncan Campbell Scott in a lengthy poem written at the time of the artist's premature death.

> I have your unanswered letter
> Here in my hand
> This—in your famous scribble,
> It was ever a cryptic fist,
> Cuneiform or Chaldaic,
> Meanings held in a mist.

The entire contents of Morris's western diary, even the marginal notes and many of the crossed-out passages, are transcribed here, so that the reader will lose nothing of the freshness of the account. Where words could not be identified, a rule represents the blank left. Doubtless there may be additional words discerned or changes made in the future, but the diaries are published here in the fullest form available at the present time, as further delay seems unreasonable. They are a truly fascinating and delightful account by a very interesting individual.

ↅ⦿

While the recording of Indian faces seems to have been one of the main drives of Morris's life, it was certainly matched by his general interest in Canadian art. Together with such artist friends as T. G. Greene, Sam Jones, John Cotton, P. Weir Crouch, and D. A. McKeller, he was a member of the Art League, and of the Ontario Society of Artists from 1905 to 1907. In 1907, determined to promote a typically Canadian art without the traditional European restrictions on subject and technique that characterized many exhibitions, Morris and other artists (such as Horatio Walker, Franklin Brownell, J. Archibald Browne, W. E. Atkinson, James Wilson Morrice, and William Brymner) formed the Canadian Art Club. Their aim was to hold annual exhibitions of Canadian painting and sculpture and to encourage other artists. Their success was possibly a stepping stone to the later success of the Group of Seven. In notebooks, which are now housed in the library of the Art Gallery of Ontario, Edmund Morris recorded the steps in the formation and the activities of the Canadian Art Club, as well as his interest in and promotion of the formation of an art museum in Ontario. When the Art Gallery of Toronto, later the Art Gallery of Ontario, came into being, Edmund Morris soon became a member of its board of directors. The Canadian Art Club arranged to hold its exhibitions there, but some members of the club disliked the growing jurisdiction of the gallery and after the death of Morris, who had been the main means of holding them together, the club collapsed.

Edmund Morris lived in a very exciting period of history for Canada, which possibly helped to inspire in him and in his contemporaries an interest in the history and the development of Canada, and a feeling of nationalism. At the time of his birth, the federal government was only four years old, and some of the present provinces did not yet exist. His father had helped to form many of the federal policies and had published *Treaties of Canada with the Indians of Canada and the North West Territories* by the time Edmund was nine. The driving of the last spike of the first trans-Canada railway and the North West Rebellion of the Indians and Métis both occurred in 1885, when he was fourteen. The greatest mass immigration to the west, brought about through an advertising scheme of the federal government under Sir Wilfrid Laurier, began in 1896, when Edmund was twenty-five. The immigrants arriving as a result of this campaign far outnumbered those brought by the first easy access of the railroad or by the gold fever, and much of the remaining prairie game disappeared. European diseases and starvation diminished the Indian population to such an extent that there was a general expectation that the remainder would soon be totally assimilated into the general population and cease to be a separate responsibility for the government. Certainly the Indians of Morris's childhood disappeared shortly thereafter.

While it is impossible to include in a book of this size all the artistic achievements or literary records of Edmund Morris, it is hoped that he will receive the recognition he so justly deserves as a portraitist and recorder of the lives of the Indians of Canada's Plains.

E. S. R.

Genealogy of Edmund Morris

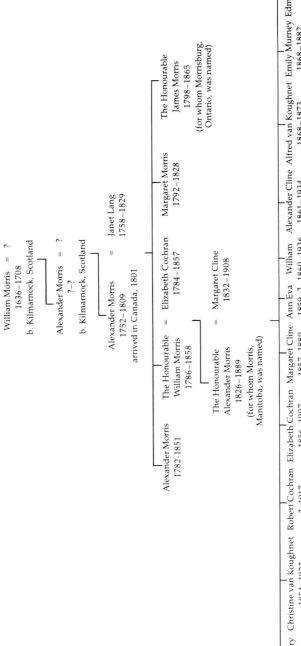

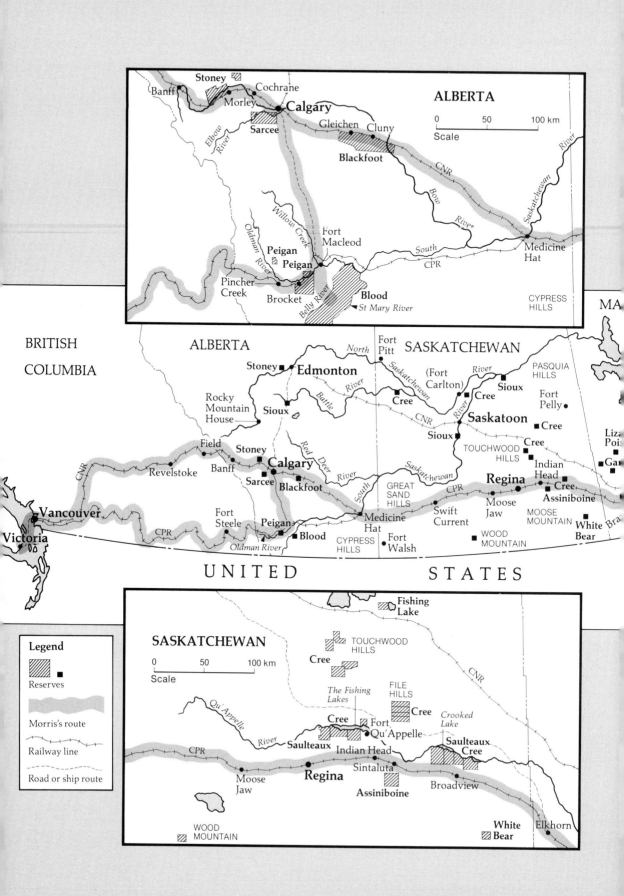

ALBERTA

Stoney
Banff
Cochrane
Morley
Calgary
Sarcee
Gleichen
Cluny
Blackfoot
Elbow River
Willow Creek
Oldman River
Fort Macleod
Peigan
Peigan
Pincher Creek
Brocket
Belly River
Blood
St Mary River
Bow River
South
CPR
CNR
Saskatchewan River
Medicine Hat
CYPRESS HILLS
MA

0   50   100 km
Scale

BRITISH COLUMBIA

ALBERTA

North
Saskatchewan
River
Fort Pitt
SASKATCHEWAN
(Fort Carlton)
River
Sioux
Cree
Fort Pelly
PASQUIA HILLS
Stoney
Edmonton
Battle
River
Cree
Rocky Mountain House
Sioux
Saskatoon
Cree
Liza Poi
Red Deer River
Saskatchewan
Sioux
TOUCHWOOD HILLS
Cree
Ga
Field
Stoney
Calgary
Indian Head
Banff
Sarcee
Blackfoot
Regina
Cree
Revelstoke
CNR
South
GREAT SAND HILLS
CPR
Assiniboine
Vancouver
Fort Steele
Peigan
Medicine Hat
Swift Current
Moose Jaw
MOOSE MOUNTAIN
Victoria
CPR
Oldman River
Blood
CYPRESS HILLS
Fort Walsh
WOOD MOUNTAIN
White Bear
Bra

UNITED   STATES

Fishing Lake
SASKATCHEWAN
0   50   100 km
Scale
TOUCHWOOD HILLS
Cree
Legend
Reserves
Morris's route
Railway line
Road or ship route
Cree
The Fishing Lakes
FILE HILLS
Cree
Crooked Lake
Qu'Appelle
River
Cree
Fort Qu'Appelle
Saulteaux
Cree
Saulteaux
Indian Head
CPR
Sintaluta
Assiniboine
Broadview
Moose Jaw
Regina
WOOD MOUNTAIN
White Bear
Elkhorn
CNR

Western Journey 1907

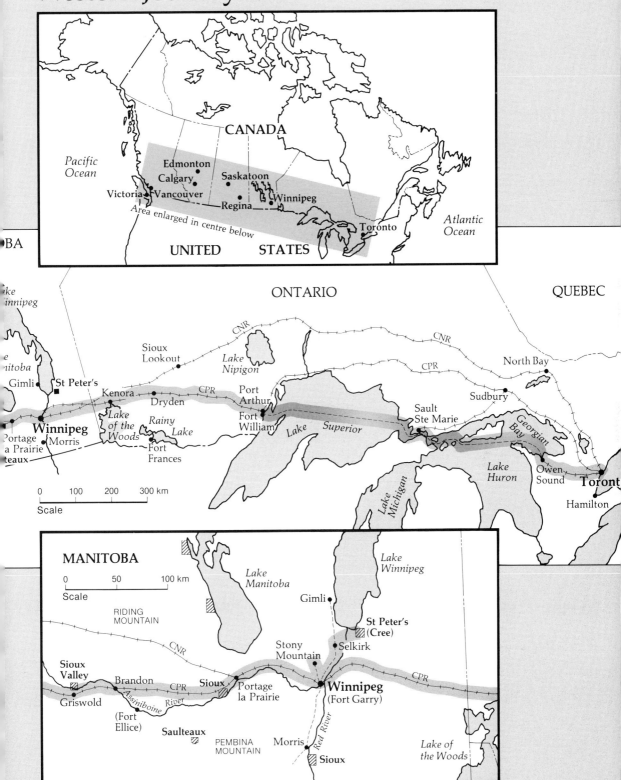

CANADA

Pacific
Ocean

Edmonton
Calgary
Victoria Vancouver
Regina
Saskatoon
Winnipeg

Area enlarged in centre below

Toronto

Atlantic
Ocean

UNITED   STATES

BA

ONTARIO

QUEBEC

ake
innipeg

e
nitoba
Gimli

St Peter's

Sioux
Lookout

Lake
Nipigon

CNR

CNR

CPR

North Bay

Kenora
Dryden

CPR

Port
Arthur
Fort
William

Sault
Ste Marie

Sudbury

Winnipeg
Portage
a Prairie
teaux

Morris

Lake
of the
Woods

Rainy
Lake

Fort
Frances

Lake   Superior

Georgian
Bay

Lake
Huron

Owen
Sound

Toront

Hamilton

0   100   200   300 km

Scale

Lake
Michigan

MANITOBA

0   50   100 km

Scale

RIDING
MOUNTAIN

Lake
Manitoba

Lake
Winnipeg

Gimli

St Peter's
(Cree)

CNR

Stony
Mountain

Selkirk

Sioux
Valley

Brandon

CPR

Sioux

Portage
la Prairie

Winnipeg
(Fort Garry)

CPR

Griswold

Assiniboine   River

(Fort
Ellice)

Saulteaux

PEMBINA
MOUNTAIN

Morris

Red River

Sioux

Lake of
the Woods

My people leave "Elderslie", Toronto,[1] for our island home in Lake Joseph, Muskoka, and I for the North West to make a series of portraits of the different Indian tribes in the North West—a continuation of those I made in the James Bay District when I accompanied Treaty Commission No. 9.[2] C.P.R. to Owen Sound then by steamer to Port Arthur. Capt. Worthington from Agra, India,[3] & young Miss _____ of Medicine Hat on board & they prove good companions.

JULY 1ST

Arrived at Winnipeg, 12 a.m., stop with my cousin Murney Morris & Mr. Darby Taylor who have bachelors' quarters.[4] The latter tells me he first came to the west on the same steamer which brought my mother and the family to Fort Garry to join my father there. One of the first things I did was to go to the old stone gateway back of the present Manitoba Club—all that is left of our old home, the Government House.[5] The high surrounding wall, the circular court, and back of our home, the HBC buildings all are gone. Too bad all had not been kept intact as an example of the early forts & used as a museum _____.

2ND
(Diary page 2)

To Stony Mountain to see Col. Acheson G. Irvine,[6] our old friend. He is now warden of the penitentiary. The old man is active and erect as ever, though he tells me when he used to visit Col. Diksen there he used to think it the most lonely spot in God's creation and now he finds himself ending his days there.[7] Mr. Campbell of Macleod afterwards told me, after the late Breed Rebellion, Irvine met Sir John MacDonald[8] and he asked him what position he wanted, that he could have anything. The Col. scratched his head and said, to guide the penitentiary!

We sat up till a late hour talking of the early days. One incident impressed me. Big Bear, the notorious Cree leader of the rebellion, found the surveyors at work, made them stop & word was sent to the police.[9] Col. Irvine at once set out on his tracks. En route he fell in with two young Bloods who invited him to their camp. Here he felt at home, as the Bloods had always been friendly with the police. They had a fire burning & presently all the braves came & seated themselves—then rising & throwing aside their blankets they stood stark naked in their war paint with Winchester rifles in their hands & gave the war dance, telling him they would follow him & kill Big Bear. But he did not want blood shed so told them he would go on alone taking Blackfoot Old Woman and another Blood buck with him[10] & would send word if he needed the others. He found Big Bear & told him he could never block the Govt. works. Irvine spoke a lot about Crowfoot, the late head chief of the Blackfoot Confederacy.[11] His son had got into trouble with a white man who chased him. The young buck turned and pointed a revolver at him & soon put him off, but the white man reported the case to the police. At the trial Crowfoot was present. He was like a king in his own country—the Blackfoot one of the most savage tribes. The mounted police had just come into the country & Col. Macleod & Col. Irvine felt the position to be an awkward one, but they passed a sentence of two months imprisonment.[12] The Chief listened to it all—then he asked if he might speak to his son. He walked up to him, then stepped back some paces & pointing his finger at him said, I

(Diary page 3)

Big Bear, Mistahah Musqua, Plains Cree chief. Pastel on paper, from a photograph. Dimensions 62.5 × 49 cm. Edmund Morris Collection. ROM HK 2448.

Photograph of the Reverend Harry William Gibbon Stocken, by George Glanville of Tunbridge Wells. Stocken was Anglican missionary for many years among the Blackfoot and among the Sarcee. Courtesy the Glenbow Museum, Calgary, Alberta, NA-1020-7.

warned you to go to three places only—the Barracks, the store and the HBC post—you went to saloons and other places where you met bad men—now go take your punishment.

At one time Irvine had many of the Dukhobors in the penitentiary.[13] They had been going about without any clothes, stark naked, looking for Christ, and would have been frozen—so the police ran them in. They would not work & refused to drink the water from the well at Stony Mountain.

The Col.'s old housekeeper, Mrs. Maclean—a breed woman—remembered my people & could not do enough for me.

3RD   Return to Winnipeg & Murney & I go to see the Lower Fort.[14] It is much as it
(Diary page 5)   used to be though the tops of the bastions have fallen in. It is no longer used as a Fort.

Met Hugh John Macdonald.[15] He is sober today. Call on the Mathesons.

3RD   Leave for Calgary. Murney comes with me. The cloud effects & the wonderful stretch of the prairies are so fine—as the clouds rise above the horizon line one feels the rotundity of the Earth. See antelope & coyotes.

4TH   Stop off at Medicine Hat, the valley is very paintable—sage green shrubs, the buffalo willow & light coloured earth. The Indian lodges,[16] some wandering Crees, grouped at the foot of the hill. I met Sir Daniel McMillan, the Governor of Manitoba, here.[17]

5TH   Arrive at Calgary. The plains nearby are covered with the Indian lodges who have come to see the fair & take part in the horse racing. I meet the Blackfoot chiefs & give them dinner.[18] Jefferys, the illustrator, Toronto, is at the same hotel.[19]

6TH   Afternoon tea at the Bishop's[20] & meet the widow of the late Col. Macleod & her daughters—they are beautiful girls.

Call on Col. Steel[21]—he tells me he was in my father's escort at the making of the treaties at Fort Carlton, Fort Pitt and Qu Appelle—he was also at the
(Diary page 6)   Blackfoot Treaty & the surrender of Sitting Bull, the Sioux leader.[22] The Col. owns farms in South Africa.

Every evening the Indians give a dance. There is a good deal of variety in it. At times they form in a circle, the men with tom tom, beating it in the centre of a group of men & women who move in a circle around the tom tom beaters chanting. At a certain point two Indians dressed alike, eagle feathers hanging down from _____ to feet & holding a wand topped with feathers, jump up & swing into the circle. There was a system both in repetition of dress & step which recalls a Japanese print I have seen.

I go to the Blackfoot Reserve. Look up Mister J. H. Gooderham, the agent,[23] who gave me the use of a room above the agency for studio. The first portrait I make is of old Sisoyake, the Cutter Woman—widow of Crowfoot, Sapo Maxika—late head chief of the Blackfoot Confederacy.[24] The Indians led me to her lodge & introduced me. Her daughter was living with her—a woman

The Cutter Woman, Sisoyake or Sisuiake, Blackfoot. Pastel on paper, 1907. Dimensions 62.5 × 51 cm. Edmund Morris Collection. ROM HK 2417.

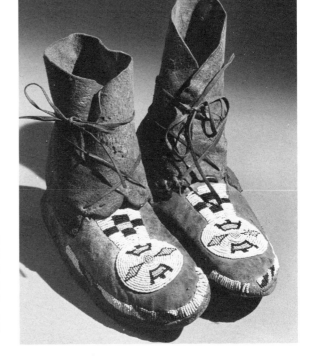

Photograph of a pair of skin moccasins belonging to the Cutter Woman. Beaded design in white and light and dark blue; red felt collar; high skin cuffs. The design on the toe matches that on the dress worn by the Cutter Woman in her portrait. Length, heel to toe, 24 cm. Bequest of Edmund Morris. ROM HK 582.

of about 40. She closely resembles her father. Crowfoot's only living son is totally blind (called Bear's Ghost)—his wife has a fine handsome young son & though both often quarrel with the old woman they are devoted to her.

(Diary page 7) Levern, a priest in charge of the S. camp Roman mission,[25] went again with me to Sisuiake's lodge to interpret for me. We found the old lady seated under a sun shelter. When asked if she would like her portrait painted, she said— but why does the white man want to paint my portrait—I am nothing by bones—and in truth the many winters have told on the old woman—but her face lights up when speaking & her smile is very pleasant. She showed me a chain of silver medals presented to her late husband by some of the Premiers who visited him, and brought out a bundle in many wrappings, which she undid, and showed an old blue velvet bonnet, which she told me Col. Irvine, called by the Blackfoot Big Buffalo Bull, Omukaistumix. She used to wear it in the Council.

The name of Irvine & Macleod is like a charm amongst the Blackfoot, & Irvine has often told me that the Indians of this confederacy were always very friendly to the police & whenever they sighted one would come riding up & shake hands—the Crees he said were different & would ride away.

(Diary page 8) Sisuiake was not Crowfoot's first wife and he had several others but he paid her most regard and she always accompanied him—the other wives attending to the horses & the duties of the camp.

I gave the old woman a shawl, a silk handkerchief for her head and some tea & sugar & this pleased her—she must be about eighty. Her face & hair were smeared with the red paint made of earth which the Indians bake. She gave me sittings for the portrait.

I had met Canon Stocken, who is in charge of the Anglican Mission at the North Camp, when he was attending a general meeting of his church at Macleod.[26] He drives me to the North Camp. It is situated in a valley, which must originally have been a lake as there are many gravel beds and high banks surrounding it here. There is the church, a boarding school & hospital—his brother has charge of the school. The Roman church has invaded his territory and has a small church which a priest visits occasionally. I had lunch with the Canon whose house is a short distance from the camp.

The next portrait was of the head man or minor chief, Weasel Calf, Apaunista, son of Sisuiake by a former husband.[27] She married Crowfoot as her second husband. He and his wife drive to the agency, gorgeous in buckskin _____ trimmed with weasel tails & beadwork. He gave me a peace pipe made of catlinite stone hung with eagle feathers.[28] Sisuiake lives *(Diary page 9)* in his house during the winter. He had signed the treaty. His face is badly marked by the effects of lupus of the lips & chin. Dr. Turner of the Anglican Mission, 1897–1900, cured him of this. At the north camp there are some painted teepees near the agency. There the Indians have encamped after returning from Calgary.

On one is the history of the owner, in picture writing—others are yellow with suns in a light yellow—again others a border of suns white on red ground—at top & bottom & from the flaps swing 2 bunches of black hair.

Weasel Calf, Apaunista, Blackfoot minor chief. Pastel on paper, 1907. Dimensions 62.5 × 51 cm. Edmund Morris Collection. ROM HK 2416.

Photograph of Weasel Calf and his wife. Edmund Morris Collection 88. Courtesy Provincial Archives of Manitoba.

Some lodges have blue suns on brown ground, with hair swinging from centre of a star—again others with a buffalo head & a _____ of badgers, beavers or bulrushes.

JULY 22
(Le Révérend
Père Levern,
OMI)

I go to the south camp—stop at the mission. Levern is in charge. Lepine & Culerier on a visit.[29] Here also is a boarding school for Indian boys & girls. From the town of Gleichen the S. Camp is a drive of 10 miles. Levern came from Brittany. He has been 3 months here, having been 7 years with the Bloods.

The senior head chief of the Blackfoot, Running Rabbit, Atsistamukkon, and his outfit are camped here, at the foot of the rolling prairie.[30] On the top of this is the coffin of his son Mikki who died 2 years ago. The old man pulled

(Diary page 10)

down his log house, built this small hut for the coffin out of it & has since led a wandering life camping here & there. They invariably do this. The Government _____ them to make coffins. They did so but will not place them under the ground, but generally on the edge of the old river bank overlooking the valley, sometimes in a coulee.

The chief clothed Mikki in his own handsome buckskin dress with beadwork & ermine. Mikki was a good looker & was made much of by the women, who would braid his long black hair & keep his boots in order. His son Horton[31] who put away his wife & married the widow of his brother Mikki. He also is good looking.* Dick Bad Boy, a grandson & a small boy live in the lodge. The chief has 2 wives, sisters. I paint him in his official uniform as chief—the blue coat with brass buttons & gold braid. Some years ago the chiefs requested to have these instead of the red coats formerly used as they were more serviceable. He carries a medicine wand was given by Governor Dewdney when Iron Shield was associated with him as head chief[32] to be used alternatively by the two men, the silver Treaty medal also, for these two as head chiefs of the South Camp.[33] He has medals from Duke of York, Lord Minto & the Japanese Prince.[34] He told me he went on the war path at 18 & took 10 scalps during his life. He now rises at 5 & works in his garden. In the evening takes off his blanket &, with only his leggings & breech clout on, smokes his pipe.

*and White
Man—who is
deaf and dumb.
He is the artist of
the tribe and
carves, in stone,
crude heads, and
colours the
skins.

(Diary page 11)

The chief named me Kyaiyii ᔨᔥᕐᕐ, sometimes ᔨᔥᕐᒡ Bear Robe, after a great Blackfoot chief he had heard of as a boy.[35] He requested me to take a message to the great chiefs at Ottawa. All the old chiefs have the same to say. They do not want any part of the reserve sold. The promise was given them at the Treaty and if broken will remain as a dark spot in our history. Canada is now in a position to give as compensation for the vast domain required by the Treaties even more than promised. The Blackfoot reserve is the pick of the land, & there are many avaricious eyes fixed on it.

Visit the Indian burial ground on the hilltop or rather on the prairie above the old river bed. Crowfoot was buried here. The Govt. put up an iron cross with the inscription—Chief Crowfoot died, April 25th 1890 aged 69—and on the other side—The father of his people. After a time the Romanists put up a fence enclosing it & other graves, but Romanists & the old sun worshippers sleep alike under one vast domain—the sky. Outside the enclosure sloping

Running Rabbit, Atsistaumukkon, Blackfoot head chief of the South Camp. Pastel on paper, 1907. Dimensions 62.5 × 51 cm. Edmund Morris Collection. ROM HK 2408.

Photograph of Running Rabbit. Edmund Morris Collection 13. Courtesy Provincial Archives of Manitoba.

down the bank is a medley of coffins, lodges, & all the equipment of the deceased Indians.

(*Diary page 12*)   Crowfoot, Sapo Maxika, was head chief of the whole Blackfoot confederacy or nation including the Blackfoot, Sik' si kau; the Piegans, Pi kŭni; and the Bloods, Kai' nah. The Blackfoot & Piegans stretched into mountains but were all dominated by him as head chief. It was his great administrative capacity which gained him this position. During Crowfoot's lifetime Old Sun was head chief of the North Camp, & when Old Sun died White Pup succeeded him.[36] Today Yellow Horse is head chief of North Camp. Crowfoot dying, he named his brother Three Bulls to succeed him.[37] He only lived for three months & the Indians were superstitious & it was difficult to get one to hold the position of head chief of the South Camp, two head chiefs dying so closely together. However, Running Rabbit was appointed and later on Iron Shield associated with him on an equal position.

JULY 26TH   I paint old Black Eagle, Sixsipita.[38] He is now almost blind. He was one of the black soldiers whose duty it was to drive all to attend the Sun dance—if any refused they would kick the key pole & bring the lodges down on their heads.[39] They used to descend on the ration house & help themselves to beef.

(*Diary page 13*)   I asked him how many wives he had. He said they had been so numerous he could not count them! Next day I went again to his lodge but he yelled, no, get out. Levern came to reason with him. He jumped up & went to the lodge of an old friend & ordered the priest out, shaking his fists. In the evening, I got his grandson Henry as interpreter & went to the old man's lodge & had a smoke with him & a talk. He then agreed to sit till the portrait was finished.

27TH   Borrowed Running Rabbit's team & with Levern as interpreter went to camp of the Head Chief Iron Shield, whom I wish to paint. Markle, the Inspector, Gooderham, Stocken all say I will never get him, but I have made up my mind to paint him. He hates the whites and opposes everything which would advance his people. When the question of a bridge was put, to cross the Bow River, Iron Shield had been at work amongst the bucks & it was downed. Running Rabbit also opposed it, preferring to swim his horses, & swore he would never cross it if carried by the Govt.

A number of young Indians, Mike Bear Hat, Joseph Good Eagle & Harry Black Eagle accompanied us on horseback. Entering the chief's big house we

(*Diary page 14*)   found him seated on his bed fanning himself with an eagle wing. He is haughty & in his bearing looks the King—listened to a long oration from him—a bunch of grievances against the present Govt. which I was to take to the big chiefs at Ottawa.[40] The main kick was about the rations which the Govt. was cutting down.

These rations were instituted by the Govt. when the buffalo gave out & starvation set in amongst the plainsmen. Now that they have adapted themselves to the grub of the white men & have their own herds of cattle, the Govt. refuses to feed all _____ Indians who can make an income by cutting the hay and working for the ranchers & only feed the aged, feeble & destitute. Iron Shield says many of the old people died two years ago for want of food. After settling questions of money he agreed to sit.

Black Eagle, Sixsipita, Blackfoot. Pastel on paper, 1907. Dimensions 62.5 × 51 cm. Edmund Morris Collection. ROM HK 2415.

Photograph of Black Eagle. Edmund Morris Collection 71. Courtesy Provincial Archives of Manitoba.

Iron Shield's adopted brother, Medicine Shield, had even more influence. Another brother, High Eagle, is the best hunter on the reserve.[41] He is employed by the ranchers to kill the wolves, which hamstring their cattle & horses. The young colts are their special prey. Sometimes in the spring a rancher loses 25 in this way.

(Diary page 15) Iron Shield has a daughter called Holy Pipe. She is the only beautiful Indian girl I have seen.[42]

28   Start the portrait of Iron Shield—all went well till late in the afternoon. This Indian work is unlike ordinary portrait work where we have sittings for two hours at a time. They are impatient & want to get it done & sit like statues, never resting—so I keep them at it according to their wish.[43] I had advised Iron Shield to rest but he would not & at last jumped up with a yell, tore off his buckskin clothes, tossed them aside & stalked away. I got my interpreter & asked the trouble. He said he heard nothing! So I _____ _____ & started away. He then got sorry & came out. I shook hands & said I would come & finish it next day.

29   Again painting the chief. All day he sat & had opposite him a large mirror in which he admired himself. He gave me some hard work.

The first room of his house is filled with _____, & the next, relatives & living room, beds encircling it. He has two wives but only allows one to stay with him. I am stopping at Mr. Van's about 2 miles from the camp. Iron Shield

(Diary page 16) lives in the house formerly belonging to Crowfoot. His mother was related to Crowfoot who used to say that he was the half of his (Crowfoot's) body. He now takes the name of Sapo Maxika but is still generally known as Iron Shield—Ixkimia Aotoni.

I got a fine red stone pipe (catlinite) from Black Water—stem & bowl cut out of the stone. This red stone is got from Pipestone, Minnesota, in the United States. It is a quarry in common use by all the Indian tribes. Most hostile enemies would meet here & feared nothing. It is also found in small quantities in Canada. Some of the old Indians telling me they get it here.

I had stopped with Van. Not far away is a party of surveyors under charge of Duff, surveying for irrigation works.

30   Return to the mission, Patrick Yellow Door driving me. The Indians all collected for their rations. Arrange to have Piiskini, A Far Away Voice or Echo, sit for his portrait.[44] He is a type of the wild savage. He came in a fine symphony of browns & oranges.

31   Drive to see an old Indian who is dying in this camp. I see a woman with her nose bitten off. This was the general custom in the early days for infidelity

(Diary page 17) towards their husbands. The case I speak of was the last practised.[45] At another lodge was an old woman with 2 thumbs on one hand. At Iron Shield's camp Spotted Calf has a finely decorated lodge, his history recorded in picture writing. Iron Shield's daughter name Holy Pipe, Na to ah ko ya ne ma ak. He has a son called Pretty Young Man. A good type here is Running Wolf.

A Far Away Voice or Echo, Piiskini, Blackfoot. Pastel on paper, 1907. Dimensions 62.5 × 51 cm. Edmund Morris Collection. ROM HK 2414.

Photograph of Father Léon J. D. Doucet, OMI, by W. J. Oliver, Calgary, Alberta. Doucet was missionary to the Indians in southern Alberta for many years and founder of the Roman Catholic mission at the South Camp of the Blackfoot reserve. Courtesy the Glenbow Museum, Calgary, Alberta, NB-16-164.

High Eagle tells of the old days. The Red Deer valley was the favourite hunting grounds of these plainsmen. Once the Blackfoot reached a high hill which commanded a view of all the neighbouring country. They saw no sight of hostiles so encamped. At night the Crees came, saw smoke rising from the hill, so crept on the Blackfoot & killed many of them. Sometimes he has seen over 200 antelope in this valley.

Paint a full length of Bear's Hat, Kyaiyi stumokon.[46] I made notes of his history. He & his brother have been at the coal mine on the reserve for 23 years.

(Diary page 18) The Blackfoot Crossing across the Bow River is close by. From time immemorial it had been a great camping & burial ground of the Indians, & here the Blackfoot Treaty (No. 7) was negotiated in 1877 by Lt. Gov. Laird, Col. Macleod & the chiefs of the Blackfoot Confederacy,[47] the Sarcees, the Stonies & other tribes. At that time they numbered (the Blackfoot) 2,000 and are now reduced to 800.

2ND AUG. Chief Running Rabbit & other Indians came to say goodbye to me before leaving the South Camp—amongst them an old Indian called Sleeping Sun. It is evening & Crow Eagle is out on the plains wailing—he mourns a son who died in January and a daughter three months ago.

3RD Return to Gleichen in the morning, in the evening a great wind & dust storm.

4TH Drive to the North Camp with the RNMP sergeant. I meet Old Calf Child— Onistaipoka—was chief of the Blackfoot, once a great warrior, medicine man.[48] He is tremendously thick through the chest & stands erect. He is nearly blind.[49] His son Joe, a wild devil of about 30, is with him[50] & his old wife, who showed me a Cree bullet wound in her arm. I arrange to paint the *(Diary page 19)* old man's portrait. I also meet Crow Shoe, a minor chief or head man, & will paint him.[51] He has a head which recalls Henry Irving's.[52]

5TH I move down to the North Camp. One word about the missions on the reserves. The Catholics or Romanists first came in 1883, & Doucet calling on Crowfoot asked if he might instruct his people.[53] He consented & they began work. Almost simultaneously Tims of the Anglican Church arrived—also went to Crowfoot, who declined to receive him, so he went to the camp of Old Sun, who allowed him to start a mission. Soon after his arrival the Chief Low Horn came with two of his daughters & offered them to the missionary & was surprised when he ordered them away. He came again the next morning & showed a roll of bills saying—these from the white men what borrows! Tims then set about investigating & tried to implicate many of the officials—he became very unpopular. The chief White Pup came to his house & told him to go back to where he came from. Tims laughed, & again White *(Diary page 20)* Pup came and told him to pack up all his belongings & they would drive them to the train & if he would not they would take him & his outfit & throw them in the Bow River—Tims left.[54] The Bishop came down & had a powwow with the chiefs.[55] Most of the chiefs left the tobacco he brought. He told them the man they were driving away he was going to make Archdeacon, but the Indians heard nothing!

A great mistake is made by the different sects by encroaching on each other's ground. If there was only one denomination on a reserve, something might be accomplished—as it is, though some conform to the usages of the church, it has no hold on them, and as an Indian enquirer put it to a missionary, when you & the others of the black robe have settled the points upon which you disagree we will listen.

These old Indians are sincere in their religion. The sun which they can see & which causes light & makes all things grow.

In the early morning & at night they are heard facing this great force and offering up their prayers. The young men have lost this faith and the other has meant nothing to them. Rev. Canon Stocken who succeeded Tims is thought highly of by the Indians & still works on though he has often thought of leaving. Last November his wife was driving home with her children & was overtaken by two Indians who were racing their horses. Her team took fright, stampeded down the hill. As they reached the bottom the wheels struck the bridge. All were thrown out & she was instantly killed. The same Indians brought the remains to the Canon & asked payment for their trouble. Though there are instances like this of the stony heart, it is not a characteristic feature of the Indians. *(Diary page 21)*

Father Doucet, O.M.I., was the first to start the Roman Catholic Mission at the South Camp of the Blackfoot, though Father Lacombe had been amongst this tribe years before as a wandering missionary.[56] Father Doucet came from Orleans in France & has been 39 years amongst the Indians; 10 years ago he removed from the Blackfoot to the Bloods. When the Police came into the country, they found him in a starving condition having lived on gophers for some days. They sat before him a hearty meal.

The priests come into much closer contact with the Indians than the clergy of other denominations, when sickness is amongst them, sleeping in their lodges. Once there was a great epidemic of fever in the west. Most of the people fled from it. Father Lacombe stayed by the construction camps & prayed with the sick & dying—he had an Anglican prayer written out & when he came to one of theirs would read it to them. *(Diary page 22)*

A Father Scullen was also for a time at the South Camp.[57] The latter was a muscular Christian as an _____. He was preaching to the natives. Some roughs gathered around & made light of it. The priest apparently said nothing but when he had finished he tore off his robe & put it on the ground, saying, there lies Father Scullen. Then rolling up his sleeves he said, Here's Pat Scullen, now come on with you—& knocked them all out.

Father Scullen travelled more among the Blackfoot than any of the missions at the time. He was much at the great camp in the Valley where Calgary stands—spoke Blackfoot fluently.

Old Calf Child sits for his portrait. Before consenting he went to his medicine bag & turning his back to me prayed to his God. He & his family are deeply interested in the work. His Sarcee woman has an inimitable laugh. Joe, the son, is a rascal—he is only lately out of six months imprisonment, & when a schoolboy was imprisoned for seducing the maid at the industrial school. He stole his wife from an older Indian. He had 3 fine boys, the eldest called Earl. When he was in prison he asked to see his wife, who had a horse ready, & *(Diary page 23)* with a yell he sprang from the window & dashed off & with his rifle kept away from the police off on the hills. Finally he gave himself up. He gave me a photo of himself made on horseback. I have finished the portrait. It rains hard, but the old man must have the promised money & the Sarcee woman, old as she is, is out hitching up the horses, & now, they go to blow it in at Gleichen. We exchange presents—I the red stone pipe inlaid with lead & a scalp decoration.

The head man Crow Shoe, Mastoitsikin drove down from his camp to be painted. His face is coloured with a red earth they use. His natural colour is more that of coffee brown. I see some of the women painted yellow with vermilion at the sides of their cheeks—some yellow over eyebrows & eyelids & just one red beauty spot. The young men pull out all the eyebrows, except a thin pencil line.

AUG. 26
(Diary page 24)

Take a run out to Calgary in time for Norman Macleod's wedding.[58] Go on to British Columbia, en route stopping at Banff for weekend. On the train I met Comptroller Fred White of the RNWMP,[59] his son Donald, Capt. Fleming, his brother Hugh & his son.

Col. White knew my father & mother at Fort Garry. He says there is a great difference today in the dealings with the Indians. In my father's day, when he negotiated the treaties & MacDonald & Galt were at Ottawa, there was a deep sympathy with the Indians and they were treated as wards.[60] He has reduced the force of the police, believing there is no need of so large a body of men in these days of peace, but warns the Govt. to be careful in reducing rations or the Indians may rise.[61] He believes the Indian question will solve itself. They are gradually dying out but would like see them intermarry with the white race. He was a great friend of Edmund or Dalrymple Clark & Frank Buchan, both of whom acted as security to my father at Garry.[62]

The Hayter Reeds are away from Banff.[63] The Whites & I stop off at Field. Here at the CPR Hotel all the waiters are Chinese in their native costume.

(Diary page 25)

How wonderful the mountains! None of our painters have yet got their spirit but some day someone will come on the scene who can do it.

Stop at Vancouver—the Indians are encamped opposite. In a great _____—all are wailing the loss of a child. In other _____ they are at work making baskets of rush, & the men betting away their earnings till the late hours. They are not to be compared with the plainsmen. Some almost look like gorillas—generations of canoeists has done the work.[64]

I see Stanley Gzowski here—he is in particularly with MacDonald & was at work on a large contract for the CPR.[65] Chinese, Japs, _____, Indians—all meet here.

Victoria comes next to Quebec in my estimation, so beautifully situated. Take a plunge in the salt water.

The Kicking Horse Pass & later on the Fraser River afford good subjects for a painter.

SEPT. 4TH

I return through the lakes & by the Crow's Nest Pass. This valley I must see again. Arrive at Calgary 5th Sept.

Calf Child or White Buffalo Calf, Onistaipoka, Blackfoot war chief of the North
Camp. Pastel on paper, 1907. Dimensions
62.5 × 51 cm. Edmund Morris Collection.
ROM HK 2412.

Crow Shoe or Face Red With Earth, Mas-
toitsiskin, Blackfoot chief. Pastel on paper,
1907. Dimensions 62.5 × 51 cm. Edmund
Morris Collection. ROM HK 2411.

6TH   Drive to the Sarcee reserve with Dr. Lafferty, 12 miles distant.[66] The agency is in a valley with a view of the Rockies. A. I. McNeill is the agent.[67] He kindly

(Diary page 26) puts a room at my disposal & I get meals at Mr. Percy Stocken's—a brother of the Canon. There is an extremely interesting man here, George Hodgson, a Scotch Cree breed. He has been with the Sarcees for 23 years & as a boy was brought up at Fort Edmonton where his father used to build the York boats.[68] He drives me to the camp of the head chief called Bull Head, Stumixotokon. His Sarcee name is Little Chief, Tçillah. He stands over six feet & is a Blood-Sarcee.[69] When we entered his lodge I was introduced & his wife placed before us a dish of Saskatoon berries. He is mourning the man he had named as his successor as head chief—Jim Big Plume, his nephew. This young man had been like a son & 9 years ago pulled him through pneumonia, sitting by his bedside at night & giving a little brandy. Big Plume died of consumption a month ago. He was sent to the hospital at Morley but as there was no hope he was allowed to die amongst his own people. The chief on this account gave away his painted lodge & lives in a dilapidated one.

     He was the youngest of six brothers—Little Chief, who was head chief, Stinking Pond, Big Plume & Many Kootenay (twins), Painted Otter & Bull Head. The 2nd, 4th & 5th were killed by the Cree & at Vermilion Creek there was a great fight. At first the Sarcees won, but Little Chief said they would fight again. This time the Crees were victors. They returned to Fort Pitt & held a great dance. The chief said they had heard in the Sarcee dance Little

(Diary page 27) Chief singing, but the song ended in a wail, & they could not account for it. It was not the chief but his youngest brother, who had the same voice & mourned his death, for the chief had been killed by the Crees, unknown to them. The chief, when dying, handed his gun to his youngest brother, naming him as head chief. Many years ago he and his band held up the Hudson Bay store at what is now Calgary. He is of a very untamable disposition & on some occasions has had to be held down by the police.

     The Sarcees have made a large pyramid of stones which is to perpetuate their wish amongst the rising generations that none of the land is to be sold. The Chief is led about by his wife. He came accompanied by a number of Indians to sit for his portrait. He was dressed all in black, even the ribbons from his medal, & kept up a wail for Big Plume—asked the agent to see that his medals are placed on the breast of a worthy man.

     Hodgson tells me one of the Sarcee legends.

In the beginning there was a man & his wife & ten young men. The Great Spirit told the young men to dress up & he would marry them.

(Diary page 28) They were surprised as they thought they were the only people, but they were led into a camp in the mountains where there were ten young girls. The eldest of them was the wisest & best looking but disguised herself as an old hag. The Great Spirit said to the youngest man, take this young girl—and so on, till there was none but the old hag left, & he said to the eldest of the young men to take that young girl. He looked & refused & the Great Spirit was angry, having done all this to try the young man, & made him a wanderer & he became known as the Old Man.

Little Chief, Tçillah, Sarcee chief. Pastel on paper, 1907. Dimensions 62.5 × 51 cm. Edmund Morris Collection. ROM HK 2410.

Big Wolf, Sarcee chief. Pastel on paper, 1907. Dimensions 62.5 × 51 cm. Edmund Morris Collection. ROM HK 2406.

Two young girls went to draw water & there appeared to them two young men, strangers who asked them to go home with them. The girls asked where they lived & they pointed to two bright shining stars but they could not follow them there, so asked them to come to their lodges. People came to see the strangers & they did many strange things & drew clothes from their mouths, so they killed them thinking they were evil spirits. For having killed his messengers the Great Spirit was angry & told the old man to build a raft. Then he made the earth & the Great Spirit made the water to come out of the ground, until the land was covered. The old man had gathered in all animals but being alone he became weary & caused a beaver to dive down to try to find earth and it was drowned. He told a duck to dive—it also was drowned. He then told a rat to dive—it was drowned but when its body floated on the waters, in its claw was found a little piece of clay. The old man took this and blew on it & it became an island. He blew again & made a plover with 2 blue rings about its neck which meant that the waters would disappear. He made it walk about the island & as it walked the land increased in size, but the old man was a wanderer alone.

(Diary page 29)

This from Inis— had he asked an Indian the name of the first man he would have said Adam!
(Diary page 30)

[The Blackfoot legend differs somewhat from this. It begins with Napi, the old man. All was water & he sent a muskrat down & it brought up clay in its claws, which he worked in his fingers & made it grow & formed land. He then out of the clay made animals & sent them out in the world & from his right side he took a rib & made a woman. From his left rib he made a boy, but the boy grew ill & the woman said she would throw a stone into the water & if the stone should float the boy would live. If it sank he would die. They watched & the stone sank & so death came into the world & so Napi & the woman parted, he going up into the mountains where Morley now stands & there he made many men. The woman went south & made a corral of women.

as related by Big Plume— Blackfoot.[70]

Long afterwards Napi was wandering & he came to this camp of women & singling the woman out, said he did not know she had all these! That he had many men & would bring them down & marry them. So the woman caused them to stand on a hill for the women to choose their husbands & she disguised herself as an old woman & came out & chose Napi, but he would not take her so she went away & dressed herself as the young girl again & came out & chose the next young man & told all the others to pass by Napi. So he was left alone & she told him to become a lone pine & he was turned into this tree & to this day the Indians point out this lone tree on the _____ River! So Napi's spirit left & went into the East & there he made the white men, whom the Indians call Nipiguins.][71]

(Diary page 31)

There is a spot near the Red Deer River which the Indians point out as Napi's bed & throughout the country there are hills & plains which mark his course.

Hodgson had followed the Blood Indians in their buffalo hunts & near the Red Deer there was a fine camp. They all got drunk & at night gave a _____ dance. One of the young girls jumped up & kissed a breed but he did not respond in the usual way by kissing her & dancing, so they all laughed. Her brother got angry & went out, got his horse ready & when she came out to gather buffalo chips he shot her dead & rushed off on horseback. Speaking of the old trading days at Fort Edmonton. The Blackfoot preferred to trade at that fort & the traders would meet them half way en route & give each of the chiefs a gallon of rum. When they reached the Fort they held a great dance which was followed by drunken day, large vats of rum being prepared & their firearms & arrows taken from them & locked up in a room. This again would be followed by trading day, the Indians still stupid from the effects of the liquor.

So much for the old mode of trading with the red man. One chief got 10 *(Diary page 32)* gallons of rum but it is said he was a wise man, would not drink himself, but sold it to the other Indians when he reached camp.

There is apparently some uncertainty as to the origin of the name Black-foot. Some hold that they wore moccasins of black fur—others that the soil of the country they passed through was black & blackened their moccasins—again others that when they came from the tundra country to the plains, a prairie fire had preceded them & their feet were blackened, & the southern tribes named them Blackfoot.

I paint Big Wolf, a minor chief or head man of the Sarcees.[72] He is married to 7TH a daughter of the notorious Cree Big Bear.

I drive over the reserve & see many encampments. The Sarcees were once a powerful tribe but their hand was against all men, & in their fights the best of this race was killed off. They are a branch of the Athapascan or Déné stock.

Snow is on the ground, cold piercing wind with rain & sleet—a disagreeable 8TH drive of 12 miles to Calgary. I have lunch with the Macleods. Norman had got a lot of duck.

Snowed all day, a foot of snow on the ground—this flattens the crops down. SEPT. 9TH

Show some of the old timers my work. They like best the portraits of Iron *(Diary page 33)* Shield, old Calf Child & Bull's Head.

I go out to Macleod, call on Superintendent Primrose at the Barracks.[73] He arranges to have one of the police drive me out to the Blood reservation.[74]

There are two ex-mounted policemen here—Anderton one of them, from whom I get a number of photographs taken long ago.[75] The Indian inter-preter, a Blood man, Tom Daly, also gave me a number.

Call on the sheriff, Mr. Duncan Campbell, whom I met at the Macleod's in Calgary.[76] He was at a dinner my mother gave at Garry for Dalrymple Clark, the adjutant of the NWMP, & his bride. Met MacKenzie, the member, & Cluny Macdonell, a lawyer who in the early days had a store at Cluny & married one of Crowfoot's daughters.[77] Macdonell holds that Iron Shield is the man named by Crowfoot as his successor, & for that reason he took the name of Sapo Maxika, but from all I can gather from the Indians, Crowfoot named his brother Three Bulls, who after his death became chief. Iron Shield was made chief by the Govt. some years afterwards.

(Diary page 34)
*Julian Ralph, when he visited the Blackfoot, was taken about by old Lereux,[79] who, though he is interesting, is not reliable.

Julian Ralph,* the writer, has said that Crowfoot, when dying, became a Romanist.[78] Doucet had asked him if he believed & he said, yes, but do not tell my people!

I questioned Doucet about this, but he would not say; Macdonell, who was present, said that he had all his medicine men about him & that rather than offend his lifelong friend Doucet, he allowed him to administer the sacrament & when asked if he believed, acquiesced but would give a sign that it was between them. Crowfoot used often to stop at Cluny (R. S.) Macdonell's house—once he was stormbound. The old man went to bed & Macdonell heard him praying all night for those out in the blizzard. Next morning Crowfoot, when greeted, lashed out—the Christians name a code of morals & are working towards a certain road, we also have a code which is equally hard to live up to, & that he believed all would meet at the same place.

I am stopping at the Queen's Hotel, one of the best kept hotels in the west. The proprietor, an ex-NWMP, Prussian, has the head teamster from the Barracks call for me and we start for the Blood reserve.[80] On the way meet Bob Wilson, the agent.[81] I introduce myself, & he asks me to return to Macleod & he will drive me down. He wants me to stay with him. There is still snow on the ground & it rains. The River Belly is too high to ford, so we have to take the luggage across in a boat.

(Diary page 35)
Wilson is well up in ethnology & has a fine library on the subject. He is a friend of George Bird Grinnell, a great authority on the Blackfoot.[82] The last time this writer was with him he took records of the Indian songs for a gramophone. Wilson says he questioned an old Blood Indian called Scalp Robe & he said he had been born when his people lived north of Edmonton. Schoolcraft, in his extensive works on the aborigines, states that he asked an aged Blackfoot where his people had come from, & he said, from the timber country to the north.[83] These timber people had no horses—they hunted & made war afoot, using dogs with travois to transport their luggage. The tribes to the south fought against the Spaniards & Mexicans & stole horses from them. In the wars more of these horses escaped & in time became wild herds that roamed the prairies. Coming against these southern Indians the Blackfoot saw them mounted & in time stole many of their horses, & thus it was they became plainsmen, but the old men still preferred to walk.

Wilson holds that the most authentic origin of name Blackfoot is as before stated that they had passed through burnt brush & their moccasins were blackened. The Indians of the plains called them Blackfoot & applied the
(Diary page 36)
name to all who came from that quarter, the Blackfoot, Bloods & Piegans.

Larry Wilson, a nephew of the agent & son of Wilson in charge of HBC post at Vermillion on Mackenzie River.[84] The young fellow had gone 60 miles farther north & started a trade with the Slave & Beaver Indians. He had been to HBC & will stop with his uncle. He is a grandson of Laurence Clark, a well known HBC factor.[85] At home we had a large buffalo robe given to my father by this gentleman.

The old chief Bull Shield, Stumixauotan, comes led by his wife to have me paint his portrait.[86] He is totally blind—has a noble old profile. His son Jack, a handsome young buck, acts as interpreter at the agency.

Joe Healey, Potaina, Blood. Pastel on paper, 1907. Dimensions 62.5 × 51 cm. Edmund Morris Collection. ROM HK 2401.

Photograph of the buffalo shield sketched by Edmund Morris. Of very thick rawhide (possibly three or more layers glued together), painted red, green, and black on the face; eagle tail feathers round rim, each wrapped at base with red cloth and sinew. Diameter without feathers 47 cm. Collected by R. N. Wilson. National Museums of Canada, National Museum of Man, Neg. # 73-3645.

Strangle Wolf, Maquaestupista, came to be painted.[87] He was gorgeous in buckskin & beadwork. When the portrait was finished, the old man was so pleased he said we were related. This the Indian considers a great compliment! We exchanged coats. I gave him a buckskin one with beadwork. He gave me a blue flannel one with ermine skins & beadwork. This was one of my best heads.

Joe Healey, Potaina, sits for his portrait. His father was a friend of Mr. Healey, the Yukon trader when at Fort Benton, who, when the old Indian died, proceeded to educate his son.[88] Joe Healey has the cunning of both the white & red men & unlike the other older Indians speaks English. Joe is over 50 now.

(Diary page 37)

24   Joe's son drives me to Macleod to draw money.

25   Bob Wilson showed me some of his treasures.

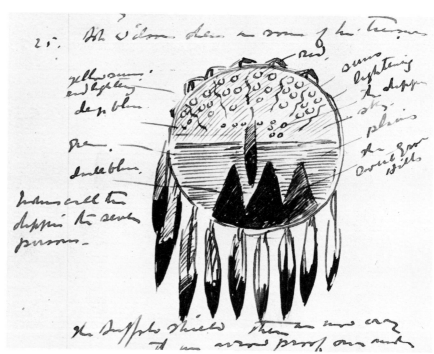

[Clockwise from top right: red, suns, lightning, the dipper, sky, plains, the Sweet Grass Hills, Indians call the dipper seven persons, dark blue, green, deep blue, red lightning, yellow suns]

The buffalo shield then as now very scarce.[89] They were arrowproof & were made out of the skin on the hump of the buffalo where it is thickest. A hole was made in the ground in which was kindled a fire. They would stretch the robe over it and the heat would make it contract & when the pegs would give out they would move the pegs closer and rub the hoof of the buffalo on it. Wilson showed this treasure to few, as he is going to bring out a work on the Indians. He has also material for the life of Red Crow, the late head chief.[90] Before he died Wilson had him come in the evenings & over a cup of tea he would relate the story of his life, W. writing it down.

From a photo Wilson took of him I made his portrait for the Indian *(Diary pages 38–39)* Department at Ottawa. He was a great _____, fearless in war & generous to his people. All disputes were settled by him. The Indians would come to his lodge with their troubles, and he would send them away satisfied. Compromise them was his rule in settling their difficulties.

The medicine tobacco was planted with great ceremony. An old man applied spells _____, singing & praying. He used the buffalo chips when planting it. This was not in common use, only on good tobacco. Old Sun was appointed for that. Amongst the Blackfoot in the spring, the whole tribe took part. If too dry he had to water it & stir it constantly. It was kept in a special medicine bag. This had lasted for many centuries. The man applied, when too old, sold his office to another for horses.

The straight pipe. In the beginning the Indians made one of reeds which is filled with their _____, but this would burn so they put clay about it, and after these follow the straight pipe cut out of stone. Finally they turned up the end. The making of their stone pipes is a long and tedious operation. Many of them are inlaid with copper and lead. In my father's collection there are two of these inlaid pipes. Later on Chief Bull Plume of the Piegans, a Blackfoot by birth, sent me a splendid example of the straight pipe.[91] It cost him ten horses & was used by the Blackfoot in their ceremonies, religious & ceremonial. It is the great Beaver medicine pipe & was used in the Great Beaver dance in the spring.

In the mound builders' ruins they found the pipe and stem but turned up—the straight pipe of the _____ _____ _____.

A young Indian whom Wilson had nursed when dying left him this blanket.

Chief Blackfoot Old Woman, Apinokŏmita, sometimes called Ermine Horses, comes to be painted. Col. Irvine had asked me to be sure & look him up. He is one of those who went with the Colonel in pursuit of Big Bear when he tried to stop the surveyors. He asked me to tell Irvine, whom the natives call Big Bull, that he was still able to ride, had a good home & many horses. Last year he & several of the chiefs accompanied Wilson to the East. In Winnipeg they were all on the streetcar.[92] It stopped & Blackfoot Old Woman got out, the rest not noticing it. When Wilson missed him he went back & found the old man camped on the boulevard where the car stopped. He was quite made up in his mind that the crowds of white people were the spirits of those who had died in the West.

(Diary page 40)

We drive into Macleod. The proprietor of the Queen's Hotel, an old ex-Mounted Policeman, was in my father's escort at Fort Pitt. He says there were 3000 Indians present, amongst these some from across the border, who tried to stir up mischief telling our Indians, Governments made treaties only to break them. At one point of the Indian manoeuvres trouble was expected, & the commissioner of the Police gave the word for them to be in readiness, for the Indians as a body rode out, with Winchester rifles in hand, dashed to the Commissioners' tent where my father stood. It proved however to be only part of their ceremony.

The fate of Charcoal, a Blood Indian, always stirs up sympathy in a westerner. He found out that another Indian was after his wife, so he kept watch & one day entering his lodge he found them together & at once shot the man dead. The police got word & were soon on his trail. The sergeant rode up to him to take away his gun & he shot him down & then fled.

E. J. B. Johnston, the great criminal lawyer, told me he holds that British law should not be applied to the Indians, as they cannot grasp its meaning. In the case of Charcoal he had it in his head that now he had killed the Indian he would be hung, & driven to desperation, shot down the sergeant. In the first instance any western jury would have acquitted him, but now that he had killed the policeman, all was up. He evaded the police for months, having as many as 30 remounts. Col. Steel, then in charge of the barracks at Macleod, found that his relations were helping him, so he put them all under arrest. They soon grew tired of prison, & Steel told them he would release them if they would give up Charcoal. The outlaw was suspicious & kept away from his kinsmen. One day he stood off from their lodge but one of them said, come on, there is no danger, & when he entered the lodge they clapped handcuffs on him. He said—it is my relatives who betray me! Their reply was that he had done wrong and the police arrested him. He was imprisoned at the barracks—his legs were paralysed from riding & he tried to starve himself to death. The only way the police could get him to eat was by promising him a smoke afterwards He was hung & met his death fearlessly. His people carried out the body.[93]

(Diary page 41)

(Diary page 42)

Not long ago 3 _____ Indians were tried for strangling a woman to death who was delirious from fever. This was a general custom at one time. They thought anyone delirious was possessed by an evil spirit.

The Hon. Edward Blake once told me that when he was Minister of Justice, 2 young Indians were tried for the murder of their old mother.[94] He inquired into the case and found that before doing so they had wept & lamented, believing her to be possessed of an evil spirit. He had the law explained to them, & they were imprisoned for a few months only, as they had been guided by a superstitious custom of their race.

Butcher, Stokinota, Peigan head chief. Pastel on paper, 1907. Dimensions 62.5 × 50.5 cm. Edmund Morris Collection. ROM HK 2409.

Crowfoot, Sapo Maxika, Blackfoot head chief. Pastel on paper, from a photograph by Professor Buell. Dimensions 62.5 × 50.5 cm. Edmund Morris Collection. ROM HK 2413.

Iron Shield, Ixkimauotani, Blackfoot head chief. Pastel on paper, 1907. Dimensions 62.5 × 51 cm. Edmund Morris Collection. ROM HK 2420.

John Three Bulls or John Drunken Chief Taking His Own Gun, Awatsiniamarkau, Blackfoot. Wearing the ceremonial headdress of the leader of the dance. Pastel on paper, 1907. Dimensions 63 × 51 cm. Edmund Morris Collection. ROM HK 2426.

Bear's Hat, Kyaiyistumokon, Blackfoot. Pastel on paper, 1907. Dimensions 62.5 × 51 cm. Edmund Morris Collection. ROM HK 2419.

Strangle Wolf, Maquaestupista, Blood chief. Pastel on paper, 1907. Dimensions 62.5 × 51 cm. Edmund Morris Collection. ROM HK 2425.

Photograph of a flannel shirt, decorated with bands of beadwork of conventionalized figures in various colours on a white background. Circular plaque applied to back and front. Decorated with ermine tails. Measures 160 cm across the shoulders, from cuff to cuff. Given to Edmund Morris by Strangle Wolf, Blood. Bequest of Edmund Morris. ROM HK 466.

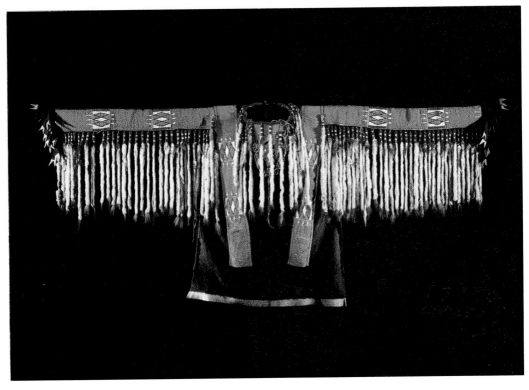

Running Wolf, Apisomakau, Peigan chief. Pastel on paper, 1907. Dimensions 62.5 × 51 cm. Edmund Morris Collection. ROM HK 2405.

Sitting Bull, Tatanka Yotanka, Hunkpapa Sioux chief. Pastel on paper, from a photograph. Dimensions 62.5 × 50 cm. Edmund Morris Collection. ROM HK 2438.

42

Bull Plume, Stumiksisapo, Peigan. Pastel on paper, 1907. Dimensions 62.5 × 51 cm. Edmund Morris Collection. ROM HK 2407.

Acoose, Man Standing Above Ground, Saulteaux chief. Pastel on paper, 1908. Dimensions 63 × 50 cm. Edmund Morris Collection. ROM HK 2402.

Sitting White Eagle, Wahpekinewap, Saulteaux medicine man. Pastel on paper, 1908. The two feathers in his cap are worn for men killed or scalped under fire in battle. Dimensions 63 × 49.5 cm. Edmund Morris Collection. ROM HK 2428.

Jack Bull Shield drives me into Macleod. Through with my work on the Blood Reserve.

Drive out to the Piegan Reserve, 18 miles distant from Macleod.[95] On the way visit Father Doucet. I had heard much about this old pioneer priest & he looked the part. He told me Brother John Berchmans would make me welcome at the old mission.[96]

The old building with its belfry where the fathers live has been occupied by the Alberta monks for many years. They give me a large room with a hole in the wall bed which recalls Europe.

Call on Mr. Yeomans the agent. He has lately come from the Sioux of Manitoba. He had met my father at the North West Angle Treaty.[97] My sisters were with him, & the lizards were so numerous they were afraid to sleep in the tents & spent the night in the carriages.[98]

Doucet has thrown his lot in with the Indians. He has a fine knowledge of the Blackfoot language. He says the old Indians had two good qualities—they kept their word & were hospitable. He went to them & they assured him his life & property were safe in their keeping. The younger ones he says are double faced.

Our conversation drifted to the early home of the Blackfoot nation. He told me the Crees named Little Slave Lake after the Blackfoot (Blackfoot, Bloods & Piegans) whom they called strangers, Ayatchiyimedok Sakahigan & the Lake of the Strangers and there is a pyramid of buffalo & antelope skulls which the Cree call the Blackfoot work.[99] They called the Blackfoot tribe Kaskiteway Esitak, The Blackfoot of the Buffalo.

He tells me the Crows occupied the country the Blackfoot now hold—& that the latter tribe used to roam far on the warpath. One old Indian told him he had been on the warpath beyond the Rockies to the ocean.

One powerful gens or rather Band of the Blackfoot, Omarketsimanex (the big dried food case people). The father of Sisoyake, Crowfoot's widow, whom I painted, was chief of this once powerful band. Over 70 years ago they went far south where there was a kindred tribe.[101] It was so far south they had always warm climate & saw negroes working in the fields. They stood this three or four years but wanted to see their own people. On the home journey they were attacked by the Snakes in Montana.[102] Her parents & most of the others were killed. A cousin caught Sisoyake then _____ up on his shoulders & rode on. Later the smallpox later broke out amongst them & carried off nearly all who were left. From a powerful band they were now reduced to a few families.

Father Doucet describing the Indians on the warpath says they went very lightly clad—moccasins, a breech cloth & a blanket strapped around their waist with a belt & no headdress, just a charm tied to their hair in front. J. W. Schultz, in his interesting work *My Life as an Indian*, says they always strapped their gorgeous war clothes to their horses, & if they had time would don them before the battle and again as they approached their camp after a victory when they rode home chanting their scalp song.[103] Doucet says

(Diary page 43)

Le Révérend Père Doucet, OMI, is ably assisted by Monsieur le Frère Jean Berchmans. These two and Père Lacombe make one think more of the old apostles than any of the black robes I have met. They have given up their lives to the Indians. There are five Soeurs de Charité in charge of the School.[100]

(Diary page 44)

(Diary page 45)

Crowfoot's heart was against the Government at the time of the late breed rebellion & if he had been near the Crees, would have joined them.[104] Poundmaker, his adopted son, the Cree head man, was another influence to draw him that way,[105] but he saw the wisdom of being loyal to the whites. He says in the early days the Chiefs were tyrants. Many Swans, the head chief before Crowfoot, used to order his men to do things & if they disobeyed would have them shot down & not a murmur from the people.[106]

He first saw old Calf Child as a medicine man at the death bed of a chief. He was masked & painted like a devil & was blowing through bone pipes to drive out the evil spirits or sickness. Both he & Weasel Calf were at one time head of the Black soldiers.

Old Eagle Flying Against the Wind, Pitamowinasi, comes to be painted.[107] He looked fine wrapped in his blue blanket with its beadwork decoration in the form of a band, brushing against the ground, with his black stone pipe in hand. He is the only Indian I have seen so far given to bald. He was ashamed of it & he would not take off the handkerchief which covered his head. I am told some would rather die than disclose their baldness.

(Diary page 46)

He showed me, by acting, an encounter he had with a grizzly bear & he showed the scars from its teeth & claws on his wrists. He pretended to be dead & after a time it left him. Also showed a large wound in his side from the thrust of a buffalo horn. I get an eagle wing fan from him.

Speaking of Rev. George MacDougall the missionary who was frozen to death on the plains,[108] Doucet says he dined with him the night before he left for the buffalo hunt, at the Calgary Barracks. MacDougall was in excellent spirits & Doucet remarked that people are often in unusual high spirits before their death. The following day they looked out & the plains were blackened by the buffalo—in thousands they came all about Calgary. Everyone was off to hunt them. The MacDougalls went with the rest & Rev. George pursued them up in the direction of Morley, meaning to strike that place for supplies & to look for an Indian who was not at the hunt and reported to be sick. He lost his way & becoming numb with the cold got confused. Had he given the horse the reins all would have come right. His body was found covered by the snow. He was a son of a former sailor on the lakes who had settled in northern Ontario, then came west to Victoria in the Territories. This missionary found it hard to forgive the Blackfoot who had stolen a stud horse from him. His sons Rev. John & David had the reputation of being simple liars—there is a saying, there are three liars in Alberta, John MacDougall is one & David two.

(Diary page 47)

Father Doucet had a close call when crossing Willow Creek in flood time. A woman was dying & he was called to administer the last sacrament. He started out in a great storm on his little black mare, came to a hill with two ravines & did not know which to take. When he came to the river it was a roaring torrent of mud & logs. He plunged in the river, & all the time the thunder and lightning. The little mare could barely keep her footing & sometimes was bent with the rushing waters. At last he reached the other side & then another struggle to climb the bank, with a good 5 miles ahead of

Blackfoot Old Woman or Ermine Horses, Apinocomita, Blood. Pastel on paper, 1907. Dimensions 62.5 × 51 cm. Edmund Morris Collection. ROM HK 2432.

Eagle Flying Against the Wind, Pitamow-inasi, Peigan. Pastel on paper, 1907. Dimensions 62.5 × 51 cm. Edmund Morris Collection. ROM HK 2423.

him before he could get shelter. This is only one of his narrow escapes. He is one of the black robe I have great regard for.

(Diary page 48) A smoke with old Eagle Flying Against the Wind in his lodge & meet Chief Bull Plume. He is a Blackfoot & was adopted by the Piegans. His movements are as restless as a panther's & he has a deep voice. Another sitting for Eagle Flying Against the Wind.

The Chief Big Swan sits for his portrait.[109] He wore a fine skin coat & his face painted yellow with splashes of vermilion. He is one of the chiefs who signed the Treaty.[110] Bull Plume & others came with him.

I also paint old Running Wolf, the oldest Piegan on the reserve.[111] He is 83 years. He is the true Piegan type. Doucet says the Piegans were not so robust a tribe as the Bloods or Blackfoot. Running Wolf came with gorgeous coat covered with ermine skin & his face painted yellow & a band of hair attached to his own. The old man is anxious to have his eldest son succeed him as chief. This is now in the hands of the Government. He spends his time now catching eagles in the mountains. The eagle plumes are valued highly for headdresses & the wings as fans; he conceals himself in a hole in the ground covered with branches & places a piece of meat on top—the eagles soaring above see this & swoop down. Then he clutches them, hauls them in & *(Diary page 49)* wrings their necks. He described all this to me in his lodge. He had heard I wanted him & had come in from the hunt & by sign language explained & then sang his eagle song.

His camp is 3 miles distant—about 6 lodges his numerous kin. In his lodge he had the _____ of eagles arranged on an altar—hung sweet grass, a row of buffalo stones at the back, & rows of eagle feathers in a _____ cleared spot.

His son Good Rider is a fine young buck.

Mr. Yeomans, who was so long with the Sioux, told me a story as related to him by Yuhaha (Bushy Tree).

When a small boy he had gone duck shooting with his quiver of arrows & strayed far from camp. He climbed up a hill but saw nothing of the camp, so got frightened & ran farther afield. Dusk came on, & as he was near a large marsh he pulled the long grass & made a little lodge for *(Diary page 50)* himself & crept in. Then night came on. He heard someone approaching, like the singing of the _____ of the medicine men. He had no fear. The steps came nearer & he distinguished them to be those of a wolf. Others came, and all through the night they kept encircling his lodge. The first comer sang to him & after a time yawned and all left but him. Then he spoke to the boy & said he guarded him from harm for he was the spirit of a departed relative & told him to go to the next hill where he would meet 2 men hunting elk & not to forget him—then he left. At dawn of day the boy went to the hill & met the men who said they were going to the bush to kill deer so he joined them. They killed several. The boy cut the tongue & heart from one of the deer & returned to his lodge. As he approached the spot a wolf crept away, so he placed them there & called out, if you are my friend it is thine—if not it will still be there when he calls.

Mr. Yeomans tells me old Antoine, John Sioux & Wanduti always open their *(Diary page 51)* speeches by telling about Governor Morris & his kind treatment of the Sioux.[112] The greetings of the Sioux—have you a glad heart & if troubled, I have a sad heart. When out in the early morning & see the sun come above the horizon they say it is the birth of morning. At the time of the Minnesota massacre the Sioux wished to form a great confederacy, sent runners with tobacco to the Indians in Canada.[113]

Doucet tells me, Weekaskoo kee say yin, the principal chief of the plains Cree, told his people to have nothing to do with the Sioux, that they wished to kill all the whites & if they entered into this alliance they would be as slaves. He did not touch the tobacco but walked away. This was significant & the runners returned to the Sioux chiefs. When my father negotiated the Treaty with the Crees at Fort Pitt in 1876 Sweet Grass had been out on the plains hunting buffalo.[114] He rode in a little later & dismounting from his horse went to the commissioners' tent & embraced my father, kissing him *(Diary page 52)* (this was an ancient custom among the aborigines). Hon. Mr. Christie & Dr. Jakes smiled at this so my father turned to the chief Sweet Grass & introduced them as his councillors whom he greatly esteemed. The chief then embraced & kissed them![115]

Sweet Grass was a Crow Indian by birth. Somewhere in the mountains in Montana a war party of Crees once heard a baby cry & they found it had been deserted or lost. They took it home to camp. Some of the Crees wanted to kill him but an old woman adopted the babe. She was very severe with him & late in life he often spoke of it & was glad of the training he got from her. He was a short man with fine head & eyes. Not long after the Fort Pitt

Treaty he was accidentally shot by his brother-in-law when examining a rifle.

The Indians all come for rations. Wolf Tail, a fine young buck, & Running Eagle, a middle-aged Indian, & Green Grass, Good Cyprus.

Brother John gives me an old medicine rattle made of buffalo skin which belonged to the late head chief of the Piegans, Crow Eagle.[116]

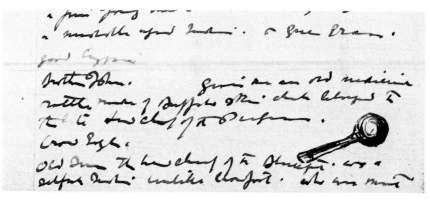

(Diary page 53) Old Sun, the head chief of the Blackfoot, was a selfish Indian, unlike Crowfoot who was most generous. When his wife died, Old Sun said he did not wish to live longer & died in a few days. His wife was probably the bravest of the Blackfoot women. In her young days she was stolen from her husband by a Cree who tied her to himself & rode off. She had a dagger concealed & waited her time & drove it to his heart, then scalped him & rode back to Old Sun. For this she always held a seat in the council.[117]

Old Sun was known to have killed a party of German immigrants who came into his country & used to show the scalp (long fair tresses of a woman). From photographs I made portraits of this chief & his wife for the Indian Department at Ottawa. They had died before I came to Alberta.

Drive to old Running Wolf's camp. He is very friendly. Gave me a weasel skin as good medicine, some root found in the marshes which I was to mix with my tobacco & his small red stone pipe made by himself. He goes tomorrow to sell his eagles. Gets a horse for an eagle tail & from 50¢–$1.00 for a good plume. One of his daughters had married a south Piegan. Three years ago

(Diary page 54) she & her husband & children were all murdered by one of the tribe. These Indians & the Bloods are a bad lot.

At Head Chief Butcher's I meet Hungry Chief whose daughter is married to the head chief's son.[118] He consents to sit for his portrait. After him I paint chief Bull Plume—he looks the warrior, had his face painted red. Chief Big Swan & others come while I am at work. They are deeply interested.

We drive to Brocket, the site of the new agency. There is an Indian burial ground close by.

Big Swan, Akamakal, Peigan chief. Pastel on paper, 1907. Dimensions 62.5 × 51 cm. Edmund Morris Collection. ROM HK 2424.

Man Angry With Hunger, Minnikonotsi, Peigan chief. Pastel on paper, 1907. Dimensions 62.5 × 51 cm. Edmund Morris Collection. ROM HK 2422.

Before I leave the reserve Chief Bull Plume rode over with a present of a grizzly bear claw which his father had always worn about his neck when fighting.

The mail carrier drives me to Macleod. He came an hour late as is their wont & I had a wild drive to catch the train for Calgary. Had to ford the Oldman River. Left Macleod 1:30 & reached Calgary that night.

(Diary pages 55–57) Campbell, now sheriff of Macleod, told me he & Smith had charged Mr. E. B. Osler & his brother, Dr. Osler, $100 transport the same trip long ago—the Dr. appreciated the fun & as his brother was putting up the money said to rush it in!

OCT. 13

David MacDougall tried to purchase a waterfall from the Stonies but they would not listen. The chief said he liked to hear the waters laughing.

*In 74, Mr. Grant of Sintaluta, when travelling near Fort Walsh, came upon 3 or four lodges, dilapidated—in them were found 7 to ten Indians in each lodge. Then as the Assiniboine chief had died of smallpox, the others fleeing from the reserve.

I go to Morley to have a look at the Stoneys. Fleetham, the agent, has made treaty payments & the Indians leave for the winter's hunt.[119] I found Mr. Fred Kidd, the trader, interesting. He has been 5 years with them & speaks the language. The wife of the agent has a large collection of Indian things—some good articles but too much of the half-breed work. Beadwork on velvet clearly has nothing to do with the early days. Kidd tells me these Stoneys when on the buffalo hunt got the smallpox. They fled* facing the northwest wind hoping the sickness would be driven back. Their course is marked by the bands settled through the country. They first came to the Rocky Mountain Fort, a HBC fort established in 1802 & abandoned in 1805, when the traders were driven out by the Blackfoot.[120] In their haste to escape they abandoned a cache of Jamaican rum. The Stonies _____ _____ abt. Oct. 10th & less, abt. 16 or 17 for the _____ came home about Xmas & NY Day had feasts in the chiefs' houses & ran out of doors with the thermometer at 30 or 40 below zero. Kidd gave me part of a stone pipe which belonged to Sitting Bull the great Sioux who had given it to chief Brule of the Moose Jaw Sioux, a branch of the Brûlés[121]—who gave it to Kidd when he left them as trader.

Joe Peacemaker's taking me to his camp & to the camp of his father-in-law chief Hunter. George Hunter was beating a large tom tom & I arouse them by singing an Ojibway song. In the evening they invited me to a dance—as dusk came on the effect was fine. Kidd's brother, Mr. Grant & others had come to see it—and as we were returning to town an imbecile methodist parson called me down for being present at the dance. He was a young man & I told him he would drive them to worse if he ever succeeded in stamping all joy & amusement out of their life. To me there was a real beauty in the rhythm of their dance—it must in a way resemble the old Morris dance of the Welsh, and in their gorgeous dresses of buckskin, beadwork & ermine skin they looked as _____ as the Highlanders.

14   Return to Calgary, & from there on to Winnipeg & Toronto.

Notes to Western Journey 1907

1. "Elderslie" was the name of the Alexander Morris family home in Toronto, at 471 Jarvis Street; the Morris family had moved into this house by 1884 and stayed on until about 1910. In 1977, the house was designated for preservation under the Ontario Heritage Act. The family summer home on Lake Joseph in the Muskoka region was built by Alexander Morris in 1888 on Morton Island, which, when he was appointed lieutenant governor of Manitoba and the North West Territories, became known as "Governor's Island". The island has been officially renamed "Home Island" and belongs to the Reverend David Luxton of Scarborough, and the house still stands.

2. Treaty Nine was arranged by commissioners from both the Canadian and the Ontario governments with the Indians southwest of James Bay in 1905 and 1906. Edmund Morris was commissioned by the Ontario government to accompany the second summer expedition and to make official portraits of the Indian leaders involved in the negotiations; while on the expedition, he also made other paintings and took photographs.

3. Research has failed to uncover any information about Captain Worthington; however, Edmund Morris would have known about Agra, India, since his older brother Robert, a graduate of the Royal Military College in Kingston, Ontario, was stationed there during a period of service with the British Imperial Army in India.

4. Murney Morris was a second cousin of Edmund Morris, being grandson of Edmund's great uncle Lieutenant-Colonel James Morris, after whom Morrisburg, Ontario, was named.

5. Government House was located at the corner of Broadway and Main streets in Winnipeg, within walking distance of the Manitoba legislative buildings; the stone gateway noted by Morris still stands, in a small park.

6. Colonel Acheson G. Irvine was commissioner in charge of the North West Mounted Police at Battleford, Manitoba, at the onset of the North West Rebellion in 1885 and was criticized for his handling of the rebellion. He was later appointed superintendent of the Stony Mountain Penitentiary, established on the Red River some 93 km (58 miles) north of Winnipeg (then Upper Fort Garry), between it and Lower Fort Garry.

7. Could this be a reference to Inspector Francis Dickens, of the North West Mounted Police, son of the author Charles Dickens?

8. Breed would be short for half-breed, and would here be in reference to the North West Rebellion of 1885. Sir John Alexander Macdonald was first persuaded to run for federal parliament in the election of 1842, as a Conservative, at the instigation of William Morris, the grandfather of Edmund Morris, and others (courtesy Queen's University Archives).

9. Big Bear (ca 1825–88), also known as the Great Bear and the Bear, Mistahah Musqua, a Plains Cree chief, was jailed after the North West Rebellion of 1885 but later released; he had a reputation as a skilful warrior and a wise leader; he was among the Indian leaders who resisted the signing of Treaty Six (see MacEwan 1971, pp. 102–13; Morris 1971, p. 193). Edmund Morris portrayed him twice, from a photograph (Royal Ontario Museum HK 2448 and Government of Saskatchewan Collection).

10. The Blood are one of the three tribes of the Blackfoot Confederacy. Blackfoot Old Woman, Apinocomita, sometimes called Ermine Horses, a Blood Indian, was portrayed by Edmund Morris on his 1907 journey (ROM HK 2432).

11. Crowfoot (ca 1821–90), also known as Crow Big Foot, Sapo Maxika (originally called Bear's Ghost—see p. 90 for a description of how he earned the name Crowfoot) was a Blood by birth but had a Blackfoot stepfather. Crowfoot became head chief of the three Blackfoot tribes. He was well known as a warrior but made peace with the Cree; he refused to participate in the North West Rebellion of 1885. Crowfoot was portrayed by Morris, from a photograph (ROM HK 2413). For further information, see Dempsey (1972).

12. The North West Mounted Police force (NWMP) was established in 1873 by the federal government of Sir John A. Macdonald, partly at the instigation of Alexander Morris, to patrol the North West Territories (which included what are now the Prairie Provinces); the first detachment, numbering three hundred, moved onto the Prairies soon after the force was established. The name of the force was changed to the Royal Canadian Mounted Police (RCMP) in 1920. For further information, see Macleod (1978). Lieutenant-Colonel James Farquharson Macleod (1836–94) was appointed the first assistant commissioner of the NWMP in 1874, and was commissioner from 1877 to 1880, retiring in 1880 and becoming stipendiary magistrate; he was succeeded as commissioner by A. G. Irvine. Macleod established Fort Macleod on an island in the Oldman River in 1874/75. He had much to do with the Blackfoot and won their confidence; Crowfoot trusted his advice. (See Haydon 1971, pp. 23, 39, 51, 63; Macleod 1978.)

13. The Doukhobors, members of a Christian sect that had its origin in 18th century Russia, began to settle in Saskatchewan in 1898 on land set aside for them under the Homestead Act. Their beliefs stress pacifism and communal living and ownership; the most rigid followers, the "Sons of Freedom", deny their members education and certain other individual rights, and express their beliefs through the removal of their clothing. The first nude parades were held in 1903, and twenty-five of the participants were sentenced to three months in jail.

14. Lower Fort Garry was built by the Hudson's Bay Company in 1830 on the Red River, north of Selkirk; the fort still stands but fell into disuse because traders favoured the junction of the Red and Assiniboine rivers, at Upper Fort Garry.

15. Hugh John Macdonald (1850–1929), of Winnipeg, was a son of Sir John A. Macdonald.

16. Tipis.

17. Sir Daniel Hunter McMillan (1846–1933) was lieutenant governor of Manitoba from 1900 to 1911.

18. The Blackfoot Confederacy was made up of three tribes at the time—Blood (Kainah), Peigan (Pikuni), and Blackfoot (Siksikau)—each having both head and minor chiefs; one chief was head of the Confederacy. These three tribes shared religion, social customs, and language, an Algonkian dialect. In the past, the Confederacy had included loosely the Sarcee and Gros Ventres as well. (See Dempsey 1979, pp. 8, 9.)

19. Charles William Jefferys, Ontario artist and author-illustrator (see Jefferys 1942–1950).

20. The Reverend William Cyprian Pinkham, Anglican Bishop of Calgary, 1886–1926 (courtesy the Anglican Church of Canada Archives, Toronto).

21. Lieutenant-Colonel Sir Samuel Benfield Steele (1851–1919), superintendent with the North West Mounted Police, joined the force in 1873 and served for thirty years; he accompanied some of Alexander Morris's treaty commissions with a police escort.

22. Edmund Morris's father, Alexander Morris, led negotiations of Treaty Four at Fort Qu'Appelle in 1874 and Treaty Six at Fort Carlton and Fort Pitt in 1876 while he was lieutenant governor of Manitoba and the North West Territories; Treaty Seven

was arranged with the Blackfoot by Lieutenant Governor David Laird, Alexander Morris's successor, and Colonel Macleod near Blackfoot Crossing in 1877 (see Morris 1971). Sitting Bull (ca 1834–90), Tatanka Yotanka, a Hunkpapa Sioux chief, after wiping out the unit of two hundred and twenty-five American soldiers under the command of General George Custer at Little Big Horn, moved his people north to Canada. During their four-year stay, the Hunkpapa Sioux were under the police protection of Major James M. Walsh of the North West Mounted Police. Walsh gained the trust of Sitting Bull and had only praise for Sitting Bull and his band's behaviour; he himself drew criticism for doing too little to speed their departure. (See Adams 1975, pp. 337–49; Haydon 1971, pp. 70–85; MacEwan 1973.)

23. John Hamilton Gooderham, federal Indian Affairs agent on the Blackfoot Reserve, 1907–ca 1914 (courtesy Public Archives of Canada).

24. Sisoyake or Sisuiake (1828–1908?), the Cutter Woman, was the favourite wife of Blackfoot Head Chief Crowfoot and inherited his treaty medal, which he had received from the treaty commissioners; during Crowfoot's life, she accompanied him everywhere and held a seat on the Blackfoot council. (See *Dic. of Can. Biog.* 1982, p. 444; Morris 1909, p. 13.) Morris's portrait of her is ROM HK 2417.

25. Reference is to Father J. L. Laverne; the Blackfoot Reserve was divided into a North Camp near Gleichen, Alberta, and a South Camp near Cluny, Alberta.

26. Canon Harry William Gibbon Stocken (1859–1955) was in charge of the Anglican Mission at the North Camp of the Blackfoot Reserve from 1885 to 1888 and again from 1895 until his retirement in 1923; his memoirs (Stocken 1976) were published by the Glenbow Museum.

27. The portrait of Weasel Calf, Apaunista, a minor chief of the North Camp of the Blackfoot Reserve, is ROM HK 2416.

28. This peace pipe may be in the collection of artifacts that Morris bequeathed to the ROM. Catlinite, a red shale containing iron oxide that the Indians valued and traded for making pipes, is found particularly in Pipestone, Minnesota, and occasionally in Canada.

29. Most of the missionary work by the Roman Catholic church among the Plains Indians was performed by the Oblates of Mary Immaculate order. Father Maurice Lépine, OMI, (1871–1946) and Father Louis Culerier, OMI, (1873–1946) both spent most of their lives working in the various parishes and missions in what is today the province of Alberta.

30. Running Rabbit, Atsistaumukkon, was appointed a minor chief at the age of 20 for his bravery in many battles, chief of the South Camp in 1890 upon the death of Crowfoot, and then senior head chief of the Blackfoot. In Morris's full-length pastel of Running Rabbit (ROM HK 2408) he holds a silver-topped cane of malacca wood received from Lieutenant Governor Dewdney, as a gift from Queen Victoria.

31. The more usual spelling is Houghton.

32. Edgar Dewdney (1835–1916), federal-government treaty commissioner in 1879; lieutenant governor of the North West Territories, 1881–82; and lieutenant governor of British Columbia, 1892–97. Dewdney was not always successful in winning the confidence of the Indians. Iron Shield (ca 1853–?), Ixkimauotani, related to Crowfoot through his mother, was appointed head chief of the South Camp of the Blackfoot Reserve by the federal government and shared this position with Running Rabbit for some years. Iron Shield adopted Crowfoot's name, Sapo Maxika, after Crowfoot's death. Portraits of Iron Shield by Morris, both dated 1907, are ROM HK 2420 and National Gallery of Canada 2030.

33. A large silver medal was given by the commissioners of the numbered treaties, on behalf of the federal government, to each Indian leader who signed a treaty. These treaties assigned the tribes to reserves with set boundaries and at the same time

granted the tribes certain privileges and regular payments from the government. Several Indians wear the medal they received in Morris's portraits; see, for example, the portraits of Running Rabbit (p. 19) and Crow Shoe (p. 27).

34. The Duke of York at that time would have been the second son of Edward VII, crowned George V in 1910. "Lord Minto" would be John Gilbert Elliot-Murray-Kynynmound (1845–1914), fourth earl of Minto, who was chief of staff during the North West Rebellion in 1885, and governor general of Canada, 1898–1904. He was sympathetic towards the Indians and urged the federal government to protect their culture and redress injustices done to them; he also pressed for the setting aside of areas as national parks and for the establishment of national archives in Canada. "The Japanese Prince" would refer to Li Hung-chang (1823–1901), who was not of royal birth but was an eminent soldier statesman and diplomat of the Chinese government of the Ch'ing Period. For his achievements Li was made governor general of Hunan and Hupeh provinces, given a minor hereditary rank and the title of Grand Guardian of the Heir Apparent, and made concurrently an Associate Grand Secretary. After 1879 he held the honorary title of Grand Tutor of the Heir Apparent. More than most higher officials of his day, Li realized that the backwardness of China in arms, communications, and modern machinery placed her at the mercy of stronger powers and retarded her economic progress. In April of 1896, Li represented China at the coronation of the Tsar; from Russia he proceeded round the world in a triumphal progress, visiting Europe, the United States, and Canada and sailing home from Vancouver in October of that year. Many anecdotes are still current about this journey. (See Hummel 1943, pp. 464–71.)

35. Kyaiyii, Bear Robe, was an early, famous Blackfoot chief. Morris signed himself by this name in his correspondence and on some of his pastels; he named his campsite on his western journeys Kyaiyii. Ewers (1945, p. 24) discusses Blackfoot pictographic signatures which served to identify the individual by name: "The lone Indian when separated from his war party or his camp could draw his signature, coupled with other pictographs indicating his recent actions, and a small arrow indicating his direction of movement, on a rock, a piece of bone, skin, or cloth and leave it in a conspicuous place where others of his tribe might find it and learn of his past accomplishments and future plans."

36. Old Sun, Natosape, was one of the three head chiefs of the Blackfoot, in company with Big Swan and Crowfoot. Big Swan died of tuberculosis in 1872 and by 1877, when Treaty Seven was negotiated with the Blackfoot, Old Sun was too old and feeble to participate actively in decision making. In 1882, at the suggestion of the NWMP, Old Sun led his followers up the Bow River, to a location that became the North Camp of the Blackfoot Reserve. (See Dempsey 1972, pp. 61, 70, 97, 145.) The location of Morris's portraits of Old Sun and his wife is not known.

37. John Three Bulls, John Drunken Chief or John Taking His Own Gun, Awatsini-amarkau, was a foster brother of Crowfoot and succeeded him as head chief of the Blackfoot (see Dempsey 1979, p. 15). Edmund Morris portrayed a nephew of John Three Bulls, named after the chief, twice (ROM HK 2426; Glenbow Museum 64.7.1).

38. The portrait of Black Eagle, Sixsipita, is ROM HK 2415.

39. The Black Soldiers were a policing force of men selected from within the Blackfoot tribe. One of their main duties was to prevent individuals from disturbing the buffalo herds by hunting alone or in any other way that would limit the success of the group hunt or allow unequal opportunity. They also enforced participation in tribal rituals.

40. This reference would be to the Liberal federal government of Sir Wilfrid Laurier, prime minister from 1896 to 1911.

41. High Eagle, Pitauspitau, was, like Iron Shield, related to Crowfoot; he was

portrayed by Edmund Morris in 1909 (Government of Alberta 0367–300–65).

42. Morris portrayed very few Indian women and this is one of the rare comments he made in his diary on the good looks of an Indian woman.

43. Morris often completed the pastel in one or two sessions, and the only mention he makes of preparing sketches is for the portrait of Little Shield (see p. 112).

44. The portrait of a Far Away Voice or Echo, Piiskini, is ROM HK 2414.

45. Grinnell (1962, p. 220) confirms this practice, stating that for her first offence of adultery the offending wife's nose and ears were cut off by her husband; for the second offence she was killed by an All Comrades policing association.

46. Bear's Hat, Kyaiyistumokon, spent five years fighting against the Crow Indians; he then returned to live among the Blackfoot where, following the advice of the North West Mounted Police, he lived peacefully.

47. Blackfoot Crossing was the only site where the Bow River could be forded when it was flooded. Alexander Morris records details of Treaty Seven negotiations (1971, pp. 245–75, 368–74). Lieutenant Governor David Laird (1833–1914), appointed first resident governor and superintendent of Indian Affairs of the North West Territories in 1876, when they were organized as a separate administrative unit, with headquarters in the territories' capital, Battleford, Saskatchewan; he held the post until 1881. When minister of the interior in the federal government, he had assisted Alexander Morris in Treaty Four negotiations; he was head commissioner for Treaty Seven, negotiated with the Blackfoot in 1877.

48. Onistaipoka—White Buffalo Calf, White Buffalo Child, Calf Child, also sometimes called Lone Chief, and called Big Charley by the British—was a war chief of the North Camp of the Blackfoot Reserve and at one time a great warrior and medicine man. Morris portrayed him in 1907 (ROM HK 2412) and in 1909 (Government of Alberta 0367–300–64). His exploits were painted for Morris on a buffalo robe and Morris transcribed the story in his diary (pp. 104–6); a robe that was part of Edmund Morris's bequest to the Royal Ontario Museum is believed to be that of Calf Child (ROM HK 460).

49. Blindness in old age, such as Calf Child suffered, was common among the Plains Indians, owing to long exposure to bright sunlight, or to venereal disease.

50. Joe was noted for having received several jail sentences. Morris left a buffalo robe with Calf Child to have a record of events in his life painted on it; Joe began the project, but, as Morris mentions later (p. 102), he proved too dilatory. Calf Child had other Indians complete the painting.

51. Crow Shoe, also called Face Red With Earth, Mastoitsikin, a Blackfoot head man, was described by Morris (1909, p. 14, no. 31) as being more than 6 ft (183 cm) tall and of fine bearing; Morris's portrait of him is ROM HK 2411.

52. Sir Henry Irving (1838–1905), whose real name was John Brodribb, was an English actor and producer, and manager of the London Lyceum; a controversial figure for his new and startling productions, he would have been well known in literary circles in Morris's day.

53. Father Léon Doucet, OMI, (1847–1942) served for many years as a Roman Catholic priest and missionary in parishes and missions in Alberta; he was the founder of the Roman Catholic mission at the South Camp of the Blackfoot Reserve. Doucet was called Little Father by the Indians.

54. The Reverend John William Tims (1857–1945), Anglican missionary, was appointed to the North Camp of the Blackfoot Reserve in 1883, but was forced to leave by the chief White Pup, as Morris describes in his diary, because Tims disapproved of White Pup's hiring out his daughters to white men. Tims went to work with the Sarcee and was replaced at the North Camp of the Blackfoot Reserve by Canon H. W. G. Stocken. Tims was an authority on the Blackfoot language, and

published a grammar and dictionary of the Blackfoot language in 1889 and a translation of the gospel into Blackfoot.

55. This would be Bishop Pinkham of the Anglican church, visited earlier by Morris.

56. Father Albert Lacombe, OMI, (1827–ca 1916) preceded Father Doucet among the Blackfoot, and spent many years among the Cree of the upper North Saskatchewan River, where he founded two missions. Lacombe was called Good Heart by the Indians. During his life, he founded the village of St Albert, Alberta (in 1861), wrote translations of several religious and educational works, drew together a manuscript dictionary of Blackfoot, and published a grammar and dictionary of Cree. His life is recorded by Hughes (1914).

57. Father Constantine Michael (Pat) Scollen, OMI, (1841–1902) was born in Ireland and came to Canada as a Roman Catholic missionary in 1862; he worked at Fort Edmonton and among the Cree and Blackfoot, 1862–81, and constructed the first Roman Catholic mission among the Blackfoot, at the present site of Calgary. He witnessed negotiations of treaties Six and Seven (see Morris 1971, pp. 183, 266, 362). He was noted as a linguist in Cree, Blackfoot, and Siouan and assisted Father Lacombe in the preparation of his Cree grammar and dictionary.

58. Norman Macleod was a son of Lieutenant-Colonel J. F. Macleod.

59. Lieutenant-Colonel Frederick White (1847–1918) was appointed comptroller of the NWMP in 1880; in 1905, he was also named commissioner of the North West Territories (courtesy RCMP).

60. Sir John Alexander Macdonald, first prime minister of Canada; Sir Alexander Tilloch Galt, finance minister in Macdonald's cabinet in 1867; Galt viewed his party's policy towards the Indians favourably.

61. Sir Wilfrid Laurier's federal government, 1896–1911, was in power during a period of economic restraint and showed little support for the expenses necessary for aid to the Indians.

62. Edmund Francis James Dalrymple Clark (1848–80), lieutenant and adjutant of the North West Mounted Police, was much respected for his services with the force. He was distantly related to Sir John A. Macdonald and a friend of the Alexander Morris family (courtesy RCMP). Clark accompanied commissioners of treaties Six and Seven, signing as witness (see Morris 1971, pp. 359, 373, 375), and was appointed to the NWMP in 1873, remaining there until his death (see Haydon 1971, p. 75).

63. Hayter Reed was assistant commissioner of Indian Affairs at the time of the North West Rebellion (see MacEwan 1971, p. 120).

64. Indians of the West Coast used yellow-cedar dugout canoes for transportation both on rivers and in the Pacific Ocean.

65. Stanley Gzowski, an engineer, was responsible for the completion of the CPR trans-Canada railroad and other projects for Sir John A. Macdonald's government.

66. The Sarcee (Sarsi) tribe are of Athapaskan or Dene stock, related to the Beaver, Hare, Yellow Knife, Dog Rib, and Chipewyan tribes (see Jenness 1977, pp. 19, 324–25); the Sarcee once lived farther north, and it is believed that they migrated south at approximately the same time as the Blackfoot. The Sarcee were friendly with the Blackfoot but an enemy of most other tribes in their more southerly settlement area; this possibly resulted from the fact that the Sarcee language, of the Athapaskan language group, was not understood by surrounding tribes. The Sarcee population was greatly reduced by constant warfare; when not in battle, the tribe lived in virtual isolation.

67. Alexander James McNeill was federal Indian Affairs agent for the Sarcee Reserve, 1897–1911.

68. York boats, pointed at both ends and with dimensions of 8.53–12.19 m (28–40

ft) length × 2.13–2.44 m (7–8 ft) width × 0.91–1.22 m (3–4 ft) depth, were used for river travel (courtesy Department of Ethnology, ROM).

69. Bull Head, half Blood and half Sarcee, head chief of the Sarcee, received the gun and authority of his eldest brother, Little Chief, Tçillah, along with his eldest brother's name. Morris's portrait of Bull Head/Little Chief is part of his bequest to the Royal Ontario Museum (ROM HK 2410) along with a buffalo robe describing the chief's exploits (ROM HK 459).

70. Big Plume, also called Old Man, Omuk sa pop, Blackfoot; distinct from Jim Big Plume, nephew of Bull Head, and from Big Plume, brother of Bull Head, both the latter being deceased at the time of Morris's western journeys.

71. Morris crossed out the lines within square brackets; they have been transcribed for reference. Grinnell (1962, pp. 137–44) relates a Blackfoot story of Creation that is similar to this version, with the addition that the Old Man threw a buffalo chip into the river. Grinnell also discusses the Blackfoot concept of Old Man as both a creator and a trickster (1962, pp. 256–58). John Maclean, an Anglican missionary who worked with the Blackfoot, described Old Man as "not the same as the Great Spirit, but a secondary creator" who "appears in legends as a good and bad being...a benefactor...full of deceit and various kinds of tricks" (Maclean 1896, p. 52).

72. Morris's portrait of Big Wolf is ROM HK 2406.

73. Philip Carteret Hill Primrose was appointed superintendent of the NWMP in 1899, first of the B Division at Dawson and then of the D Division at Fort Macleod (see Haydon 1971, pp. 36, 214, 365).

74. The Blood Reserve is located in southern Alberta, east of Fort Macleod; the tribe had moved from north of Edmonton in the 1800s.

75. Edmund Morris recorded in a notebook (now in the Department of Ethnology, ROM) the paintings he made and sold; these records indicate that Morris drew portraits of several deceased Indian figures from photographs.

76. Duncan Campbell was sheriff at Fort Macleod in 1887, the sheriff being an official appointed by the attorney general and not having police duties (courtesy RCMP).

77. R. S. MacDonell, who once owned a store in Cluny, Alberta.

78. Julian Ralph, an adventurer, wrote a report of his travels (Ralph 1892). He spent several years travelling in western Canada.

79. Jean L'Heureux, a French-Canadian voyageur and adventurer, spent many years among the Blackfoot and learned the Blackfoot language; he was signator of the Blackfoot Treaty (see Morris 1971, p. 373) and served on many occasions as interpreter, for example, at treaty negotiations (see Morris 1971, pp. 253, 260) and when the adventurer Julian Ralph travelled among the Blackfoot (see Ralph 1892, pp. 28–30, 34–35). He is commented on by many contemporary authors since he presented himself as a priest to the Blackfoot, even though he had no training, and performed many religious rites among the Indians. The Indians saw him as a priest, giving him the name "Three in One" (see p. 121). Dempsey (1972, p. 83 n.) gives details of L'Heureux's life.

80. This former NWMP officer, proprietor of the Queen's Hotel, was part of Alexander Morris's escort when the latter administered Treaty Six at Fort Pitt in September 1876.

81. Robert Nathaniel Wilson, federal Indian Affairs agent for the Blood Reserve, 1904–11 (courtesy Public Archives of Canada).

82. George Bird Grinnell (1849–1938) was author of several books on legends, stories, and the way of life of Indians (e.g., Grinnell 1962).

83. Henry Rowe Schoolcraft lived among Indian tribes for thirty years and was author of a number of books on his travels and on his studies of Indian customs.

84. Traders at the Vermilion Post received furs from a large area farther north. The Slave (Awokanak) and Beaver (Tsattine, or dwellers among the beavers) Indians, both peoples of Athapaskan linguistic stock, inhabited the upper waters of the Peace River and the Mackenzie River system. When trading posts were built along the two rivers, the Slave changed their whole pattern of life in order to obtain trade goods; instead of following an annual cycle in search of fish and moose meat, they turned to trapping fur-bearing animals as their livelihood. The Hudson's Bay Company valued the Beaver for their skills in hunting and trapping.

85. Laurence Clark, chief factor of the Hudson's Bay Company at Carlton House, was present at Fort Carlton treaty negotiations (see Morris 1971, p. 181).

86. Morris's portrait of Bull Shield, Stumixowotan, Blood chief, is ROM HK 2427.

87. Morris's portrait of Strangle Wolf, Maquaestupista, Blood chief, is ROM HK 2425.

88. As a result of his education by the Yukon trader in Fort Benton, Montana, Joe Healey, Potaina or Potina, spoke English. He adopted the name of the trader; his portrait by Edmund Morris is ROM HK 2401.

89. Such shields were "made from the thick hide of the buffalo bull's neck, shrunken over a fire in the ground, and trimmed into a circular form about 18 inches in diameter" (Ewers 1945, p. 24). The decorations on the buffalo shield illustrated by Morris, from Robert Wilson's collection, are typical and were "symbolic medicine paintings intended to protect the shield owner in war" (Ewers 1945, p. 24). This shield is now in the collection of the National Museum of Man.

90. Red Crow (ca 1830–1900), Mekaisto, head chief of the south Blood, signed Treaty Seven at Blackfoot Crossing (see Morris 1971, pp. 259, 372). His life story has recently been published by Dempsey (1980).

91. Bull Plume, Stumiksisapo, a Blackfoot who was adopted in early life into the Peigan tribe and who became a chief of that tribe, was one of the four Peigan chiefs who recounted his exploits in designs on a buffalo robe (ROM HK 461) that Edmund Morris left with the tribe. Morris portrayed him twice (ROM HK 2407; Art Gallery of Ontario 655).

92. The chiefs travelled with Robert Wilson beyond Winnipeg to Ottawa and Toronto.

93. Haydon also describes the arrest of Charcoal (1971, pp. 182–85). In October 1896, Charcoal, alias Bad Young Man, killed another Blood Indian, Medicine Pipe Stem, for tampering with his wife. This incident and Charcoal's desire to kill Red Crow, who was chief of the Blood at the time, were reported to the NWMP; in a chase that ensued a NWMP sergeant was shot to death. Charcoal was finally turned over to the police by his brothers Left Hand and Bear's Back Bone, with whom he had taken refuge, and was tried and executed. His life was related by Dempsey (1978).

94. Edward Blake (1833–1912), lawyer, was premier of Ontario in 1871/72, and then entered federal politics in the Alexander Mackenzie administration, serving as minister of justice from 1875 to 1877. Blake gave lighter sentences than was customary for acts that were viewed by Europeans as misdeeds but were performed as a consequence of the offender's religious convictions.

95. In Canada this tribe is the aputoksi-pikuni, or north Peigans; in the United States it is the amiskapi-pikuni, or south Peigans (see Dempsey 1979, p. 29). The three tribes of the Blackfoot nation once lived farther north, but migrated southwards into the territory occupied by the Crow. The Peigans preceded the Blood and the Blackfoot in this migration and spread over a wider area. The Peigan Reserve in Canada is on the Oldman River, west of Macleod, Alberta.

96. Brother John Birchman was stationed at the Roman Catholic mission on the Peigan Reserve; the Peigan Indians called him "Our Brother".

97. Mr Yeomans was federal Indian Affairs agent for the Peigan reserve; the North West Angle Treaty referred to was Treaty Three, signed with the Ojibwa at Fort Frances, Ontario, in 1873 (see Morris 1971, pp. 44, 45).

98. See the genealogy on page 9 for names and dates of Edmund Morris's sisters and brothers. Evidence that Christine van Koughnet Morris accompanied Alexander Morris on the journey for the signing of Treaty Three is found in her signature on the treaty, the text of which is printed in Morris (1971, p. 325). The second eldest sister, Elizabeth Cochran Morris, was also probably present—both sisters signed Treaty Five (see Morris 1971, p. 348).

99. A reference to Lesser Slave Lake, called Lake of the Strangers by the Cree; the pyramid is located near Great Slave Lake and is believed to commemorate the southerly migration of the Sarcee tribe from their parent tribe, the Beaver. Dempsey (1979, pp. 36, 72) believes this separation took place long before the arrival of fur traders, citing a reference from 1772/73 by Matthew Cocking to them as a distinct tribe of "Equestrian Indians".

100. Les Soeurs de la charité, or Grey Nuns, a religious order active in the care of the aged and infirm, worked with the Oblates of Mary Immaculate order of priests at Roman Catholic missions on the Plains.

101. This may be a reference to the Atsina, who according to tradition were once of the Arapaho, and who also spoke an Algonkian dialect; historically the Atsina tended to ally with the Blackfoot, their neighbours (for further information, see Kehoe 1981, p. 280–81). They were known to other Arapaho as Hituena, "beggars" or "spongers"; whence the tribal sign, commonly but incorrectly rendered "belly people" or "big bellies"—Gros Ventres, distinct from the Gros Ventres of the Missouri.

102. The name Snake was applied to many different bodies of Shoshonean speaking tribes, particularly those of eastern Oregon.

103. James Willard Schultz (1859–1947), an American adventurer from St Louis, Missouri, lived for many years in Alberta among the Blackfoot as one of them, moving camp, fighting in battles, and marrying a Blackfoot woman. Morris refers to pp. 47, 51 of Schultz (1907); Schultz was author of several other books (e.g., Schultz 1962).

104. Crowfoot was approached repeatedly by emissaries from Louis Riel, and his younger tribesmen were keen to join the Cree in the revolt, but he kept them under control and remained loyal to the Canadian government (see MacEwan 1971, p. 87); he knew that the Indians depended on the government for financial support now that their traditional lifestyle was no longer possible.

105. Poundmaker (1826–86), Pee too kah han or Oo pee too cah hay an a pee wee yin, died of consumption in 1886 shortly after serving a jail term for assisting in the North West Rebellion of 1885 (see MacEwan 1971, p. 114); he was buried on a hill near Blackfoot Crossing, Alberta, near the grave of his adopted father, Crowfoot. In 1967, his grave was moved to the Poundmaker reserve near Cut Knife, Saskatchewan (see Sluman 1967, p. 301), and in 1972, it was marked by the framework of a large tipi. Edmund Morris drew portraits of Poundmaker in 1907 (ROM HK 2444) and 1909 (Government of Saskatchewan Collection).

106. Before becoming head chief of the Blackfoot Confederacy, Many Swans, Akka Makkoye, was chief of the North Camp.

107. Eagle Flying Against the Wind, Pitamowinasi, a Blackfoot adopted by the Peigan tribe; Morris's portrait of him is ROM HK 2423.

108. The Reverend George McDougall, a Methodist missionary, set up the first Methodist mission in Alberta, at Edmonton in 1871, and the second, on the Bow River, northeast of Calgary in 1873. He froze to death near the Bow River mission; a small white memorial church stands on the site of that mission. McDougall acted as advisor to the Indians for the negotiations of Treaty Six at Fort Carlton and Fort Pitt (see

Morris 1971, pp. 172–75). One of his three sons, John McDougall, continued his missionary work in Alberta.

109. Big Swan, Akamakal, was one of the Peigan chiefs who recounted his exploits in designs on the buffalo robe that Morris left with the tribe (ROM HK 461). Morris's portrait of him is ROM HK 2424. Dempsey (1979, p. 30) mentions that by 1882 Big Swan was among those Peigans who had success as farmers, particularly in growing potatoes.

110. Reference is to Treaty Seven, signed in 1877 at Blackfoot Crossing.

111. Running Wolf, Apisomakau, a Peigan chief, son of the former chief Iron Shirt and grandson of former chief Sun Bull, was well known for his knowledge of traditional eagle-hunting rituals. Morris's portrait of him is ROM HK 2405.

112. Antoine Hoke, a Sioux medicine man, was portrayed by Edmund Morris in 1908 (ROM HK 2437). Reference is to Edmund Morris's father, Lieutenant Governor Alexander Morris; two reserves were established for the Sioux in 1874, and one in 1876 (see Morris 1971, pp. 276–84).

113. Reference is to the Battle at Little Big Horn, Montana, in 1876 between General George Armstrong Custer, with his unit of 225 men, and the Sioux, under the leadership of Sitting Bull and other chiefs. The furor resulting from General Custer's defeat led to the Sioux's fleeing to Canada for asylum (see MacEwan 1971, p. 131).

114. Sweet Grass, Wee kas koo kee say yin, was a Crow Indian adopted into the Plains Cree in Saskatchewan; he became the principal chief of the Plains Cree and was an influential and respected leader. He refused, as Edmund Morris describes, to take part in the Sioux scheme to annihilate all Europeans. On the advice of Father Scollen, Alexander Morris sent for Sweet Grass, who was on a hunt, to attend the making of the Fort Pitt treaty; Sweet Grass led the negotiations in a friendly manner, and encouraged other Cree leaders to sign the treaty, asking only that the buffalo be protected (see Morris 1971, pp. 183, 190, 191, 229). Edmund Morris relates the circumstances of Sweet Grass's death, which occurred a few months after the signing of Treaty Six (see pp. 125, 140–42). In 1909 Morris portrayed Sweet Grass from a photograph (Government of Saskatchewan Collection).

115. Alexander Morris also records this incident (1971, p. 189). William Joseph Christie, chief factor of the Saskatchewan District of the Hudson's Bay Company, served with Alexander Morris as commissioner for Treaty Six (see Morris 1971, pp. 170, 177). A. D. Jackes, MD, was secretary to the commissioners for treaties Five and Six (see Morris 1971, pp. 180, 348, 357).

116. Probably a reference to Brother John Birchman; Crow Eagle, Mastepitah, Peigan chief, signed Treaty Seven (see Morris 1971, p. 373) and a photograph of him is included in Dempsey (1979, p. 29).

117. Unistaipoka, the wife of Old Sun, was one of the very few Blackfoot women to be allowed to wear three feathers and to sit on Blackfoot councils. Photocopies of Edmund Morris's portraits of Old Sun and Unistaipoka, made from photographs in 1907 for the Department of Indian Affairs in Ottawa, are in the Provincial Archives of Manitoba, but no originals have been located.

118. Butcher, Stokinota, Peigan, born in Montana and belonging to the family of an earlier Peigan head chief, Eagle Tail, became head chief, successor to Crow Eagle; he was one of the Peigan chiefs who portrayed their life events on the buffalo robe that Edmund Morris left with the tribe (ROM HK 461). Morris's portrait of Butcher is ROM HK 2409. Hungry Chief or Man Angry with Hunger, Minnikonotsi, was also Peigan; Morris's portrait of him is ROM HK 2422.

119. The Stoney are Assiniboine (Assiniboine is an Ojibwa term meaning "those who cook with stones"), who in turn are, by tradition, a branch of the Yankton Sioux. With the growth of the Hudson's Bay Company, the Assiniboine took up the

opportunity for business in supplying pemmican to Company traders; bands scattered, from their earlier settlements, westwards to concentrate on buffalo hunting on the Prairies, and western groups became known as the Stoney (see Kehoe 1981, p. 284). Their reserve is near Morley, Alberta. Thomas James Fleetham was federal Indian Affairs agent for the Stoney Reserve, 1904–11.

120. Reference is to Rocky Mountain House, Alberta, a Hudson's Bay Company trading post.

121. Brûlé was a general term used in the Canadian West to describe people who were Indian or part Indian; the Métis were known as the bois-brûlé, for example (courtesy Saskatchewan Archives Board). Brule was also the name of a subdivision of the Teton Sioux, who in turn were a division of Siouan people (see Kehoe 1981, p. 283).

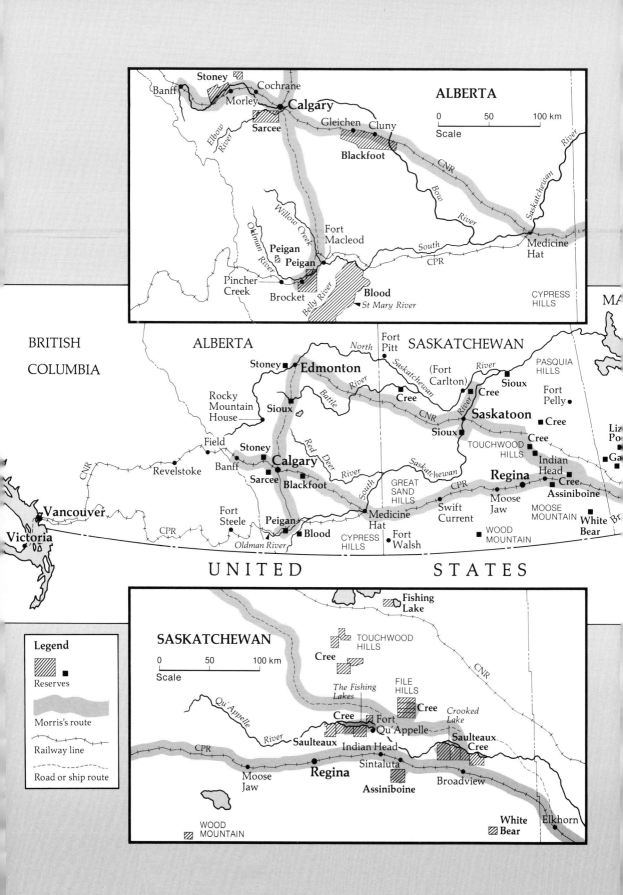

Western Journey 1908

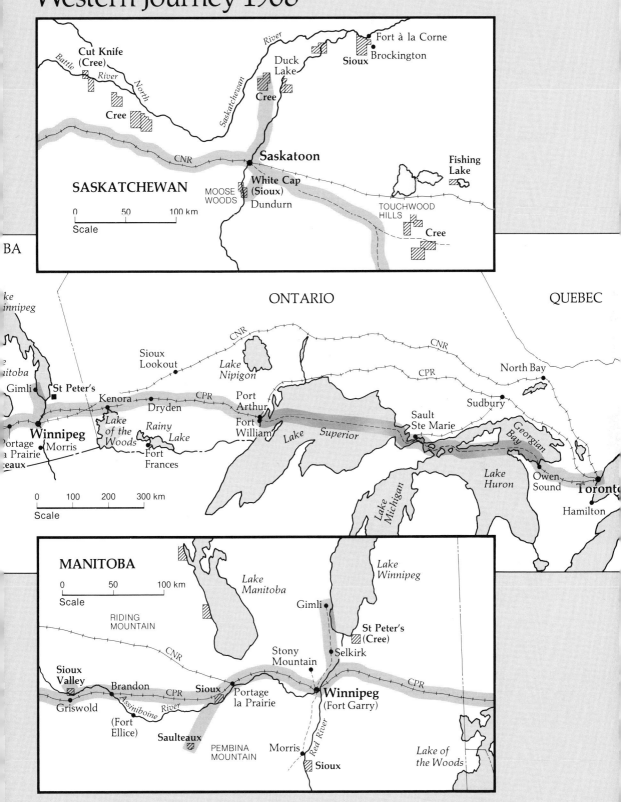

SASKATCHEWAN

Cut Knife
(Cree)

Battle
River

North

Duck
Lake

Cree

River

Sioux
Brockington
Fort à la Corne

Cree

Cree

Saskatchewan

CNR

Saskatoon

White Cap
(Sioux)

MOOSE
WOODS

Dundurn

Fishing
Lake

TOUCHWOOD
HILLS

Cree

0   50   100 km
Scale

BA

ONTARIO   QUEBEC

ke
innipeg

itoba

Gimli   St Peter's

Sioux
Lookout

Lake
Nipigon

CNR

CNR

CPR

North Bay

Kenora

Dryden

CPR

Port
Arthur

Fort
William

Lake   *Superior*

Sault
Ste Marie

Sudbury

Georgian
Bay

Owen
Sound

Winnipeg

ortage
a Prairie
eaux

Morris

Lake
of the
Woods

Rainy
Lake

Fort
Frances

Lake
Michigan

Lake
Huron

Toronto

Hamilton

0   100   200   300 km
Scale

MANITOBA

0   50   100 km
Scale

RIDING
MOUNTAIN

Lake
Manitoba

Lake
Winnipeg

Gimli

St Peter's
(Cree)

CNR

Stony
Mountain

Selkirk

Sioux
Valley

Brandon

CPR

Sioux

Portage
la Prairie

Winnipeg
(Fort Garry)

CPR

Griswold

Assiniboine   *River*

(Fort
Ellice)

Saulteaux

PEMBINA
MOUNTAIN

Morris

Red River

Sioux

Lake of
the Woods

Left Toronto CPR 26th June & the steamer "Manitoba" at Owen Sound. Arrive Port Arthur 28 at 12. Go on to Winnipeg 8:30—arriving 29th at 10, stop at Corona Hotel.

Call on Mr. Laird, late Lieut. Governor of the North West Territories—now in charge of the Indian Office[1]—& with him go over the course for me to take. I found many of the men I hoped to see have passed away.

Poor Darby Taylor very ill & much changed.

The Manitoba Club purchased one of my Indian portraits & I presented another—the portrait of Iron Shield, the other was Strangle Wolf.[2] The members all like them. At the club I meet D. H. Macdonald of Fort Qu'Appelle who had gone to St. John's College with my brothers.

Went to Selkirk & out to the St. Peter's Reserve. Saw chief Prince, who had gone to the Soudan as a chief voyageur.[3] He wore two Egyptian medals. He looks the breed & has a grey moustache.

The Indians have a picturesque village by the river—all living in houses. The nearness of the town of Selkirk is disastrous. The young men spend all their time in the poolrooms—& bars. They are to be removed farther north tho' it is optional with them.

Go on to Gimli, the Icelandic settlement on Lake Winnipeg,[4] from there to Clandeboye & hunt up the chief John Prince, who with others was present at my father's funeral.[5] It was he who when someone present asked if they came by accident said, "no the great spirit called me here to be by the side of my friend." He is now very aged & is life councillor. He was very pleased to see me. I took some photos of him.

Am returning to Winnipeg for the Col. Irvine had come in to see me.

Out to Portage la Prairie—Jack Birnie drives me to Yellow Quill's reserve, 30 miles distant—arriving at Indian Smoke, I find all away, the Chief having gone to a dance given by some far away chief & will not return for a month, so I have to drive the 30 miles back over a rough road—cold & dark before we reach town. Many years ago this same month my father had gone over the same trail to settle disputes & allot land to this Saulteaux band.[6]

Go on to Brandon. Many Indians have come for the fair. The Pipestone Sioux, the Griswold Sioux & Saulteaux.[7] Meet the noted Sioux Old Antoine, a medicine man who had been a leader in the Minnesota massacre, & Wanduti who wears a King George medal. Antoine said my father told him they might live on this soil in peace & see their children & grandchildren growing up about them & it had come true.

The Indians dance every night.

I go on to Broadview & stop at the home of Mrs. Magnus Begg whose husband was agent to the Blackfoot[8] & her father Rev. John MacDougall, the missionary. From here drive out to the Crooked Lake agency, about 9 miles. Mr. Millar is agent & Mr. Saywell, a relative of General Brock, is clerk.[9] I board with him. The Indians are all assembled for the Treaty payment.

I had written Mr. Millar I was coming to paint the portraits of some of the best types to be found, but he could not make out my lengthy plans & with hair standing up & eyes protruding asked the clerk who this man was who was coming to make portraits for the Indians. He was relieved when he found out my mission. I arranged with the agent to let them have a dance. It was very fine. Each band had a pole erected & they formed around them & danced. They placed a seat for myself & the agent & the leader of the dance presented me with a fine headdress with eagle plumes from head to foot.

Old Peter Hourie, the son of an Orkney soldier who had fought at Waterloo and a Snake Indian woman brought up by Mr. Baird, a chief factor of the H.B.Co. Hourie had been present at the Treaty my father made at Fort Carlton & was interpreter for General Middleton.[10] His son Torence captured Louis Reil.[11] At night the scouts keep up a continuous song in the Indian encampment.

I paint Acoose, Man Standing Above Ground. He is 61 years—his father still lives, kept by the priests, though he is 103 years. His mind is quite clear & I talked with him in French.[12] He is blind & his skin looks like parchment. His name was known far & wide in his time.[13] Acoose was the fleetest of the Saulteaux. He used to compete with the whites in races & always outrun them. He went to moose hunt once & fell in with 9 elk. His bullets had slipped through his pocket so he ran them down the first day then drove them 60 miles to his own camp at Goose Lake & killed them. This brought him renown in his tribe.[14] His great grandfather & his mother were half-breeds. Penepo Resiell, his brother, has blue eyes—a fine type of athlete whom I saw play football. Active as a youth, he wore long braids of hair & a brass decoration tied to the scalp lock. Acoose's son Paul is coming to the fore in races—at Winnipeg _____ ran against _____ the Englishman.

Drive down to the Roman Mission. The view of the Qu'Appelle Valley & Crooked Lake is very beautiful & here are many subjects for landscape. I look up Nepahpenais, Night Bird, sometime chief of Cowessess Band of the Saulteaux.[15] He agrees to come to be painted & gives me a present of his fire bag of buckskin & beadwork. These are called fire bags, they used to carry the tobacco, & flint & punk with which they ignited fire. He was once Presbyterian but the Romanists got his wife & family to join their church & he finally went with them. He is 74 years of age. At 18 he joined a war party & counted 3 coups. He was in 7 battles—once in Inkster hunting the buffalo his party was surrounded by 700 Sioux.[17] Though they only numbered 46 they held out for 2 days, killing many Sioux, & only losing two of their men. The Sioux gave up the fight & they escaped. Another time the Sioux swept down on their camp & stole 200 horses. They used to go on the warpath by way of Red River & as far as Little Devils's Lake across the border.

I have a house at my disposal for a studio and regularly every morning I hear old Peter Hourie coming with his big walking stick & he stays till I stop work, interpreting for me.

(Diary page 61)

They fought—84 Sioux killed, 4 Saulteaux the _____—half breeds. It lasted all day.

18TH

(Diary pages 62–67)

Mrs. Padgett is wrong in referring to them as deer.

20TH

Against a Sioux war party—he joined them & went from Red Lake,[16] he & others, for Palmesan came, making 98 men—going to Quills Reserve, Goose Reserve, & Mission Reserve—approaching the river, they heard the shots of the Sioux ring chasing the buffalo—one chased a buffalo towards river, & they killed him. He visited the Mandan tribes— a friendly visit.

Across the border near Missouri River.[19] They had 60 guns. As the camp moved after the buffalo they saw a large camp of the Sioux. Before being seen they _____ about, trotting quickly to a table land, & unhitched. They sent 3 half breed scouts who neared the camp. They heard the Sioux in council— would make peace with the half breeds & go to camp & kill all. 2 of the scouts spurred their horses. They surrounded the third & killed him—the others told all.

He tells me they always went on foot on the war path because they could easily hide from the enemy. They painted their faces because it concealed their change of colour & hid faces. They never carried their war clothes.

(Diary pages 68–69)

He has a pension from the Govt. but the house they gave him is in a hole in the ground & this worried the old man who would like to look out upon the horizon.

The Indians are encamped in a large circle. At night three or four Indians on horseback ride up & down the centre of the camp as guards & keep up a continuous chant. This is a very old custom—though it is becoming obsolete.

Walter Ochopowace, the hereditary chief of these Crees & grandson of Loud Voice who signed the Treaty, comes with a beadwork decoration for a horse's head.[18] His brother Jack sells me a straight pipe, which belonged to Loud Voice, & also his gorget. Sold his own war pipe, but before I got up to leave the lodge he said, wait—and asked me to sit down.

It was dusk & we encircled the fire in the centre of the lodge. He had sweet grass burning & held the stem of the pipe over this, then pointed it to the heavens, then to the Earth and to the four cardinal points, chanting the while—Every night my fathers do this—and as he was so much moved, I told him not to part with the pipe, but keep it in remembrance of his fathers.

There is here a very astute old medicine man, Wah pe kine wap, Sitting White Eagle. The Indians pass by the white doctors and go to him to be cured. He comes to be painted.[20] He is 70 years—in his day was a great warrior. At 12 he got in with a war party against the South Blackfoot. He was in 5 battles with the Sioux, 5 with the Blackfoot, 5 with the Blood, and 5 with the Crows. On some occasions he was the only Saulteaux with the Crees in their frays. He has killed many men in a hand to hand fight with many thrown aside their guns. He says the black beads on his coat stand for shots fired at him which took no effect—bulletproof.[21] He and others were once captured by the Piegans. There were hundreds of Piegans all about & in broad daylight he came out, walked straight out of the camp, the others following him, & not one Piegan saw that man! He tells me they never kept scalps for more than 2 months, then would select a nice spot & bury them. Both he & Nepahpenais tell me the Sun Dance has nothing to do with making braves but is a religious ceremony & they torture themselves to carry out a vow made to the sun.[22] An Indian becomes a brave when he takes a scalp while under fire of the enemy or by killing a man in battle. Sitting White Eagle is a son of As gun rn shep. The last claims a Saulteaux by a Swampy woman who belonged to the tribe of Cut Nose Chief, who was party to the Treaty made by Lord Selkirk.[23] His people came from Lake Manitoba & Lake Winnipeg. Going to war at 12 he saw fighting & at 20 he was in a fight—one of the hostiles got shot through the leg & fled to his lodge. He followed him up & scalped him—for this he still wears a feather in his bearskin cap. The other feather is for another encounter—a Sioux levelled his gun at him. He threw his away & the Sioux did the same & both engaged with scalping knives. He killed the Sioux & took his scalp.

Lt. Col. McDonald, with Peter Hourie as interpreter, brought a number of these Indians to the East in 1886, and I remember them calling upon my father at _____ & my brother Wm. & I saw them off at the train.[24] The party consisted of Mis to was is, O'Soup, Ka kn wis ta hah, Atakakoop, Flying in a

Man Sitting in the Middle of the Sun, Nowwekeshequappew, Saulteaux. Pastel on paper, 1908. Dimensions 62.5 × 50 cm. Edmund Morris Collection. ROM HK 2429.

Photograph of a catlinite pipe with wooden stem, given to Edmund Morris by Sitting White Eagle. Stem is decorated with brass tacks and strings of small red, yellow, and light green beads. Total length 78 cm. Bequest of Edmund Morris. ROM HK 210.

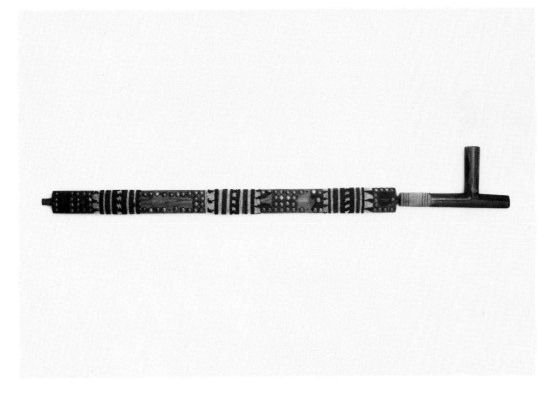

Circle. Peter Hourie tells me interesting details of this trip & of a visit he made to Great Falls, Montana. Walter Ochopowace is my last model at this reserve. Besides this portrait from life I have made many photographs as I have such exceptional chances & its services will be invaluable. One I took of the medicine man Sitting White Eagle. He raises his fingers to the heavens, looks upwards! and to the horizon.*

I drive into Broadview with Mr. Millar, the agent. Stop overnight, going on to Sintaluta in the morning & from there drive to the Assiniboine agency. Mr. W. S. Grant is agent here, a stout gentleman.[26] He was at one time in the Mounted Police & with my father at Fort Ellice.[27] He has been many years with the Assiniboines & a short interval with the Crees at Hobbema—5 years. After lunch he drove me to the camp of the chief Carry the Kettle.[28]

The Assiniboines once had heard questions about Indian Head, which drew its name from the skulls of those who died of smallpox & were left on the hilltop about 90 years ago.[29]

They were called wat a tapan cause, men travelling in canoes made of skins. When the Treaty was made by my father at Fort Qu'Appelle in 1876 this band was off hunting the buffalo[30]—so Mr. Laird dealt with them later on, at Maple Creek or Fort Walsh. In 1882, they were sent to Qu'Appelle and thence to Sintaluta Reserve. The same fall they all went off after the buffalo & were reluctant to return. The police rounded them up & sent them back in boxcars. As luck would have it, the cars went off the tracks & upset. Some got badly injured—& pandemonium reigned. They believed the engineer did it purposely & wanted to kill him. The chief's wife got her arm broken & he threatened to shoot the engineer. Old Sharp Tooth—or The Wasp—on the warpath with an axe, threatening right & left. This old boy lived to be 120. Little Mountain was in the thick of it. He was a bad actor having killed some whites in the States & the American Govt. had $500 on his head.

There are tribes of the Assiniboines at Moose Mountain near Carlisle[31] & these used to be at constant warfare with the Sioux. Living near the border they crossed often—St. Anne & Morley.[32] They have similar legends of the origin of the Earth as the Blackfoot & other races, but instead of Napi it is Inktomi.

Chief Chag a kin, Carry the Kettle, tells of his adventures at war & the buffalo hunt. He is like an actor & by his sign language I could follow without the interpreter. A big number of Indians come with the chief & crowd around to see how the portrait is made—till I have to order them away.

The night before, young Grant & I took a walk & came upon the Council lodge. They were all assembled & I fixed on the men to paint. The most striking is Big Darkness, The Turtle, an old man, & The Runner, younger brother of the chief.[33] I now found the reasons of the Council. They were making _____ & put the questions to me: to get 25% duty taken off the horses which they get as presents from the kinsmen in Montana. Horses under a year old come free—but for others to come the duty they have to part with sure to make up this amount. The next, they wanted a stud horse for the reserve. They had not spoken to Grant about this. He will get a stud for them.

Photograph of Carry the Kettle. Edmund Morris Collection 35. Courtesy Provincial Archives of Manitoba.

The Spring Man, Kahmeeusekahmaweyenew, Cree. Pastel on paper, 1908. Dimensions 62.5 × 50 cm. Edmund Morris Collection. ROM HK 2433.

The chief got his name when a small boy. His people had crossed the border near the mountains (Rocky) after the buffalo—he strayed away & got lost. When they found him he had a little copper kettle which he carried for water & cooking in. He killed his first hostile when quite a young fellow. Killed two only. They do not count the men shot in a fight—only those they kill & scalp while under the fire of the enemy.

Once he & his brother, the late chief The Man Who Took the Coat, went off to the Blood reserve to steal horses[34]—but were discovered & surrounded by the Bloods & his brother was made prisoner, he escaping—but he was uneasy about his brother, so drew his blanket about his head & walked up to a Blood woman & asked where they had taken the Assiniboine. She pointed to a lodge and as he came near it a big Blood came out—he asked him where the Assiniboine was, & then entered the lodge. He threw aside the blanket & sat down. The Bloods thought this very brave of the young fellow & made friends & gave both him & his brother food—& the Blackfoot came & saw him.

He used to roam the prairies & plains from Lake Winnipeg to the Rocky Mountains after the buffalo & has many wounds on his body from enraged bulls. He told of one [hunt]. When the ice was still in the ground he was out riding & came across a herd of buffalo. He had nothing but his knife, so singled out a heifer, but his horse was afraid & he could only urge it near enough to stab the beast in the haunch & it kicked, nearly killing his horse—he got it by stabbing it in the ribs. He killed seven grizzly bear.

The chief's father was called the Conjuring Old Man—he had once killed & taken a coat from a Blackoot & called his son The Man Who Took the Coat (Jack). The Runner, another son, lately shot another Assiniboine over some love affair, & on this account the agent did not want me to paint him.[35] These Assiniboines met some time ago & arranged that once a year they would hold a great dance to keep up the old customs and dresses. The squaws spent a year making beadwork dresses. Graham, the inspector, got word of it & stopped them promptly.[36] The missionaries & agents hold that these dances are as intoxicating to them as whiskey. Doucet told me that after some of the dances the men get the look of wolves.

I bought two of their beautiful dresses—one from the Runner, a complete outfit, and a coat from Frank Walking Sun. They are solid beadwork with the old-time designs.

A daughter of the Conjuring Man married Thomson, a civil engineer & onetime scout for the Police. The marriage was an unhappy one & _____ finally shot herself. Her sons Archie & Jim, the first a clever fellow & Jim a handsome boy.

The late chief, The Man Who Took the Coat, at the time of the breed rebellion, offered to supply scouts for the Police but they did not wish to stir up the tribes.

Mr. Grant had to drive the Chief, the Thomson boys & their sister & Mrs. Aspdin* and her three daughters. Her husband was an Englishman who came to the west [& riding alone on the plains was overcome by the heat or was ill, & was found by a Sioux girl who took him to her father's lodge &

nursed him. He recovered and rode off, but could not forget the kindness of the young Sioux girl, & searched her up again, & married her.] He became agent to the Assiniboine at Sintaluta & then not long ago in British Columbia. [Mrs. Aspdin is still beautiful and has all the bearing of an aristocrat.] One of her daughters is the prim English type, the other the western type.

She makes beautiful work with porcupine designs on buckskin. She would not consent to be painted. Before I left they got up a house party in full dress.

An old man called The Cris came to the agency. We were all seated around. He remained quiet & then broke silence by the ejaculation, I from nothing! He then told us he had just returned from Montana with several horses but had given them all away to his sons & relatives. This is a custom when the Indian gets up in years. He gives all his possessions away and relies on his people to look after him. Some have different views on this, as for instance old Slow Coming Over the Hills & the Blackfoot.[39]

I get Jim Thomson to drive me to the station & take him on to Broadview. Hire a horse & we start for the reserve, but when well out on the plains, he for ten minutes kicking on the dashboard, puts his hoofs through my portrait case & then stampedes—a narrow escape. We take him back to Broadview & get another horse.

That evening Mr. Millar drives me through the beautiful Qu'Appelle Valley to Greyson[40] & from there we take train to Balcarres & drive to the File Hills, where we are the guests of Mr. W. M. Graham, the Inspector of Agencies in this district.[41]

The Indians are gathered from Touchwood Hills & the other reserves & all encamped about the small lake.* Many painted lodges. The Thunderbird on some & on others, the particular spirit the owner worships. I select the one I will paint.

Mr. Graham drives me to see his colony of schoolboys—as soon as they are old enough to get married, he removes them from their old quarters & starts them on farms. It is proving a good success.

Drive to the Qu'Appelle Mission where Rev. Father L'Hougonard, O.M.I., is in charge.[42] This is the finest of all the missions I have seen—run like a military institution. It is a 21 mile drive to Lebret from File Hills—four miles from Fort Qu'Appelle. Father Hougonard told me of an incident which happened in 1876. Food gave out & he had sent to Fort Ellice for 20 bags of flour. The Sioux had lately taken refuge in Canada—great swarms flushed with the success of Custer's defeat & they were in a starving condition. They got word of the arrival of his carts with flour.

One morning looking out from his log cabin he heard the ass bray, & filing along the opposite bank a long procession of warriors coming on the trail at the foot of the hill.* This file of horsemen came to his cabin. As they approached two dismounted & led the horse of the leader. It was the famous Sitting Bull. He spoke seldom but with authority—sitting erect on his horse

The Assiniboine, with others of Moose Mt., were to locate about Wood Mt. & Ft. Walsh, after the buffalo. The Assiniboine now of Sintaluta were once large in numbers. The smallpox scattered the tribes. Chief Long Lodge of Sintaluta, after his death his band was amalgamated with Jack's band, who became chief of both. Mr. Grant made Carry the Kettle chief on death of his brother.

5TH AUG.
*Two old chiefs, Muscopetung and Mascowegaiass, camped here. Good types, too, Keewist, Buffalo Bull, Eagle Cap, & Day Bird.

8TH

9TH

(Diary page 78)

*_____ with breech rifles & some with top boots.

he demanded the flour. Hougonard told him he knew they were in distress as the buffalo had left & offered them some 10 bags of his flour. In exchange they gave him gold watches, riding boots & shirts they had taken from the American soldiers in the late massacre.

He gave Graham a rail resembling a speech of the late Chief Piapot. He (*Diary page 79*) wound up his speech saying when the Treaty was made it was provided the land was to be theirs & certain things granted as long as the sun shone & men walked with two legs! Then the Great Spirit sent along a man with one leg (Graham) so that it might be broken.

Mr. Graham suggested to me a subject for a painting. At Moose Mountain he came upon a group of cowboys with horses screened by a bluff. It was dusk. They had stolen them & hit the trail for Prince Albert not knowing that Graham had bought one, & it was afterwards identified by Father St. Germaine as his favourite horse.

At File Hills I had met young Glen Lyon MacDonald,[43] a grandson of the old Factor Archibald MacDonald & I spent a few days with his people at Fort (*Diary page 80*) Qu'Appelle. Many landscape subjects here,[44] back of John Archer's house— the lake is black with duck.

From Frank Dumont, a nephew of the noted rebel, I hear the history of Almighty Voice. He is the breed who was with Sergeant Colbrook when he was shot.[45] Almighty Voice, a young Cree of about 20, had stolen a steer from a rancher & was arrested by the police & worked a yr. at Duck Lake. During the night one of the police left the room leaving the key in the door, & returning, the Indian was off. Colbrook got Dumont & started off on the trail. Towards night snow fell. They found the tracks & hearing the report of a gun, they soon came on the Indian with a young girl he had eloped with, seated around a fire cooking a prairie chicken. The Sergeant rode up & said, come along. The Indian said no, & put a discharge of powder in his double barrelled gun, dropping to his knee & levelling it at the policeman. Dumont said, no don't shoot, & he rose & walked backwards going that way about a mile—every now & then dropping to his knee & levelling his gun.

(*Diary page 81*) Almighty Voice came to a bluff & the Sergeant told Dumont to go around it & head him off. In a moment the Indian was on his knee & shot the Sergeant dead, the bullet entering his heart & coming out of his neck. He fell with a small revolver lying in his hand. Dumont then rode off for help & the Indian escaped. What followed is given in my notes. Dumont said Almighty Voice, as soon as he had got out of prison, had gone to his people. His old mother warned him that he had done enough mischief but he said, they will never take me alive. After his escape from Colbrook months went by before they again tracked him up—and it took the force from Regina to finally blow up the bluff where he was entrenched with 2 companions. Many lives were lost. At the trial scene, his old mother was a witness & joined in singing his death song. Then she dressed him in a gorgeous native dress & so buried him.

(*Diary page 82*) Besides the collection of Indian relics I am making myself, I am getting many for Mr. B. E. Walker, C.V.O., & sent on some cases to him.[46]

Dan Wildman, Stoney. Pastel on paper, 1908. Dimensions 63 × 49 cm. Edmund Morris Collection. ROM HK 2435.

Peter Wesley, the Moose Killer, Stoney chief. Pastel on paper, 1908. Dimensions 62.5 × 50 cm. Edmund Morris Collection. ROM HK 2441.

Left File Hills for Saskatoon. I heard that White Cap, the Sioux rebel whom my cousin Col. Merritt captured in the late rebellion, was still living. With difficulty we locate the Reserve.* It is in a flat marshy _____. I stop with a French family called Genereux, a widow with 5 boys. The old chief is dead— his sons survived him but Charles Eagle is the leader. Young Willie Flying Buffalo from Prince Albert Sioux is a good type—but he will not be painted, so I return to Saskatoon. I found them drying the native corn. This is a very paintable subject. The women preparing it & it hung on poles—with a background of the silvery buffalo willow, the hills, reds, blues, & yellows of the corn make a fine play of colour.

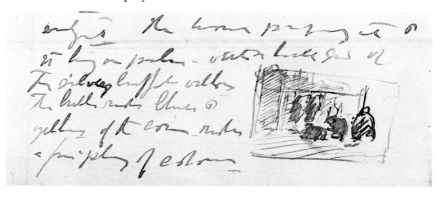

(Diary page 83) Drive to Dundurn with Fred & Olive Genereux & take train to Saskatoon. Go on to Duck Lake & stop overnight with Mr. Mitchell, the trader who figured in the late rebellion.[47] He has a beautiful house here & his wife has a very fine collection of Indian relics.

I drive out to the Duck Lake Agency with Jack McArthur, the eldest son of the agent.[48] We pass the spot where the lst shot of the late rebellion was fired.
    These Indians had given my father trouble at the Fort Carlton Treaty & were the first to join the breeds.[49]

I paint Kah mee use kom mee kah we in, the Spring Man.[50] He was in the last fight with the Blackfoot & took part in the half-breed rebellion. He leads the _____ life of a teamster. Old Cha ki kum was upset at not being the lst called on—he came all dressed up, gun in hand.

(Diary page 84)   Splashing Water was at one time Poundmaker's councillor & went with Big Bear to Prince Albert to hold a council. He took part in the rebellion & fled to the States, residing there 10 years. He was the messenger the Chief Beardy sent to learn the terms of the Carlton treaty—see *Treaties of Canada with the Indians of Manitoba & the Northwest Territories* by my father.[51] P. Cha ki kum once had long hanks of hair below his waist. Graham gave me a photo of a Nut Lake Saulteaux with his hair in great braids trailing on the ground.[52]

Mr. McArthur is a highlander from Nairn. He wants me some year to join him & go to Trout Lake, Fort à la Corne, & other places where he pays the Indians.

The Feather, Meguinis, Cree. Pastel on paper, 1908. Dimensions 63 × 49.5 cm. Edmund Morris Collection. ROM HK 2446.

Photograph of Father Albert Lacombe, OMI, Roman Catholic missionary among the Cree and Blackfoot. Courtesy the Glenbow Museum, Calgary, Alberta NA-518-2.

While at Kirkcudbright in Selkirkshire, I had heard from an old servant of the late Earl of Selkirk that he had been stolen from his father by the Indians. This electrified McArthur who had never heard it.

(Diary pages 85–90)

On the 8th I go on to Edmonton, a beautiful spot, make a sketch of the old HBC Fort where the Parliament Bldgs are to be erected.[53]

These Crees were implicated in the Rebellion of 1885, robbing the Hudson's Bay stores near Penoka.[55] They seized the Govt. Provisions & helped themselves but did not take up arms.

Go to Hobbema—Cree agency. The chief Ermine Skin refuses to sit for his portrait & left his camp—to Wood Mt. His father, Jean-Baptiste Piche came from Terre Bonne, Quebec[54]—of a good family but was wild & has a trade with the Indians, leading their life, & married a Cree woman, daughter of the chief, & had several sons. 2 of them became chiefs: Ermine Skin & Bob Tail.

Son Grandeur Monseigneur Légal, évêque de Saint Albert.

Drive to the camp of an old warrior & medicine man, Kn un biso. He is a fine specimen—tall & erect with a mass of grey hair. He has some Cree, Saulteaux & Blood in him & his grandfather was a white who married a Blood woman & his mother was also a Blood.

Only get one portrait at Hobbema. A young Belgian priest, a good mission, has trained the pupils of the school to play stringed instruments faultlessly.

*After leaving Calgary I stop off at Griswold & drive out to the Sioux. I paint Old Antoine—would like to get Wanduti but he is away. The agent seems to hate himself & the whole world, so it is not agreeable. There is an Ojibway missionary here.[60] I go on to Rothwell & stop at Indian Smoke at Mr. McKee's, who is in charge. Saw _____. A son of the Gambler[61] acts as interpreter and we go to the log house of Yellow Quill.[62] I paint his portrait. My father had negotiated with him in 1876. He lost

Went on to Calgary & from there to Morley. The agent has seemed to resent my coming—but I care not. I paint the old chief the Moose Killer, generally called Peter Wesley.[56] The old man when asked to sit said, yes, if he will give me a nice young white girl. His old wife sitting near chased him with a log & he laughed, clapping his hands. Paint also Dan Wild Man[57] & then go on to Banff to CPR hotel. Meet the mining experts who have a special car, & Mr. Ian Nairn, whom I had met in Glasgow, has me to dinner on this train. Had taken a holiday & end up with the Piegan Reserve to see my old friends there.

Père Lacombe, the pioneer missionary of the West, the Bishop of Mistre, Bishop Légal, came on a visit to Father Doucet—glad to meet Père Lacombe.[58] He had known my father. The chiefs all came to see us. Lacombe had not seen old Running Wolf for many years—he stood regarding him & then placed his hand on the old Indian's head & said, *pacem vilex*. Both are near their graves.

I drive up to Brocket with Father Lacombe. He told me about the chief Sweet Grass. The Crees had been on the warpath & hearing a cry went in the direction & found a babe in the grass—one of the Crows. They took him home & he was adopted by a Cree woman. He had no name—he wanted to make one for himself and while still a boy started off alone with his bow & quiver of arrows. He travelled on many days and one morning when he awoke he saw from his place of hiding a big Blackfoot appear with a herd of horses. He drew his bow & taking good aim killed him & then stampeded the horses. The camp heard the yell & followed in hot pursuit, but he had the best horse and after some time they fell off. He travelled on to the Cree camp leading the horses and as he neared his people he called out, come my brothers come, & waved in his hand a bunch of sweet grass he had pulled when the Indian had fallen. He told the tribe to help themselves to the

Antoine Hoke, Sioux medicine man. Pastel on paper, 1908. Dimensions 63 × 49 cm. Edmund Morris Collection. ROM HK 2437.

Yellow Quill, Auzawaquin, Saulteaux chief. Pastel on paper, 1908. Dimensions 63 × 50 cm. Edmund Morris Collection. ROM HK 2403.

horses. They now called him Sweet Grass & made him a chief—& in time he became the most influential of the Plains Crees.

I have spoken of this chief before in connection with the Treaty my father made at Fort Pitt, and earlier of his refusal to join the Sioux. Père Lacombe baptised him into the Roman faith—& he before all his people told of the wild bad life he had led & renounced it.

Père Lacombe returns to his _____ at Pincher Creek. He allows old Lereux to live here _____ _____ as his mode of life & tho' much is said against him, the Blackfoot swear by him and his treatment of them at times warrants it. Once they were in a starving condition & saw coming over the plains a caravan of red river carts.[59] They prepared to fight thinking it was the Crees— but it proved to be Lereux who had heard of their distress & brought supplies to them. At that time he was in such destitution he lived in a hole in the ground.

I return to Calgary* & from there to Winnipeg & Toronto, having this year visited the Crees, Saulteaux, Assiniboine, Sioux, Stoneys, and Piegans.

Notes to Western Journey 1908

1. David Laird had been chief commissioner making Treaty Seven with the Blackfoot in 1877.

2. The Manitoba Club is still open in Winnipeg; the two portraits by Morris, of Iron Shield and of Strangle Wolf, are still housed in the club.

3. Chief John Prince, Swampy Cree/European, at the St Peter's Reserve, was the son of Cut Nose Chief, and was related to Henry Prince (Red Eagle, Miskoo Kinew), who was chief on the same reserve at the time of Treaty One negotiations in 1871 with the Cree and Ojibwa of southern Manitoba (see Morris 1971, p. 35); he was a veteran of the Boer War.

4. Gimli, Manitoba, was established in 1875 as one of a series of Icelandic settlements on the west shore of Lake Winnipeg.

5. Alexander Morris (1826–89) was buried in Mount Pleasant Cemetery, Toronto.

6. Yellow Quill (ca 1833–?), Auzawaquin, a minor chief of the Saulteaux, was one of the band leaders who signed Treaty One in 1871 at Lower Fort Garry; this treaty was organized by Alexander Morris's predecessor as lieutenant governor of Manitoba and the North West Territories, Adams G. Archibald. Yellow Quill and his band were dissatisfied with the reserve provisions under the treaty; Alexander Morris was appointed to settle the misunderstandings and revise the treaty in 1875–76 (Morris 1971, pp. 129–31, 134–42). Edmund Morris returned on his way back on this journey to portray Yellow Quill (ROM HK 2403). The name of the Saulteaux (Sauters or Sotoos), of French origin, refers to a western branch of the Ojibwa.

7. Sioux from Pipestone, Minnesota, and from the reserve in Griswold, Manitoba.

8. Magnus Begg (1853–1904?) was federal Indian Affairs agent for the Sarcee at Blackfoot Crossing from 1884 to 1901; he was later transferred to the Cree reserve (courtesy Public Archives of Canada).

9. The one Indian Affairs agent with a similar name in the records Public Archives of Canada is Matthew Millar, at Duck Lake agency, 1904–14. Sir Isaac Brock (1769–1812), major general in the British army, was hero in the defence of Upper Canada in the war of 1812.

10. Peter Hourie, Mosquito Hawk (courtesy Queen's University Archives), an interpreter, was among those who signed Treaty Six at Fort Carlton (see Morris 1971, p. 357). Sir Frederick Dobson Middleton (1825–98), major general, was in charge of operations during the North West Rebellion of 1885.

11. Louis Riel, the Métis leader of the North West Rebellion of 1885.

12. Acoose, Man Standing Above Ground, was chief of the Sakimay (Mosquito) band of Saulteaux at Crooked Lake; Edmund Morris portrayed him in 1908 (ROM HK 2402) and in 1909 (Government of Saskatchewan Collection). Morris would have had a knowledge of French from the three years he spent studying in Paris, 1893–96, and from having lived in a small artists' colony in a Quebec village for a few years (courtesy Queen's University Archives).

13. Morris left a space at this point for an additional word or two—perhaps Acoose's father's name.

14. Paget records the same story of Acoose's run (1909, p. 87).

15. Nepahpenais (1832–1920), Night Bird, a former chief of the Cowessess band of the Saulteaux in the valley of the Qu'Appelle River, was a respected buffalo hunter and a kindly leader; he had been an employee of the Hudson's Bay Company for many years (courtesy Saskatchewan Archives Board). Edmund Morris portrayed him

in 1908 (ROM HK 2436) and in 1910 (Government of Saskatchewan Collection). There is a third portrait in the Winnipeg Art Gallery (WAG G–29) and a fourth in the Glenbow Museum (57.6).

16. Possibly Upper or Lower Red Lake, Minnesota, south of Lake of the Woods. Many crossed-out passages interrupt the text of this note leaving the sequence of remaining sections unclear.

17. Morris wrote the number "2000" above this line; its reference is not clear.

18. Walter Ochopowace, of Algonkian and Cree blood, was hereditary Cree chief of the Ochopowace band of the Cree. The Ochopowace Reserve is located about 16 km (10 miles) northeast of Whitewood, Saskatchewan, on the CPR main line. Edmund Morris made portraits of Walter Ochopowace in 1908 (ROM HK 2447) and in 1910 (Government of Saskatchewan Collection). Loud Voice, Ka ki sha way, a former Cree chief and medicine man, signed Treaty Four at Fort Qu'Appelle in 1874 (see Morris 1971, pp. 81–83, 334); Paget (1909, p. 117) attributes his name to his practice of ventriloquism. The horse's head decoration was part of Edmund Morris's bequest to the Royal Ontario Museum (ROM HK 239).

19. The Mandan, a Siouan tribe, once lived in easterly region, according to their tradition; they speak of a migration westwards in their historic era, up the Missouri River. Their villages were permanent assemblages of earth-covered log structures; they "were intensive agriculturalists" (Lowie 1963, p. 23) and cultivated maize among other crops. These villages became market centres, evidenced by items such as dentalium shells from the Pacific coast found at village sites. The tribe suffered severely from smallpox.

20. Sitting White Eagle, Wahpekinewap, was of a Saulteaux band in Saskatchewan and was a great warrior and medicine man. Morris's portrait of him is ROM HK 2428.

21. The black beads are visible on Morris's portrait of Sitting White Eagle.

22. The Sun Dance was a religious ceremony performed by the Plains Indians. During illness, battle, the death of relatives, or other stresses, an individual would make a vow to the sun to perform this ceremony. Although the ceremony differed from tribe to tribe, there were certain common aspects: it was held in the summer, before a tribal assembly, with elaborate preparations; it was characterized by special costumes, prayers, dances, and music, and by acts of self-torture. (See Lowie 1963, pp. 177–79.)

23. Peguis, Cut Nose Chief, Swampy Cree, was one of the five Indian chiefs who sold their right to lands the Earl of Selkirk wanted for his Red River Settlement. Thomas Douglas Selkirk (1771–1820), fifth earl of Selkirk, established colonies for the evicted crofters of his clan in Scotland on lands he bought in the New World, including those in Prince Edward Island and Upper Canada. He obtained 464 400 sq km (116 000 sq. miles) in what is today Manitoba, Saskatchewan, North Dakota, and Minnesota—with a northern boundary of 52°30' between Lakes Winnipeg and Winnipegosis and 52° extending east and west from them, and including the Assiniboine and Red rivers (see Morton 1939, pp. 535–36)—in 1811 and 1817, by purchase from the Hudson's Bay Company and by treaty from certain bands of Saulteaux and Cree. The Red River Settlement extended south from Manitoba into present-day Minnesota and North Dakota. (See Morris 1971, pp. 13–15, 299–302.)

24. The Canadian government brought a group of western chiefs east to join eastern chiefs at the unveiling of a monument to Joseph Brant at Brantford, Ontario. Among the group were five from the Blackfoot Confederacy, including Crowfoot, and four Cree chiefs, including Star Blanket. (See Dempsey 1972, p. 201.)

25. Morris's portrait of Man Sitting in the Middle of the Sun, Nowwekeshequappew, Saulteaux, is ROM HK 2429.

26. William Samuel Grant was appointed agent in 1906 for the Assiniboine Reserve

at Sintaluta, and remained there until his death in 1911; he was replacing Thomas W. Aspdin, who had retired; Grant's earlier appointments as agent were at Indian Head, 1886–97, and Hobbema, 1897–1906 (courtesy Public Archives of Canada).

27. Fort Ellice was built in 1831/32 as a trading post for the Hudson's Bay Company on the Assiniboine River, about 8 km (5 miles) below the mouth of the Qu'Appelle River; by 1860 its trade had greatly declined and it was closed about 1885.

28. Carry the Kettle, Chagakin, said to have been one hundred and seven years old at his death in 1923, was Assiniboine chief at the Carry the Kettle Reserve, about 16 km (10 miles) south of Sintaluta, Saskatchewan, on the CPR main line. He was short, but of noble bearing, and was friendly and popular with the members both of his tribe and of many other tribes. (Courtesy Saskatchewan Archives Board.) Edmund Morris describes the origin of the name Carry the Kettle (p. 72); see also MacEwan (1971, pp. 51–57). Morris portrayed Carry the Kettle in 1908 (ROM HK 2440) (Morris 1909, p. 20, no. 50) and in 1910 (Government of Saskatchewan Collection).

29. The Assiniboine's language is a dialect of the Dakota Sioux, but, by tradition, they are a branch of the Yankton Sioux, a prairie-oriented Sioux. They lived in the midwest, on the Minnesota border and in southern Manitoba, but hunted also to the north into the boreal forest. They were among the main suppliers of furs to the French trade; at the conclusion of the Seven Years' War in 1763, the Hudson's Bay Company and independent traders took away the Assiniboine role as middleman in the fur trade. A new business developed: supplying pemmican to trading posts and brigades of canoes. (See Kehoe 1981, p. 284.) The Assiniboine began to concentrate upon buffalo hunting, and scattered bands hunted all the way to the slopes of the Rockies. The western groups became known as the Stoney. Indian Head, Alberta, was named by European settlers when they found the bones of dead Indians in what had been a burial ground.

30. Treaty Four at Fort Qu'Appelle was negotiated in 1874, not 1876.

31. Carlyle, Saskatchewan, named after Thomas Carlyle.

32. It seems that this sentence is about two separate events. The Assiniboine, originally from the south themselves, crossed the border from Manitoba and Saskatchewan into the USA to fight the Sioux. At the time of the smallpox epidemic, the Assiniboine moved northwest in a attempt to escape the plague; Morris probably mentions Lac Ste Anne and Morley, Alberta, in this latter context.

33. Big Darkness, Opazatonka, a former minor chief of the Assiniboine in Saskatchewan, was deposed by the federal government for leaving Canada without the government's permission (see Morris 1909, p. 20). Edmund Morris portrayed him twice, in 1908 (ROM HK 2439) and in 1910 (Government of Saskatchewan Collection). The Runner, Een gana, also Assiniboine, was the youngest brother of Carry the Kettle and lived on the Carry the Kettle Reserve.

34. Jack, the Man Who Took the Coat (?–1892), Chiwicanocahco, was former chief of the Assiniboine and older brother of Carry the Kettle.

35. The agent would be William Samuel Grant. Edmund Morris did portray the Runner in 1910 (Government of Saskatchewan Collection).

36. Inspector James F. Graham, of the NWMP, signed Treaty Three of the North West Angle and Treaty Four at Fort Qu'Appelle (see Morris 1971, pp. 325, 341, 342).

37. Piapot or Payepot (ca 1816–1908), called Flash in the Sky in his youth, was chief of the Cree reserve at Fishing Lake; he had several confrontations with the NWMP during his life and spent fourteen years as a captive of the Sioux (see MacEwan 1971, pp. 93, 101). A portrait of him by Edmund Morris is in the Government of Saskatchewan Collection).

38. Thomas William Aspdin (1854–1906) was farmer-in-charge of the Assiniboine Reserve near Sintaluta from 1897 to 1901, and then agent for the same reserve until

1905 (courtesy Public Archives of Canada).

39. Edmund Morris's portrait of Slow Coming Over the Hill, Itspeeotamisow, an old Blackfoot, is ROM HK 2418.

40. Greyson, Saskatchewan.

41. William Morris Graham, inspector of Indian agencies for the Qu'Appelle inspectorate, 1904–18 (courtesy Public Archives of Canada); distinct from the NWMP inspector James F. Graham.

42. Father Joseph Hugonnard, OMI, (1848–1917) came to Canada from France as a missionary, joined the Roman Catholic mission near Fort Qu'Appelle in 1874 as an assistant, and served in the area of what today is Saskatchewan.

43. Glen Lyon McDonald was son of John Archibald McDonald and grandson of Archibald McDonald (1790–1853), chief factor of the Hudson's Bay Company (courtesy Saskatchewan Archives Board).

44. Landscapes by Edmund Morris are in various private collections, and public collections including those of the Ontario Government, the Glenbow Museum, the National Gallery of Canada, the Norman Mackenzie Gallery, the Art Gallery of Ontario, the Art Gallery of Hamilton, and the Women's Canadian Historical Society.

45. Frank Dumont, an officer of the NWMP, was related to the Métis rebel Gabriel Dumont (1838–1906), who was one of the prime instigators of the North West Rebellion (see McKee 1973, pp. 25–32). Almighty Voice, Ka kee manitou wayo, Cree, killed Sergeant Colin C. Colbrooke (courtesy RCMP) of the NWMP on 29 October 1885; the lengthy chase that ensued before the NWMP arrested him is described by Haydon (1971, pp. 174–81).

46. Sir Byron Edmond Walker, Commander of the Victorian Order, (1848–1924) was banker and president of the Bank of Commerce, 1907–24, and wrote a history of banking in Canada (Walker 1909); he sponsored many cultural and art organizations. Walker appreciated the value of Indian artifacts; he donated to the Royal Ontario Museum the collection that Edmund Morris gathered for him.

47. Mitchell, a trader at Duck Lake, had a large quantity of provisions and ammunition in his store when it was attacked by the half breeds and Cree on their way to protest at Fort Carlton, and the first shots of the North West Rebellion were fired during the Indians' encounter with the NWMP at Duck Lake (see Haydon 1971, p. 133).

48. James McArthur, federal Indian Affairs agent at Duck Lake, 1903–12 (courtesy Public Archives of Canada).

49. Fort Carlton is now Carlton. Alexander Morris had difficulty in arranging negotiations with the Willow Creek band, under chief Peter Beardy. They were encamped at Duck Lake at the time the treaty was being made at nearby Fort Carlton and refused to join the other Cree, not only because they were unwilling to accept the sale of Indian lands to the government, but also because Beardy had a vision telling him the treaty should be signed at Duck Lake. (See Morris 1971, pp. 182–84.)

50. The portrait of Spring Man, Kahmeeusekahmaweyenew, of the Willow Cree band, is ROM HK 2433.

51. Splashing Water, Chakikum, of the Willow Cree band, returned to Canada after a ten-year exile in the USA, when the Canadian government offered amnesty to participants in the North West Rebellion. Morris's portrait of him is ROM HK 2433. Alexander Morris does not name the messenger from the Willow Cree (see Morris 1971, p. 184).

52. An Indian from the Nut Lake Reserve, north of the Quill Lakes, Saskatchewan.

53. The oil painting based on this sketch is in the Glenbow Museum collection (55.39).

54. Terrebonne, P.Q., on the north shore of the St Lawrence River.

55. Ponoka, Alberta.

56. Peter Wesley, the Moose Killer, was a Stoney chief, once a great hunter; Edmund Morris's portrait of him is ROM HK 2441.

57. Edmund Morris's portrait of Dan Wildman is ROM HK 2435.

58. Bishop Émile Légal, OMI, (1849–1920) worked among the Blackfoot between 1881 and 1890; he was the author of several manuscript linguistic and ethnological studies of the Blackfoot. Légal was bishop of St Albert, Alberta.

59. Red river carts were two-wheeled ox carts made of wood held together with rawhide, and with high sides of vertical poles; they were used primarily by the Métis at first, but then by the Hudson's Bay Company and settlers of the Upper Fort Garry area.

60. This missionary would have been the Methodist Henry Bird Steinhauer.

61. There were two native leaders called the Gambler. One signed Treaty Two, the Manitoba Treaty. The reserve for his family, the Tanners, is on the Assiniboine River in western Manitoba. The other Gambler, Otakaonan, was in Pasqua's band in Saskatchewan and negotiated with Alexander Morris during the Qu'Appelle Treaty (see Morris 1971, pp. 97–114). Edmund Morris seems to be referring to the former, who lived in Manitoba.

62. This is Yellow Quill, Auzawaquin, whose band was absent when Morris went to see them on his way west.

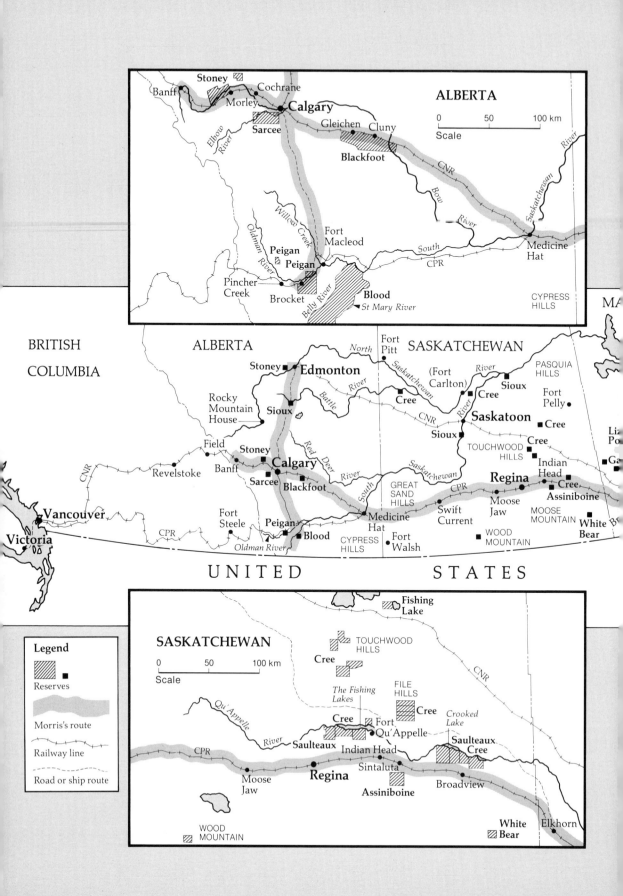

ALBERTA

Stoney
Banff
Cochrane
Morley
Calgary
Sarcee
Gleichen
Cluny
Blackfoot

0   50   100 km
Scale

Elbow River
Willow Creek
Oldman River
Fort Macleod
Peigan
Peigan
Pincher Creek
Brocket
Belly River
Blood
St Mary River

CNR
Bow River
South CPR
Saskatchewan River
Medicine Hat

CYPRESS HILLS

MA

BRITISH

COLUMBIA

ALBERTA

North
Fort Pitt

SASKATCHEWAN

PASQUIA HILLS

Stoney
Edmonton

Saskatchewan River

(Fort Carlton)
Cree
Sioux

Fort Pelly

Rocky Mountain House

Sioux

Battle River

Cree
Saskatoon

Field
CNR
Revelstoke
Banff
Stoney
Sarcee
Calgary
Blackfoot

Red Deer River

Sioux

Cree
TOUCHWOOD HILLS
Cree
Indian Head
Regina

Li
Po

Ga

Vancouver

Fort Steele

Peigan
Blood
Oldman River

CPR

Medicine Hat
South
Saskatchewan River

GREAT SAND HILLS
CYPRESS HILLS
Fort Walsh

Swift Current
CPR
Moose Jaw
Cree
Assiniboine

MOOSE MOUNTAIN
White Bear

Victoria

CPR
UNITED   STATES

WOOD MOUNTAIN

Legend

Reserves

Morris's route

Railway line

Road or ship route

SASKATCHEWAN

0   50   100 km
Scale

Fishing Lake

TOUCHWOOD HILLS
Cree

CNR

Qu'Appelle River

The Fishing Lakes

FILE HILLS
Cree
Crooked Lake

Cree
Fort Qu'Appelle
Saulteaux
Indian Head

Saulteaux
Cree

CPR
Moose Jaw
Regina
Sintaluta
Assiniboine
Broadview

WOOD MOUNTAIN

White Bear
Elkhorn

Western Journey 1909

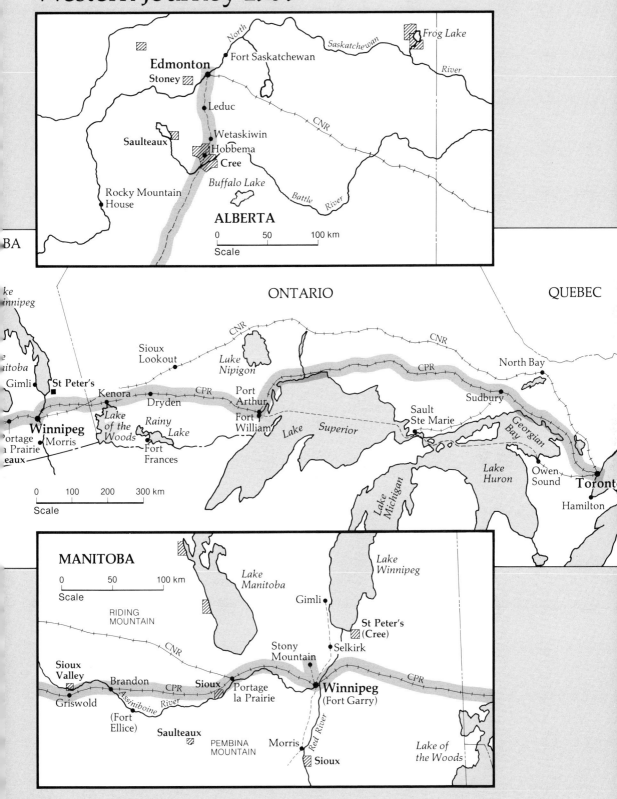

North Saskatchewan River

Frog Lake

Edmonton
Fort Saskatchewan
Stoney

Leduc

CNR

Wetaskiwin
Saulteaux
Hobbema
Cree

Buffalo Lake

Battle River

Rocky Mountain House

ALBERTA

0   50   100 km
Scale

BA

ONTARIO

QUEBEC

Lake Winnipeg

Manitoba

Gimli
St Peter's

CNR

Sioux Lookout

Lake Nipigon

CNR

North Bay

CPR

Kenora
Dryden

CPR

Port Arthur
Fort William

Sault Ste Marie

Sudbury

Georgian Bay

Winnipeg
Morris
Portage la Prairie
eaux

Lake of the Woods

Rainy Lake

Fort Frances

Lake Superior

Lake Michigan

Lake Huron

Owen Sound

Toronto

Hamilton

0   100   200   300 km
Scale

MANITOBA

0   50   100 km
Scale

RIDING MOUNTAIN

Lake Manitoba

Lake Winnipeg

Gimli

St Peter's (Cree)

CNR

Stony Mountain

Selkirk

Sioux Valley
Brandon
Griswold

CPR

Sioux

Portage la Prairie

Winnipeg (Fort Garry)

CPR

Assiniboine River

(Fort Ellice)

Saulteaux

PEMBINA MOUNTAIN

Morris

Red River

Sioux

Lake of the Woods

My people leave for Isle _____, Lake Joseph, Muskoka.[1] I remain in Toronto to settle my affairs with the Ontario Govt. Place labels on the collection of portraits & get my cheque of $2500.00 for the last series of 25.[2] I have been appointed a member of the Council of the Toronto Art Museum—we have at last got a good gallery to make a start and before leaving I called a meeting of our Canadian Art Club & proposed that we use the Museum for our annual Exhibits instead of altering the old Court House, still keeping apart as a separate organization from the Museum & other Societies.[3] Present at the meeting—Homer Watson, D. R. Wilkie, E. Atkinson, J. Russell, Curtis Williamson, J. Arch. Browne, E. Morris, Walter Allward & Horatio Walker—& A. P. Proctor wrote approving of the move.[4] It was carried & we get club rooms over the Imperial Bank for a rendezvous for the members.[5]

Leave for Winnipeg, travel by rail. The Exhibition of Art now on in this city is execrable. I told Mr. Martin, Mr. Atkins & others this,[6] & that our Club would not exhibit in Winnipeg until they provided a suitable gallery. The Law Society of Manitoba has had a portrait painted of my father as first Chief Justice of Manitoba, for the Court House. I sent a photo taken just before he left the East for Winnipeg, but they have had it painted from the large photo I had Inglis make for the Govt. House from one taken after his return to Toronto in 1879,[7] so that it represents him as an older man, when he was Chief Justice. They would have been wise to consult me as the artist. See Sheriff Inkster. He was appointed by my father & is one of the few left who was in his Council.* Spend a weekend with Col. Irvine at Stony Mountain. He is in a larger house now.

(Diary page 92)

*His mother, a
half breed lady,
danced with Sir
John Franklin at
Fort Churchill—
his father, a
Highlander, was
one of the Sel-
kirk settlers.[8]

(Diary page 93)

I go on to Regina to see Hon. Walter Scott, the Prime Minister of Saskatchewan, re a series of portraits for the Province.[9] Fortunately find him at his office late that night & have a long talk with him on art matters. He will bring the matter of Indian portraits before his ministers. I suggested his Ministry commissioning Proctor the sculptor to make statues of buffalo for either side of the entrance of the Parliament Bldgs & for the prison.[10] He favours the Indians & writes the author Brian Maxwell of Montreal about it. He talked to the Indians of an art committee for the province. Stopped off at Brandon to see the Sioux. Met old Antoine & Wanduti. Get some of the beautiful transparent woven beadwork—beautiful as the art of Persia. I go on to Gleichen (named after Count Gleichen a former director of the CPR & a relative of the late Queen). Clouds of mosquitoes cover the plains—it is impossible to work,[11] so I go on to Banff, stop at the CPR hotel. I meet Mr. Rutherford, Prime Minister of Alberta, & he gives me an order for 5 portraits for the new Parliament Bldgs at Edmonton.[12] He will bring the matter of further work before his ministers. I brought Proctor's name before him, suggesting an equestrian group of wild animals of Alberta for the grounds of the Bldgs. Talked over the work of the portrait painters. He proposes to have his cabinet painted. The Hicksons, Henshaws from B.C. & others at Banff.

I meet Tom Wilson, an ex-police & guide in the mountains—he got his feet frozen in climbing one of the mountains. He has a remarkable collection of books on Western History.

The Mounted Police hold that Inspector Dickens, son of the author, showed the white feather at Fort Pitt.[13] Wilson upheld him—said he relied on MacLean's judgement when he asked him to relinquish the Fort, for they were far outnumbered by Big Bear's force & MacLean & his family voluntarily became prisoners of war in Big Bear's camp.[14] One of MacLean's daughters, Mrs. Padgett, has written a book, *People of the Plains*.[15] Father Doucet says Dickens had never recovered from the sunstroke he got while in India & was of a very unmilitary-like bearing. He died a hard death in Chicago. Wilson says he never suspected trouble till he was in the thick of it. Young Brewster has a good library of western books, as well as Wilson. Tom Wilson comes on with me to Morley. _____ Scott is selling out to young Dan MacDougall. The Stonies hold a dance that evening in honour of some Cree visitors. Some are almost nude. Old English had painted his face pure white. They had an _____ of cut boughs & the old men were seated in a circle against this. As the sun got low the play of colour was intensely brilliant, yet not at all discordant. One old warrior recounted his deeds—at each pause in his speech the young men would once strike the tom toms.

(Diary page 95)

(Diary page 96)

I return to the South Camp where I encamp. The old Indians as cordial as ever. The first portrait I paint is of High Eagle, Pitauspitau, the best hunter of the Blackfoot. He is brother of Iron Shield. In the evening we met in the lodge of John Drunken Chief and with my interpreter questioned High Eagle & Drunken Chief about the gens or bands into which the Blackfoot are divided.[16] George Bird Grinnell, the New York author, long intimate with the Blackfoot, in his work *Blackfoot Lodge Tales*, systematically classifies their gens, as he calls them.[17] I spoke of it to Canon Stocken, at first he discounted it. Grinnell is more familiar with the southern Blackfoot & Piegans—but I gave Stocken the diagram High Eagle made & he revised it by questioning other Indians. In looking into the matter he says they are more of the nature of bands than gens.

(Diary page 97)

High Eagle's diagram of the camp before Treaty time.

1. 2 commmunal tents.

(Diary page 98)

2. Etsikinox, Those Who Wore Moccasins. The late Head Chief Sapo Maxika, Three Bulls, & c. belonged to this band.

3. Omuketsimanix, The Big Dried Food Case People. Sisuiake belonged to this. _____ _____ _____ _____ _____/_____ _____ .

4. Ai suk ko yo ke kox, The Camped Anyhow People. This name was given up & _____ _____ adopted after Treaty times.

5. Pakh ski yox, Hitting in the Face. This was the former name of the band. They were since 1887 known as Akus tsi yox. Stumix o to kan pi, Bull Turning Round, was a prominent chief of this band. Spotted Eagle also belonged to it.

6. Api kai yix, Skunks. Pi tau pi kis, Eagle Rib, was the last of its chiefs—_____ & Three Guns who originally belonged to the Etsikinox was one of this group.

7. Mo ta to si mix, Many Medicine Men. The late Head Chief Old Sun

(Diary page 99)

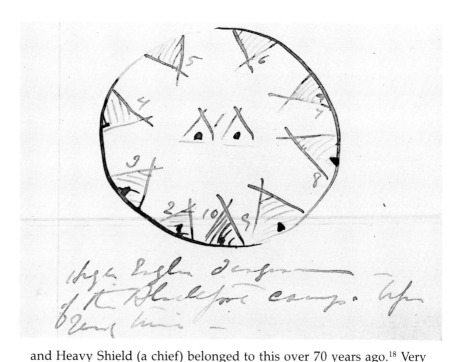

and Heavy Shield (a chief) belonged to this over 70 years ago.[18] Very few remain today are associated—perhaps three, Frank Tried to Fly is one of them.[19] He is son of Old Sun. Wolf Carrying used to be one.

8. Sai yex, or Cruel Crees. The last important chief of this band was Ponokaistumik, Elk Bull, with whom was associated Omuk sa pop, Big Plume.* Crow Shoe is now the principal one.

9. Pakh si na ma yix, Stinking Guns. Good Looking Child & others.

10. Mio pi ni nia nix, Strong Whips. Calf Child, the war chief—Bear Hat & Calf Bull.

High Eagle & Drunken Chief tell me about Crowfoot their uncle. They say his father & mother were Blood Indians* who settled with the Blackfoot when Crowfoot was a young man. The father was called _____ Head—he was not a chief. Crowfoot got his name in this way. Some Blackfoot horses had been stolen & a party was got up to search. It was in the winter, & he found large tracks in the snow & exclaimed, a Crow[20] (Father Doucet says he killed this Crow Indian who was a giant—old Indians telling him that an ordinary sized man reached only to the top of his leggings). So he was called Crowfoot—before that he was known as Bear Ghost.* We sat in the lodge till a late hour talking on these things.

I get John Drunken Chief to show me Poundmaker's grave. He was Crowfoot's adopted son & died when on a visit to him in 1886. Wm. Brigmann, the artist, was present when he was buried & helped to lower him into the grave. The grass has all fallen in & the wooden cross decayed—a mass of strawberry bushes conceals all from sight. I get John Drunken Chief to fill it in with earth & have 2 cartloads of stones from the Bow River & we built a

*Big Plume had a following of 70 lodges, & before the smallpox in 57–8, 200 lodges.

(Diary pages 100–103)

*A Blood Indian lately bore his name Sapo Maxika—probably a relation as they have no family names.

*The name his blind son bears.

See Brigman letter to _____.

Spring Chief, Ninauksiskum, Blackfoot chief. Pastel on paper, 1909. Dimensions 63.9 × 50 cm. Government of Alberta 0367-300-66.

Photograph of Running Rabbit (*left*) relating his story as illustrated on the buffalo hide (ROM 977x1.3). Edmund Morris Collection 196. Courtesy Provincial Archives of Manitoba.

*Which I found decayed—for he had been baptised in prison & Father Doucet read a prayer when he died. Poundmaker left a son Gabriel. He also is dead.

*By Mrs. Padgett, whose grandmother was one of the Dog Ribb (Dene) Indians. She is related to the Campbells & Murrays—half breeds.

Poundmaker— Peĕ too kah han, literally a taking in or the person who had a taking in, referring to buffalo corral.

(Diary page 104)

mound, & I inscribe his name on a slab with the old Indian cross representing the four cardinal points + & the cross of the Roman Church † * for [Doucet had baptised him]. Poundmaker was one of the greatest of the red race. I remember once going into my father's office at home. It was at the time of the rebellion. He was reading the newspaper & looked distressed. I asked what troubled him & he said, they have imprisoned Poundmaker.

After we had marked the spot of this old warrior, on the same evening I got by post from the Indian Department the book *People of the Plains** with my portrait of Poundmaker reproduced in it.[21] John Drunken Chief asks me to write on a slab to mark the last camp of his uncle Crowfoot. The circle of stones with the small circle for the fireplace is still there. It was in a beautiful spot on the prairie above the cut bank of the Bow overlooking the valley & the Blackfoot Crossing. The Indians always encamp in beautiful places. The Indians will mark for me the spot where the Blackfoot treaty was made in 1877.

I have brought four buffalo robes which belonged to my father to have records made by the Indians in picture writing.[22] I already have the history of Bull's Head, the Sioux Head Chief[23]—and another records the history of the Piegan chiefs. Running Rabbit, one of the Head Chiefs of the Blackfoot who was an old warrior, now paints his history on one of these robes for me. He works early & late at it & groans over the hard work. He looks fine in négligé costume while at work.

His son Horton translated the picture writing.

1. When I was 17 I joined a war party against the Crees. We came on a camp. The men were all off after the buffalo. We killed all the women except one young girl whom I took captive.

2. Join with a war party into the Cree country. We sighted the enemy who entrenched themselves in a hole in the ground. I killed one of them & took his scalp.

3. A large war party went to the Crows. A big fight followed. We killed a lot of them.

4. Again in the Crow country we are surrounded by a large number. They killed one of the Bloods. My horse was wounded. I jumped on another but got a wound from an arrow before I got away.

5. We fall in with the Crees—a big fight. The Crees held up blankets suing for peace.

6. Again met the Crees. We drove them into a lake. They had difficulty running through the mud & we killed them all.

7. Again met the Crees. I killed the chief Handsome Young Man.

8. Represents the Crees he killed—a spear, war pipe, & war club, & powder flask taken from the Crows.

9. An encounter with the Crees.

10. Horses he took from the Crows.

11. He killed 4 grizzly bear.

12. The buffalo hunt. Hunts out Crees who had stolen 4 horses, he took them all back.

Big Darkness, Opazatonka, Assiniboine chief. Pastel on paper, 1908. Dimensions 63 × 49.5 cm. Edmund Morris Collection. ROM HK 2439.

Night Bird, Nepahpenais, Saulteaux chief. Pastel on paper, 1908. Dimensions 63 × 49.5 cm. Edmund Morris Collection. ROM HK 2436.

Photograph of a skin shirt, with fringed sleeves; notched round neck and at base; oval perforations near base; sleeves and body decorated with applied heavily beaded bands. Measures 153 cm across the shoulders, from cuff to cuff. Given to Edmund Morris by Night Bird, Saulteaux. Bequest of Sir Byron Edmund Walker. ROM HK 587.

Carry the Kettle, Chagakin, Assiniboine chief. Pastel on paper, 1908. Dimensions 62.5 × 50 cm. Edmund Morris Collection. ROM HK 2440.

Splashing Water, Chakikum, Cree. Pastel on paper, 1908. Dimensions 62.5 × 49.5 cm. Edmund Morris Collection. ROM HK 2443.

Walter Ochopowace, Cree hereditary chief. Pastel on paper, 1908. Dimensions 63 × 49 cm. Edmund Morris Collection. ROM HK 2447.

Photograph of a horse's head cover in two pieces. Cloth outlined in orange cotton; heavily beaded with two holes for ears outlined in blue and yellow and two for eyes outlined in red. Length of bottom 39 cm; height 37 cm. Given to Edmund Morris by Walter Ochopowace, Cree. Bequest of Edmund Morris. ROM HK 239.

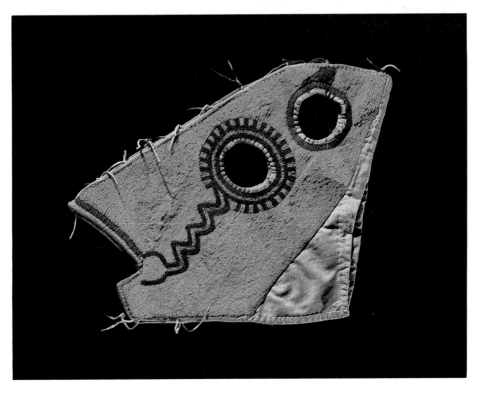

Wolf Collar, Makoyo ki na si, Blackfoot medicine man. Pastel on paper, 1909. Dimensions 63.9 × 50.1 cm. Government of Alberta 0367-300-62.

Photograph of a buffalo hide that belonged to Alexander Morris and that was given by Edmund Morris to Running Rabbit, Blackfoot, for illustration; showing events in Running Rabbit's life. Dimensions 190 × 170 cm (approx.). Bequest of Edmund Morris. ROM 977x1.3.

Photograph of a roach. The long tapering central section is woven of short deer hair dyed red, white, and yellow; the long black and yellow fringe is probably of horse hair. Blackfoot. Length 60 cm. Probably given to Edmund Morris by Walter Ochopowace, Cree. Bequest of Edmund Morris. ROM HK 484.

Landscape of Old Fort Edmonton. Oil on canvas, ca 1910. Dimensions 85.1 × 112.3 cm. Courtesy the Glenbow Museum, Calgary, Alberta, ME.55.39.

Star Blanket, Cree chief and medicine man. Pastel on paper, 1910. Dimensions 63.8 × 50 cm. Collection of the Norman Mackenzie Art Gallery, Gift of Mr Norman Mackenzie, 53-83.

I paint the portrait of Spring Chief, Ninau ksis kum.[24] He is a headman or *(Diary page 105)* minor chief & son of the late head chief Three Bulls. He is a fine strong specimen.

The Head Chief Running Rabbit and his outfit all move off to the two AUG. 15 _____ ranches where they will work. The Indians are all scattered haying so I get Spring Chief to drive me to Gleichen & have Wolf Collar, Makoyo ki na si, a medicine man, come to the agency to be painted.[25] He is now catechist in the Anglican Church but in his young days had been in several battles—& killed a number. When the portrait was finished he requested me to put certain marks on his face—the sun & 2 green moons on either side of his face. These he had always worn in battle. He and two others were once riding on *(Diary page 106)* the plains & were struck down by lightning. He was unconscious, or dead as he expressed it, for two hours & saw these marks. The other 2 were killed.

I drive to the North Camp and stop with D. L. Brereton, the farm instructor.[26] 22ND He comes of a good family, is a son of Judge Brereton & a relative of the Beresfords. In his young days was a cowboy. I go to the lodge of the war chief, old Calf Child. The old man says he is always glad to see me. He showed me an old cap which had belonged to his father, Lone Chief, a chief & renowned warrior. He handed me a present of his father's brush made out of the tail of a buffalo. Said many had tried to get it but he had kept it to this day & it was for me. It was used to brush away mosquitoes.[27]

Again meet the war chief & arrange for sittings. He asked me to be seated, 23 then got from behind him something wrapped in many wrappings—he *(Diary page 107)* partly unwound them & holding it directly in front of him, addressed it—and it apparently answered. He said he had asked it if it was good for him to be painted & if I was good & it had said yes. I showed some curiosity, & he turned it around. It was a crude being of a man—large mouth & eyes, grey hair & painted red. His Sarcee woman, who is very ill & always on her back, now was greatly excited while this was going on. He deceives himself by ventriloquism.

Calf Child comes of a race of warriors. His father, Lone Chief, was counted next to Crowfoot & was liked by all the tribe. Calf Child's woman was a Sarcee whom he took when a girl. Her father, a chief, was called White Buffalo Hoofs.

Brereton was night herding beef for I. G. Baker & Co. who had the contract of *(Diary page 108)* selling beef for the agencies.[28] This farmer of Fort Benton, Montana, had a fur trading post at the junction of the Bow and Elbow rivers, close to the site of Fort Calgary, when the Mounted Police came into this country & it was this from which erected the Fort. Calgary at that time was known by several names—The Mouth, The Elbow, The Junction—& when the detachment came, Fort Brisebois after the Inspector. Col. Macleod called it after his early home in the Highlands, Calgary, which in Gaelic means clear running waters.[29]

Brereton tells me Crowfoot held absolute sway over his people. Once some of the Blackfoot were camped near the Bloods. They got whisky & in a dispute one of the Bloods was killed. Crowfoot called for the murderer & himself shot him down. Another time a prairie fire was sweeping down

(Diary page 109) towards the camp. The Indians saw it but did not move. Crowfoot, coming out of his lodge, looked out & at once ordered all to go & fight it. They never questioned his word but obeyed. At the time of his last illness he told the people not to mourn, that he would die & in three days come to life. He had a trance. They would not let the Dr. of the reserve feel his pulse but he placed his hand on his ankle & found that he lived. After the 3 days he came to, but it was the beginning of the end. When he died the whole nation seemed stunned, even the dogs seemed to know—not a sound was to be heard. They buried him underground but his brother, Three Bulls, said he heard him kicking up the dust so they compromised & raised the coffin nearer the surface.

This summer High Eagle & Iron Shield had a visit from a breed who proved to be an uncle. Near Edmonton there lived an Englishman married to

(Diary page 110) a Cree woman. They had three boys, who one day went hunting bird's eggs—they got a number & went around a lake to look for more, leaving the youngest brother till their return. Coming again, he had gone. They searched but could not see him so ran & told their father. He & a party came & examining the ground, found foot marks on both sides of the boy's tracks but could not follow them up, & the old man died still regretting the little fellow. It was this summer one of the elder sons came to the Blackfoot. He told High Eagle of this incident & he became curious & enquired particularly about markings on the boy which proved him to be his father, adopted into the tribe. He had _____ a Blackfoot woman, & _____ a great warrior. He was killed in one of their battles.

Iron Shield and High Eagle had adopted a brother, Heavy Shield, an older man—his squaw stabbed him to death.

(Diary page 111) Brereton tells me the Blackfoot at the time of the breed rebellion of 1885 were not loyal but they knew the whites were all powerful (both Doucet & Cluny MacDonell confirm this).[30] He says they had crossed the border & had got ammunition & arms from Joe Kipp or Dupines Crull.[31] They had cached this in the ground & were armed to the teeth & had got extra cases for the ammunition. In July they held a great sun dance. The southern Blackfoot & Piegans were present & the Chief of the Gros Ventres. They had a plan cut & dry. Had the last battle of the Crees been successful they intended to take the beef herd, then slaughter the whites as far as the mountains. After that go to the assistance of the Crees. They had runners out & the news of the defeat of the Crees was brought to them sooner than by wire. The sun dance at once broke up & they returned to their different homes.

(Diary page 112) Painted the portrait of old Calf Child. His old Sarcee woman, ill as she is, came, looking ghostly as death. They all approved of it.

The old man is too blind to record his own history on the robe so he relates it to his son Joe who starts, but he proved too dilatory, so the old man takes it to another camp & gets several at work.[32]

High Eagle, Pitauspitau, Blackfoot chief. Pastel on paper, 1909. Dimensions 64 × 49.8 cm. Government of Alberta 0367-300-65.

Poundmaker, Oo pee too cah hay an a pee wee yin, Cree chief. Pastel on paper, from a photograph. Dimensions 62.5 × 50 cm. Edmund Morris Collection. ROM HK 2444.

Peter Erasmus a veteran interpreter spends the morning with us translating the history for me.[33] Calf Child speaks Cree & relates it in Cree to Erasmus. It runs as follows:

I When young I started off with a war party. My father told me—my son you are a fine looking man, don't spoil your good looks by being a coward. You have a fine horse. Mount him, take your war clothes with you, and try & be first. Above all, try & capture some horses & take a scalp. This is how a man proves himself to be brave.

(Diary pages 113–114)

We were coming near the country of the Crees. I was sent out as a scout with three others. We saw a Cree & forced on our horses. I came up to him first—I [had a six shooter & shot him three times] shot & killed him & took part of his scalp—the others took the rest. I took his horse.

II We the Blackfoot are encamped at the Hand Hills, Red Deer Valley—a party of five of us. I had the same black horse. We went on to the Nose Hills but sighted none of the enemy and rode on to the Eye Hills south of Fort Pitt.[34] Here we spied a Cree with others out hunting. We gave chase. My horse was the swiftest. I overtook him, shot him & took his scalp. We came back to our camp at Flag Hills further down, north of Battle River. Here we held a scalp dance. _____ _____

_____ _____ _____ _____ _____.

III I formed a party of eleven for a raid. Starting off we rode night & day. We came upon a number of Cree women cutting wood & rushed on them. I was ahead and, as I came up to them, jumped off my horse & led it. One of the women struck out at me with her axe. I guarded the blow but got wounded in the head. I got hold of the axe & smashed her head in. Shots were exchanged, & hearing it the Crees came rushing down from camp. We rode off. I was forming a rearguard & called out for them not to go, so we turned back & had an encounter—& the Crees fled.

IV We started off a war party—a great number. We met the Crees at the Eye Hills, many of them. We fought—our party was to the south & the Crees to the north. We had made a fort out of branches & the Crees came at us in it. I now had a large horse, a swift mare, & getting restless rushed out naked & mounted my horse. One man came out to meet me. I ran against him with my horse & knocked him down & took his gun & arrows but did not kill him. 2 of our party killed, & three Crees.

V In the morning early, when at the Knee Hills in my lodge, my Sarcee woman called out, I think we are attacked by the Crees. I ran out naked as I was & jumped on my horse. The Crees had surrounded us. I got amongst them. A man came to meet me, he was on foot. I got hold of his scalp & gun, took both & killed him on the spot. We killed eleven Crees, none of us killed. I had been counted brave before, but I was now named by the tribe one of the braves.

VI We are camped by a creek [near the Hand Hills]. The Flat Heads surprised us.[35] Our scouts had been out but had seen nothing. The Flat Heads are all mounted. We chased them to another creek [somewhere near the Red Deer]. They jumped off their horses & left them & came on

Nose Hill is the highest hill or rising on the prairies. Of that lovely Hand Hill close to Red Deer—high, say, for any—it is a long ridge. Flag Hills (near Wetaskiwin). Travel at night—finally they got in day _____ sleeping, some woke. At day break _____ _____ not stopping long _____ _____ _____.

(Diary page 115)

This must have been a war party of Flat Heads, for they were for fine horses.

(Diary page 116)

Calf Child or White Buffalo Calf, Onistaipoka, Blackfoot war chief of the North
Camp. Pastel on paper, 1909. Dimensions
63.9 × 50.1 cm. Government of Alberta
0367-300-64.

Photograph of Calf Child examining Edmund
Morris's portrait of him. Edmund Morris Col-
lection 526. Courtesy Provincial Archives of
Manitoba.

to fight us. We dismounted & met them. After a time they turned & fled. I overtook one (painted on robe red). He made to strike me with his gun but I shot him, took his guns & scalp—that ended the fight. The women all liked me for this!

VII At Battle River there are many, about 40, lodges of us camped near Buffalo Lake. A war party of Crees—Big Bear, Little Pine, & Poundmaker, & their following came upon us at night. We had made a sort of fort of brush. Father Lacombe & John Lereux were in the camp. Lacombe spoke in Cree to them telling them to go away but they would

Three Ponds.

not & he was struck by a bullet. It was a hard fight & lasted all night. I went outside the enclosure, fighting them, & my Sarcee woman stood within singing the war song. I had my war bonnet of buffalo horns & ermine skins.

(Diary page 117)

I took 2 scalps. The fight lasted till daylight, then the Crees fled. 3 women & 2 men of our people killed. We counted 5 Crees killed.

VIII 12 Crees on a horse stealing expedition. We found these men in camp. I jumped on my horse & chased them & got in amongst them. I ran against one of them & knocked him down. While I was fighting him a Cree from behind jumped on my horse to kill me, the others firing all the time. I held him & rode hard to camp & threw him down amongst the lodges & told the women to kill him. None of them—Poundmaker, Big Bear, Piapot—ever did this. I was now made war chief.

IX I took some of our party off. We spied 5 Crees sitting on the edge of a wood, three women & two men. I told my men to wait & I would go & see. I shot some of them, & my men coming up killed the others.

I captured the horses and took a buckskin horse with a red cloth around its neck and gave it to my Sarcee woman. She was glad.

(Diary page 118)
In the Cree country, Sas-katchewan.

The five Blackfoot Hills get their name from this (near Lloydminster).[36]

We are sitting near the lodge where his old Sarcee woman lies ill—she calls out—he is not telling you half that he did. The old chief says—she was brave & often out with me.

X Near the Cypress Hills we came on a party of Crees in a coulee.[37] We attacked them—they were some of Piapot's band. We are Blackfoot, Blood & Piegan all together (I am to the right on robe). I killed a Cree but got a bullet wound through my chest.

These are only a few of his experiences. He had been in 32 fights against the Crows, Flat Heads, Nez Percés,[38] & Crees. He even told me of a party of them going into the country of the Crows. They were discovered & chased by the Crows. One of the party had a bad horse & was lost. He dismounted & seeing

(Diary page 119)

a wolf's hole, enlarged it & crept in unseen. A Crow in pursuit came on ahead. As he came up, the Blackfoot threw the earth which surrounded the hole in the horse's eyes. It reared & threw the rider off, breaking his neck. The Blackfoot then mounted & escaped.

Calf Child, Unistaipoka, White Buffalo Child or Calf—it was the name of his grandfather who handed it over to him when he was a young man. He in turn gave it to his son, Joe, and takes the name of his father, Lone Chief—but he is generally known as Calf Child. The British used to call him Big Charlie. In the wars, before Crowfoot rose by his administrative power to be Head Chief, he took second place to Calf Child. Father Doucet first saw him at the deathbed of a chief. He was naked & painted like a devil & was blowing through bones to drive out the evil spirit or sickness. I got from the old war chief his 2 old medicine bags made of buffalo skin—he has 2 later ones. Before parting with them he took out from each a hawk wrapped in cloths & a large piece of birch bark that had belonged to his father. Some picture writing was scratched on it. At the time of the fight with Big Bear, Poundmaker, Piapot & the others his Sarcee woman got a bullet wound through her arm.

(Diary page 120)

Heavy Shield's grave is on the gravel ridge near the present farm instructor's home. It is the oldest grave on the reserve. He was a powerful Indian in the old days.

Photo taken in 19___.

Heavy Wood, son of Old Sun, is buried on the prairie near the cut bank of the Bow. His son bears the name of his ancestor Heavy Wood & has many of Old Sun's relics, though Frank Try to Fly has the copy of the treaty & most of the charms.

The name Frank Try to Fly but Could Not came in this way: a Blackfoot had a dream that he was a bear & could dive into the Bow River & appear at the other side. He gathered the people & jumped in. Came up nearly drowned & they hauled him out. Again he had a dream—that he could fly. He told the people but they laughed & recalled his other dream, but he insisted so they gathered on the high cut bank, & he jumped into the air & falling to the bottom was smashed.

(Diary pages 121–123)

Old Peter Erasmus is a most interesting character. When the big Cree Treaty was made in '76 the Indians had got him for their interpreter and my father meeting him also had him act as government interpreter. His headquarters were Smoke Lake and at the time of the rebellion his influence was a good one there with James Seenum, the chief.[39] His father, a Dane, came with 2 others from Denmark & settled in Manitoba, marrying a Swampy woman. They wanted Peter to go into the church. He translated the Gospel of St. John into Cree but never intended to take the black robe. He for a time acted as interpreter to for Rev. Thos. Wolsey, who was missionary to the Stonies before Rev. George MacDougall and P. was associated with Rev. Mr. Rundel in preparing his Cree dictionary. _____ works of Evans the missionary.[40] He acted as guide to the Palliser expedition, 1857–58, crossing from Carlton to the north of the Bow River where Morley is & into the Blackfoot country.[41]

Speaking of the MacDougalls, he says of John MacDougall was a sister [*sic*] of Revs. Robert & Egerton Steinhauer.[42] Their father, an Ojibway Indian from Rama, was adopted by a German gentleman, by name Henry Steinhauer, who gave him his name. He became a missionary & founded the Fish Lake Mission.[43]

Old Man Big Plume calls Rev. John MacDougall his son-in-law & through Rev. Canon Stocken sent him a present of a dollar.

He was out hunting the buffalo when the Indians sent for him.

Pakan, James Seenum, stopped the Riel flames from spreading west— White Fish Lake, Smoke Lake. Erasmus is covered with scars he got in various feuds.

Western Journey 1909 / 107

Mr. Brereton tells me about Scraping Hide. In 1895, his child was ill & died. He imagined he had a grudge against Wheatley, the farm instructor, & as is unreasonably the case with the Indian when on the warpath, the first white man he comes across is good enough for his vengeance.[44] About 10 or 11 at night he went up to the Wheatley's house but finding no one there went on to the house of the rationer F. Skinner.* He was resting at the time.

*Frank Skinner, the issuer of rations on the reserve.

Scraping Hide knocked at the door. He came out & asked what he wanted in an abusive manner & called him down. The Indian turned upon him saying, "You will do as well as the other man. I'll kill you as I would a beef steer"—shooting him through the eyes.[45] He went out to the stables, took out Skinner's horse & saddle & rode through the camp, calling threats to certain Indians he had grudges against. He met Spotted Calf & his wife on the road & told them what he had done & that he would be on the hill in the morning where his child was buried, that he wanted to die there. The Indians sent now to Magnus Begg, the agent, who notified the police. Supt. Marshall & three police came down. Begg, Cluny MacDonell & the police went into a coulee near the hill where the Indian was standing. After they had sent a scout asking him to surrender he said he would die there rather than be taken alive. He got up on front of Crowfoot's grave & danced & sang his death

(Diary page 124)

song. Marshall shot but missed him. After exchanging several shots the Indian's gun got jammed. Hiding behind Crowfoot's grave he hung up part of his dress, which misled the police & gave him time to slip down the hill & off across the flat.

About 3 o'clock, Big Baldwin, & MacDonell saw Scraping Hide coming along holding his rifle & chanting.[46] Baldwin shot & broke his arm. He struck into the underbrush. About 4, the police sighted him along the river bed. They got on his tracks & shot him down while climbing the river bank.[47]

Brereton also gave an account of Deer Foot, the noted Blackfoot runner. He once broke into a house near Calgary. The police got on his trail, captured him & locked him in a car house. He found an axe, burst the door & threatened the guard with the axe. He then ran down the CPR track. The

Returning to the agency, I paint Water Chief, one of the minor chiefs.

other police had followed a bunch of Indians & returning along the railroad, met Deer Foot, tried to stop him & he again threatened with the axe. The sergeant tried to intimidate him & shot off his big toe. He bandaged it up & told him to shoot straighter next time. He ran on to Beaupre's store at Gleichen, then escaped on the reserve.[48]

(Diary page 125)

A carload of men were sent from Calgary to trace him up, 40 or 50 police from Calgary. While they were searching the reserve, Deer Foot & his wife were across the border. The next word of him, he had shot his wife through the hand in a quarrel. He finally surrendered later in the fall. He got a sentence of six weeks. He took to drinking hard & finally died of tuberculosis.

SEPT. I am encamped on the plains, Kyaiyii Camp.[49] The spot was a favourite one of the buffalo. There are several sloughs and many buffalo wallows on all sides of my tent, and their trails lead down to the valley of the Bow River, deep cut in the ground. I find a subject for a fine landscape & the Indians marvel when I introduce the buffalo into it. An Indian camp is quite near. Water Chief, son of Little Person & adopted son of his brother Yellow Horse, the head chief, is here.[50] Old Slow Coming Over the Hill, the oldest man on *(Diary page 126)* the reserve; he has the largest lodge in the camp. See his old stooped figure with staff in hand, walking far over the plains. He has a herd of 200 horses & will part with none of them. He believes when he dies he will go to the happy hunting grounds & will have all those horses & be again young. He has two eagle wings & expects to live till they break in two. The thought seems to prolong his life—he is very ancient.

When I arrived he came & sat taking it all in—then got active, carrying in my outfit & arranging it for me. I paint the wife of Water Chief. She is a rather good looking woman.[51]

I have as cook Jack Bergess, a young Irishman of 27. He had been through the South African war, & his brother was shot down by his side in a coulee by the Boers. He is full of stories of the war & the west—is good company. *(Diary page 127)*

The Indians come & tell us Sun Calf, an Indian of 45, is at large on the reserve 14TH & coming our way. He had been imprisoned at Calgary when I first came this summer. He had, in a drunken brawl, smashed his brother's face with an axe. He was needed at Strathmore as a witness. The police brought him down, & when returning he got in one side of the car & out the other & escaped handcuffed. The Indians hold that he is possessed of evil spirit & can break asunder the handcuffs. They advise us to take in our axes.

It is late & old Slow Coming Over the Hill keeps up a continual chant in which the coyotes join. The Indians watch tonight.

Chief Spring Chief, Little Shield & Bob Poor Eagle come to see me. Spring *says his father Three Bulls. Chief* was in the battle with the Crees when they were driven into the lake. Given in picture writing on Running Rabbit's robe[52]—he was stabbed by one *(Diary page 128)* of the Crees but killed him.

Crowfoot led the Blackfoot on a raid to the Snake Country. They came upon a large camp of the Snakes. Crowfoot told them to be quiet & wait till they slept—they then swept down on them & killed nearly all, even the women & children. Only a few escaped, the horses having stampeded. 5 Blackfoot were killed.

The Thunder Woman is famous in the tribe. When a little girl she went with a lot of women to gather berries & big bear carried her off—she kept perfectly still & after a time walked out of its den & the people all marvelled, thinking she had been killed. She is related to Little Shield.

Spring Chief when a boy, over 20 years ago, joined the buffalo chase with bow & arrows & killed one, but _____ old Cree came at him & demanded the buffalo. He said, take it.

When Poundmaker came to the Blackfoot, the Crees were still at war with them & he went back & told them to make peace. *(Diary page 129)*

Crowfoot had lost a son in the wars & coming upon Poundmaker, who closely resembled him, went to his mother, a Cree woman, & said, he is my son, & the woman told him to follow Crowfoot.

Three Bulls with many others out hunting the buffalo. They got seven—six got away. One of them he chased up to a cut bank, not seeing it. The buffalo jumped over & his horse, a swift one, had just time to turn quickly & saved both. Another time he chased a buffalo bull. It got enraged & rushing at his horse cut it in the belly. He fell off his horse. He had a blanket over his loins & rolled into a creek, & the buffalo followed up & licked him with its tongue. He recovered consciousness & saw the buffalo by him. It licked him again & Three Bulls grabbed its tongue. Terrified, it ran off, but wounded him with its horns.

(Diary page 130)   150 Blackfoot on the warpath—meet the Crees & fight—they found Cree women gathering wood. Three Bulls captured one of them & told the Blackfoot not to kill her, but one called him crazy, saying that some Blackfoot had been killed & asked what he would do with the woman. So Three Bulls killed her & took her scalp. They killed all the women. The Crees heard the shooting & said the women must all be killed. There was 2 feet of snow on the ground—all the Crees had snowshoes. The Blackfoot had none & said, let us turn away, they will kill us all, let us run to the cut bank. But in doing it 50 of the Blackfoot were killed. The Crees were afraid to follow.

I question Spring Chief about chiefs before Crowfoot. Many Swans was his predecessor. (Head of the Confederacy. Erasmus met him in 57/8. He was a power—is buried somewhere near Edmonton.) Before him there ruled two chiefs over all, Three Suns and Chief Bird. They say Three Suns was cruel & *(Diary page 131)* he was afflicted with some disease. They say the Crees gave him bad medicine.

Crowfoot told Gov. Laird at the time of the Treaty he was head of all and to make Old Sun, who was a minor chief, head chief of the North Camp.[53] Cluny MacDonell tells me the North & South Camp refers to long ago. Those of the North Camp hunted about the Saskatchewan & those of the South Camp to the south & across the border.

Three Bulls told his son Spring Chief about a young Crow Indian, a chief, and another chief, a Snake. The Crow had taken a woman as a wife & the Snake had a girl, but the Snake was paying attention to the wife of the Crow, & he watched. She went to get water. The Snake was there & he picked up a pebble & put it in his mouth & threw it to his Crow girl, & she did the same. This is a kiss. The Crow chief said he would see which was the best looking. He knew he was & told the Indian so. Early in the morning he told her to paint herself & dress up & he sent her over to the Snake, but when she came to him the Snake removed the colour & put the Snake design of a chief's wife & sent her back. Her husband ushered her back to the Snake & declared war.

(Diary page 132)   When the Mounted Police came into the country the Blackfoot lodges were all grouped together. They all went after the buffalo—killed a lot & then started to butcher them. One went off & returned saying the Crees had sighted them. These Crees, eleven of them, had made two holes in the ground & got in. An old Blackfoot who spoke Cree said he would confuse them by telling them only Crees were there. They would not listen & were going to shoot him but told him to go away. He said they were all crazy, that they were Crees in the camp. They then came out & found they had been outwitted. The Blackfoot took them to a high butte. Here they smoked. All the Blackfoot came around & shot at the ground where a young Cree was sitting smoking. The Crees ran & the Blackfoot killed them all. This happened when the police had come but the Indians had not heard of their

arrival. This was in Sept. 1874. They had heard of the fighting & had *(Diary page 133)* entrenched themselves by throwing up earthen works—Col. Macleod, Col. Irvine, Capt. Denny & 5 men.[54] Macleod asked for the Head Chief & Crowfoot came & conferred with them. He told them the land was his but he would keep the peace. He asked them to go where Calgary now stands.

Spring Chief drove me through the sand dunes—Ghosts Coulee—we came to a slough & in the centre of it were piled coffins—the lids damaged & the skeletons gaping out. Others on the rising ground of the sand hills, scrubby willows all about. It was a gruesome sight. The Irish lad was dumbfounded.

I remove my camp from the old buffalo wallow to the sand dunes to paint a picture of death lodges. Jones, the farm instructor, told me he once rode through them & came upon a new death lodge.[55] An Indian was standing *(Diary page 134)* guard with a gun in his hand. He would look at the lodges of his brothers & then at the sun—and as it neared the horizon, said, "Is slow in going down." The entrances all face the east, closed by branches.

The Indian camp moved north. Swarms of horseflies came when they left, a horrible pest and an enemy. Jack swore he saw a ghost from the _____.[56] I looked—it was an unfortunate deserted dog in the last stages of mange. All this I think proved too much for Jack. We went to Gleichen for supplies & he went on to Calgary.

Moved my camp to the plains where Spring Chief & Little Shield are camped. I paint portrait of Little Shield.

Drive into Gleichen to meet my friend A. P. Proctor, the sculptor. He had 29TH come out from New York, stopping at Montreal & Regina. It was an awful night, stormy & wild. He is out after big game but will join my camp for a *(Diary page 135)* while.

I move camp to the valley of the Bow. All along the cut bank are old buffalo 30 trails leading to the river. There is splendid variety in the grasses & shrubs in the sand dunes which are close to hand. My camp is not far from old St. John's Mission, now deserted as it was found to be too near the Romanists.[57]

Spring Chief drives us through the sand dunes. 31

Three others join us & we drive in the sand dunes. They get 19 prairie chicken OCT. 1ST & Proctor kills 15.[58] I made some sketches.

Drive to the camp of the head chief, Running Rabbit. He & his wives were 2ND preparing their winter house, filling it up with clay between the logs. The chief has a number of sons: Duck Chief, Big Nose, Last Medicine Man (d., *(Diary page 136)* father of Dick Bad Boy), Mikki d., White Man—deaf & blind, Horton. The chief was called when a young man Last Medicine Man, later White Buffalo Lying Down, & after this Running Rabbit. He gave Mikki the 2nd name. Proctor makes a sketch of the cut banks.

3RD Peter Erasmus, my father's old interpreter, & Dick Bad Boy drove down to see me. Duck Chief & Calf Son came, too. Peter says in 1857, they started for Battleford, travelling a month, and all the way passed through vast herds of buffalo which opened apart to let the red river carts pass through & this as far as the mountains.[59] He says the grizzly bears, black bears & others lived on the plains. John the Buffalo, an Indian, told him he had seen a grizzly grapple a buffalo by the horns & break its neck. They had their dens in the cut banks, & he has often seen them stretched out on the ground in the shade.

(Diary page 137) Make more sketches of the death lodges & of Little Shield _____ for this
4TH picture.[60] He became anxious as the sun got low. They fear ghosts.

5TH Pack up & drive to Gleichen—rearrange our outfits & take train for Macleod. Proctor goes to Pincher Creek & from there to Twin Butes after the mountain
6TH sheep,[61] & I go to Brocket & drive to the old agency on the Piegan Reserve— stop with my old friend Father Doucet.

7TH The chiefs all drive down to see me. I gave them presents—Running Wolf, a staff from Ceylon; Butcher & Bull Plume, medals; & Big Swan, a flag.
    I have a long talk with the chiefs. Running Wolf tells me the Bow River had been called by the early tribes Swift Current, because before it was frozen hard the buffalo in crossing broke through the ice & were drowned in the
(Diary page 138) swift current. Running Wolf's generation named it Big River, & the younger generation called it the Bow. The Blackfoot Crossing was a rendezvous for all tribes because it was the only spot they could cross when the river was swollen by the floods.
    Running Wolf's father, Iron Shirt, was head chief of the Piegans; after him came Bull's Head, Stumixotokon, who gave the name to Col. Macleod—at the Treaty of '77. He said he was too old & handed over the head chiefship to Eagle Tail, who lies buried on top of the hill near the slaughter house, his son North Axe by his side. When the rebellion broke out, Eagle Tail was old & did not want trouble. He kept loyal. Red Crow of the Bloods was most loyal & as he had the following of the Bloods, this all had weight with the crafty Crowfoot. North Axe succeeded his father & died young. Then came Crow Eagle followed by the present chief Butcher, a relative of Eagle Tail, former chief.
(Diary page 139) Bull Plume is very aggressive & annoys the older chiefs, interrrupting them. I had to tell him I heard only Running Wolf for he had an ancient story. The old man began:

> About 200 years ago two medicine men of our tribe came from the north, the Bow River was so high they could not cross. One of them sat down and, resting his pipe in the river, began smoking. The river parted and the dogs with their travois passed over. It was in the days when they had not yet got horses. He told the other medicine man to go to the opposite bank and smoke in the same way & the river parted still more and his people all crossed.
> The names of these medicine men were "Weasel Heart" 2nd, and "All

Thought He Was Holy".[62] The same two medicine men one day had been in the brush on the river bank making bows & arrows. One looked into the river & saw a lodge. He said to his friend to look but he saw nothing. Then All Thought He Was Holy said he would go and see what it was. Weasel Heart said, no the river is too low, but he would not listen. He got a log and on it floated to the spot where he had seen the lodge. Just as he got there he let go the log & went down. The lodge was there and no waters about. He went in and an old man* told him to take a seat, that he would give him the lodge & all. The old man's lodge was painted yellow.* Another lodge painted black he gave to Weasel Heart and sent a message for him to come down. All Thought He Was Holy passed out, the waters not troubling him, & told his friend to go down & the old man would give him the black lodge. The old man taught them the buffalo song & by singing it the buffalo at once came about their lodges. This song is still sung by the Blackfoot and two lodges are still painted like these water lodges by the descendants of these medicine men.

(Diary page 140)

*The chief of the water people.

*A buffalo bull's head painted on one side and a cow's head on the other.

This was told to my old friend Running Wolf, who related it to me, by his father, the head chief Iron Shirt, who died an old man & had been in three sieges of the smallpox, so he had seen many years.[63]

Joe Scott, son of a trader who lived on this reserve, by a Piegan woman, *(Diary page 141)* interpreted for me. He had come from the Bloods. After my interview I get him to drive me out to the old Buffalo pound of the Piegans. It is in the Porcupine Hills near the spot which Col. Steel had marked as a natural fortress for the people of Macleod in case of the tribes' rising in 1885. A very wild spot & it will supply me with many motifs.

They used to drive the buffalo over the steep perpendicular wall of rock, & in the natural pound below the buffalo horns are three feet thick. Flint arrowheads are found there in quantities.

High up in this wall of rock is a small grotto & here are the bones of an Indian doubtless killed by a maddened bull. Not far from this is a large boulder looking like an altar. Ages ago it had dislodged itself from the ridge of rock above. Its course down the ascent is still marked. This rock was an *(Diary page 142)* ancient burial ground of the tribe's—only one or two bleached bones remain on top but Father Doucet says when he first came, there were many remains of Indians on top, with all their belongings. He says cowboys scattered them but I think it was the work of storms for bones are deep in the ground all about and on the surface of the ground. I picked up an elk tooth, many old beads, arrowheads & c. It is _____ to reserves. In one of the coulees not far from the Oldman River is another group of huge rocks & this has been used recently as a burial spot.

The graves in the sand dunes of the Blackfoot were different. They had pitched the death lodges in a group of willows. I found many signs of old lodges, nothing left but the bones & some of the poles rotted away.

My friend Proctor is a great hunter. His father, a Canadian, had gone to Colorado mining, & the son afterwards went to Montana & lived the life of *(Diary page 143)* that country. At 16 he killed a grizzly bear & a bull elk in one day. Later he was hunting the pumas or mountain lions in the Rockies. He had wounded one but it got off. Next day it snowed, & as he was walking, stirred up blood & traced the animal, but as he went he passed a scrubby overhanging tree & heard a great growl—turning he saw the puma two feet away with its mouth open. He had not time to shoulder his gun but stuck it in its mouth and fired.

He could hardly accustom himself to our peaceful Indians after the Indians of Colorado & Montana & always had his gun ready, expecting trouble. I named him the Parson—& the Indians at once took it up.

8TH   We all drive to Brocket. It is Treaty payment—all the Indians present. I take the names of those I will use for models.

(Diary page 144)   In the afternoon they have sports—riding horseback, & the Treaty money soon goes in betting. Water Chief of the Blackfoot & a handsome young buck Arthur White Elk came, also some Bloods. After, they will all go to Macleod & Pincher to have sports & spend money on clothes & c.

I have lunch with Mr. Black, the clerk.[64] He is an old timer & was for a long time with the Bloods. He tells me, the chief Blackfoot Old Woman, whom I painted, once had a dream that he was to go and live alone in a desolate spot. He did this and while there dreamt he was to return & kill his four wives, one a year. He came to his lodge & told them this. They gave themselves as a sacrifice to the sun.

(Diary page 145)   In a book called *Where the Buffalo Roamed* are some reproductions of Paul Kane's pictures—*The Buffalo Chase* & c.[65] Father Doucet, who has witnessed many buffalo hunts, says they are trash & does not count him an artist. In reality Paul Kane was an adventurer & explorer, but his works have a value and in craftsmanship they are better than the other Indian painter Catlin.[66]

George de Forest Brush, the New York painter, has done some excellent work—*The Aztec & the King* & c.[67] He lived amongst the Indians for a time & Proctor tells me he is again going to take up Indian work after a long lapse. He was a pupil of Gerome's and these early pictures show the influence.[68]

Father Doucet tells me Crowfoot was cunning as a fox & crafty, & that Governor Dewdney (who began life as a prospector & was uneducated) was like a child in the hands of Crowfoot.[69] He was without tact & wanted to get the Blackfoot to fight the Crees, which showed an absolute lack of under-*(Diary page 146)*   standing. Crowfoot in his heart would like to have wiped out the whites, but he was powerless. They had no means of support & the Govt. was funding them.

Mr. T. C. Wade of Victoria, the lawyer who was employed to investigate the Alaskan boundary dispute, in going over records in England, found that there was a secret agreement between the British & American governments to kill off the buffalo as that was the only way they could control the aborigines.[70]

During the Rebellion of 1885, Doucet had seen Crees encamped on the Blackfoot Reserve hidden in the bushes along the Bow River. They were trying to stir the Blackfoot up.[71]

Doucet remembers old Munroe. He at one time lived on the Piegan Reserve & married a Piegan woman. His 2nd son was a good buffalo hunter—once when alone was surrounded by a number of plains Assiniboine & killed them all.[72]

In going over a trunk of old letters of my grandfather's, his brother wrote to him in 1816, from Brockville on the St. Lawrence River, that the Indians were encamped on the island & he expected them in to trade. Grandfather, going to the military settlement on the Rideau with the disbanded troops after the war in 1816, got the Indians to work for him. These Indians of the Ottawa Valley called him The Rising Sun—Shakeishkeik. From him my father learned to have a deep sympathy for the red men. He was elected in 1821 by the settlers to represent them in the Provincial Parliament, & was a member of one or other branch of the Legislature for thirty years, & held offices of Receiver General & President of Her Majesty's Executive Council.

(Diary page 147)

My cousin James Morris, Q.C.,[73] had a flint arrowhead he had picked up on the land where my great grandfather Alexander Morris lived in 1806–9, Elizabethtown (Brockville).*

*having come there from Montreal. He had come to Canada from Scotland in 1801, & travelled between Montreal & Glasgow.

Going back to old Munroe, as he was known in Alberta—J. W. Schultz, the trader, in his most interesting work—*My Life as an Indian*—devoted a chapter to him—The Story of Rising Wolf—for that is the name the Blackfoot gave him, Mah kwo i pwo ahts. Hugh Munroe's father, of the same name, was a colonel in the British army & his mother, a member of the LaRoches, a noble family of French émigrés, bankers in Montreal & large land owners in that vicinity. Hugh was born on the family estate at Three Rivers,[74] it was in July 1798. At 15, he, 1813, entered the service of the Hudson's Bay Company & went to Mountain House near the Rockies.[75] Thousands of Blackfoot were encamped about him wanting to trade for goods the flotilla had brought. As yet the company had no Blackfoot interpreter, their speech having first to be interpreted into Cree & then into English. Many of the Blackfoot proper, the North Blackfoot, spoke good Cree, but the more southern tribes of the confederacy, the Bloods & Piegans, did not understand it. The factor entailed Munroe to live a time with the Piegans & learn their language, also to see that they returned to Mountain Fort with their furs the following summer. Word had been received that following the course of Lewis & Clark, American traders had been yearly pushing farther & farther westward & had even reached the mouth of the Yellowstone about the eastern line of the vast territory claimed by the Blackfoot as their hunting ground.[76] The company feared this competition; Munroe was to do his best to prevent it. He left the fort with 800 lodges of Piegans—about 8000 souls. Doucet knew him at Edmonton; he was an old man then and had gained his freedom from the company. He after that acted as interpreter on the Piegan Reserve and later crossed the border. He had a numerous family.[77]

(Diary page 148)

(Diary page 149)

A son of Dr. Bright, the discoverer of Bright's disease, came to Alberta as a cowboy, leading their wild life.[78] His father was coming to see him, so the day he arrived, he rounded up the cattle of the great Cochrane ranch on his bit of land. The old man was greatly impressed with his progress & sent him a good annuity! A son of another distinguished man Dan Morrison, the artist & writer, was also a cowboy in Alberta. He was noted for killing calves & taking only the sweetbreads to eat!

(Diary page 150)
Senator Cochrane who owned the Cochrane ranch was once riding on the plains with a friend.[79] He saw an Indian approaching, dressed in grey flannels, & said, here's an Indian dressed as well as a white man. As the buck passed he remarked, yes, & why in hell shouldn't I be!

I often regret the Cochranes sold the ranch—it is now owned by the Mormons.[80] J. A. Cochrane, the eldest son, is married to my sister Eva. She and Margaret, Mrs. Malloch, were twins.[81] At the Indian Treaty made by my father, the Crees named them (E. A.) Tabis Roo Amikook—Equal to the Earth, (M.) Tabis Roo Kiyick—Equal to the Sky.* They called my father Kitchioki-mow—the Great Chief.

*When they named the twins, then young girls, they gave them each an elk tooth which was good medicine & was to bring them good luck.

The Blackfoot called Jerry Potts, the guide of the Mounted Police, Bear Child.[82]

Erasmus, my father's interpreter, his mother was a brother [*sic*] of the 1st native Anglican clergyman ordained. His name, Henry Budd. He was brought in from York Factory by West[83] & was adopted by an English gentleman who provided him funds to be educated. He worked among the Indians at The Pas as a catechist. The nephew, Peter Erasmus, left his home for Fort Edmonton & acted as interpreter for a Methodist minister—then

(Diary page 151)
went as guide for the Palliser Expedition. After that he was interpreter with Rev. Geo. MacDougall at Pakan, or Victoria, on the Saskatchewan.[84] This minister afterward went to Morley about 67. Then came the Treaties & Erasmus was interpreter. He is now 76 & is studying the Blackfoot language.

While with Palliser's expedition, there was a large camp of Blackfoot in the Red Deer Valley at Hand Hills, 150 lodges. One of them stole 2 of the horses. The interpreter refused to go after them & Erasmus volunteered. He rode up to the lodge where the horse was & untied it. The Indian came out & they had a struggle. He shot at Peter, but his gun _____ _____ _____ off. A great crowd of Indians came around him. Fortunately the Head Chief Many Swans came out of his lodge & with his quirt drove the Indians away, saying he would never shed white man's blood.

Erasmus had driven down & had dinner at my camp. My friend Proctor, the sculptor, was with me. Our camp was beautifully situated on the plain at the foot of the Sand Hills with a grove of trees to the back & Indian lodges not far away. The old man said, what would the Governor say if he could see you!

(Diary page 152)
In September while the Ministers were in council a fire broke out in the west wing of the Parliament Bldgs., Toronto.[85] The library was totally destroyed. Rare books & manuscripts which can never be replaced all went up in smoke. Sir James Whitney replied to my wire that the portraits were all saved.[86] I afterwards heard that one of the first things the Ministers did was to see that the portraits were saved, taking a personal hand. Some of the series of Indian

Slow Coming Over the Hill, Itspeeotamisow, Blackfoot. Pastel on paper, 1908. Dimensions 62.5 × 51 cm. ROM HK 2418.

Installation view. Edmund Morris Collection of Indian Portraits and Artifacts at the Canadian Art Club, 57 Adelaide St E., Toronto, 29 March to 17 April 1909. Collection of Edward P. Taylor Reference Library, Art Gallery of Ontario. Gift of Edgar J. Stone, 1953.

portraits—last year's work—were stored in the basement till my return when I was to inspect the hanging. The whole wing was burnt to the ground.

The Indian work of Catlin, the first painter to go among the native tribes, in 1830 had a similar narrow escape. Catlin spent many years among them, going to the most savage tribes, and was the first to describe them. He

(Diary page 153)

painted heads & wrote a book describing them. He went to France & found a purchaser for his collection but an American officer, hearing of it, said they were quite false & his account untrue. It was a _____ libel & lost the painter the sale. He was now in great poverty & an American Quaker advanced him money on the collection which he stored in his house.[87] The house was burnt but the portraits uninjured. They are now in the White House at Washington. Others were purchased by a nobleman in England & recently offered for sale.

When the Governor General Lord Minto visited the Blackfoot he told them his wife had the blood of the Algonkians in her veins, for she is a descendant of Pocahontas, the Indian maid who saved the life of Capt. John Smith, the discoverer of Virginia.[88] The present Governor General, Earl Grey, is a brother of Lady Minto's.[89] The Japanese Prince Lie Hung Chang also came to the Blackfoot.[90] He was surprised and told them they did not belong to this continent but were his people—that they resemble most strongly a wild tribe of Chinese in the interior of the country. He gave all the chiefs medals.

(Diary page 154)

The Indians chose isolated huge rocks to place their dead out of the reach of the coyotes & other wild animals, but the great storms generally scatter them.

There is no doubt that many Indians are buried alive. They are always in great haste to put the shroud of blankets & wrappings about them & hurry them away.

When Crowfoot was dying all the medicine men were in his lodge with their old rattles of buffalo skin. They got on one side & the women on the other, chanting. As I said before, he went off in a trance & the Indians would have buried him, for as soon as he became unconscious the report of a gun was heard & they had killed his best horse. Fortunately, a white doctor was present.

When he really passed away the medicine men all helped themselves to his belongings. Doucet tells me some Indians, if they recover from the hands of the medicine men, are as when they first came into the world—bare to the skin.

Last year I had left a buffalo robe with the Piegans to be painted & it arrived in time for my Exhibition of Indian Portraits & loose collection of objects & Indian objects of art, held in the Gallery of the Canadian Art Club, the old

(Diary page 155)

Court House, Toronto, last March.[91] Mr. B. E. Walker, C.V.O., opened this Exhibition with an address. The press spoke well of it. The closing night I gave a smoker, inviting my men friends. Horatio Walker & Proctor came up from New York for it. As we were breaking up I struck the tom tom & Proctor & I gave the war dance!

See Father Doucet's letter.

On the Piegan robe I spoke of is recorded incidents from the lives of the chiefs Running Wolf, Big Swan, Butcher & Bull Plume. Doucet sent me a translation. He says the Indians came to see it. They said all was true except the scene Bull Plume made. He is a great talker & boasts but has a good intellect & had he been educated would have made a good lawyer.

William Brigman, P.R.C.A., writes me an account of the burial of Pound-maker & of the Sun Dance of the Blackfoot. He was with them in 1886.

In July I called on Père Lacombe who with the other clergy was attending a meeting in Calgary. The son of Ermine Skin, the Cree chief, had come from Hobbema to see him, a good-looking Indian. The Rev. Père says he has only one thought now, his home which he is founding for old people. He had before started a home for the half breed children but they burnt it down. His life is being written.[92] *(Diary page 156)*

On the way out I called on Mr. John MacDougall of Lockport, Manitoba. He has an interesting collection of fragments of pottery found in the vicinity of the Red River—on them are various designs.

At one time Col. Irvine made up his mind he would write a history of the RNWM Police. He and another officer met, they got talking of the old days, refreshed with Scotch, & the hours slipped by. The Col. looked at his watch in the early hours of the morning & exclaimed, by Jove! Extraordinary & we've written nothing. This was repeated several times with the same result. He has Mr. P. Turner living with him now & engaged on the work.

Erasmus told me the word Bungee applied to the Indians about Lake Winnipeg & is derived from the Ojibway word Pungee, meaning a little.[93] They used to sell baskets & brooms made of the fibre of the ash tree and would say give me a little—Pungee.

In *Gunner Jingo's Jubilee*—Major General T. Bland Strange, late of the Royal Artillery & who had a ranch adjoining the Blackfoot reserves & led troops in the last rebellion, refers to a young fellow he had with him amongst the Blackfoot as a son of Governor Morris.[94] He is wrong here—my brothers left Manitoba in 1878 & have never been west since—except William, the eldest, who was in the Quebec Cavalry & took supplies to the Governor General's Bodyguard in 1885, but was never in Alberta, & could not speak Blackfoot. I met Genl. Strange's son, a rancher who was selling out & after a visit to England proposed to settle near Edmonton. The General had been at the Citadel, Quebec, & was much liked by his men. He now lives retired in England. *(Diary page 157)*

Col. Irvine had two volumes of his letters to his sisters bound. Last winter he burnt them but Mrs. Irvine had before taken extracts. The old man thought his time was up last winter.

One disease, the white plague, tuberculosis, is playing havoc with the native tribes. Before the coming of the whites it was unknown to them. Now the doctors hold that about 70% of them have it in some form or another.[95] Fomerly leading the free roving open air life & living in their lodges summer & winter with a current of air constantly passing, & plunging in the cold rivers made them a strong hardy race. Food was the strong meat of the buffalo. The Govt. has exhorted them to build houses but it proves false. The same was experienced with the Crofters in the Highlands of Scotland. Their old homes were full of air holes & they were free from diseases, but in new homes with windows & doors tightly closed they soon fall sick & die. This should have the closest attention of the Department, & some form of *(Diary page 158)* ventilation introduced. It is useless employing doctors to cure them & make many reports unless the root of this evil is got at. Again, one consumptive living in these tiny log cabins with many soon spreads the disease. It attacks them in its most virulent form. Flat Dagger, a fine young Blackfoot, was carried off in his full strength. Jones, the farm instructor, was going to see him but a friendly Indian told him not to, that he wished to take someone on the long journey—but Jones went & as he reached the lodge they were carrying out the body. Many of them become blind—trachoma brought on from granular lids.[96]

Old Running Wolf, the Piegan chief, when a young man was once out among a hostile tribe, the Kootenays.[97] He wore on his breast a medal he had got from an American & he thought this would protect him. The Kootenays all attacked him. He ran to the lodge of the chief & caught a little child up & held it to his breast. This touched the chief, & he protected him.

(Diary page 159) R. S. MacDonell, or Cluny as he is called, told me there was a batallion of
9th Battalion, French Canadian soldiers stationed at Gleichen & more at Cluny during the
Quebec Rebellion.[98] The Indians indulged in bravado & looked with contempt at the
Volunteers. French who were of much smaller stature.

When the Piegan chiefs came to see me this time, their minds were greatly troubled as the Inspector Markle has arranged to sell by auction a portion of the reserve near Brocket on the CPR. Nothing could be done without the consent of the majority. Numerous meetings were called & the majority always opposed. After a time the chiefs & their following grew weary of being continually asked to come & a meeting was held when the majority of those present voted for the sale. They are off to Macleod & will probably employ a lawyer. The present Government seems determined to break the reserves. On the Blackfoot Reserve an irrigation ditch was put through the reserve against the wish of the chiefs. If it was a Government work it would be different, but it is the Southern Alberta Irrigation Co., & Sifton & McClintock are the grafters.[99]

(Diary page 160) See in Grinnell's *Blackfoot Lodge Tales*—Two War Trails—p. 89.[100] Father heard from the Crees a different version relating to Kom in a kus mound. The Crees were entrenched in the ground completely surrounded by the Blackfoot & were dying of thirst. The chief said he would take chances & ran with a kettle to the spring for water. He dashed out & when he filled the kettle he held it up high & took a deep draught. A Blackfoot bullet pierced the kettle & went through his eye, coming out through the temple. He put his thumb over the hole in the kettle & rushed back with water for his companions. He was a brave Cree chief. Doucet remembers him with a cloth which he always wore over his eye.

Col. Irvine has a collection of Indian relics. Sheriff Inkster has the best necklace of grizzly bear's claws which Sitting Bull used to wear, & George Allan has the collection of relics which Paul Kane made. Canon Stocken has loaned his collection to the Banff Museum.[101]

Many of the Piegans came to see me. I questioned the old chief Big Swan & Head Chief Butcher & the other Indians who accompanied them—Bad Boy, Many Robes, Side Hill & others—about the leaders of the Blackfoot & their people long ago. They tell me the first who led them against the other Indians was called "The Boy". He & his people chased the buffalo from where Pincher Creek stands to the timber country about the present city of Edmonton & they went into the country of the Crows. After him came Sun Bull, the war chief or leader—and he was succeeded by Kyaiyii, a great war chief, rich in horses & robes. It was after him the Head Chief of the Blackfoot named me. Old Hugh Munroe, called by the North Piegans Wolf Talk, married one of their women, the Fox Woman, a near relative of Iron Shirt, the Head Chief & father of the present chief Running Wolf. Munroe was always with the Piegans both in their hunts & fights. He spoke good Blackfoot & Cree.

14TH

(Diary page 161)

He was rich in robes—his brother was called Many Mules because he had got many of these animals.

The Blackfoot called Father Lacombe Good Heart, Father Doucet Little Father, & Brother John Birchman (van Zieghen) Our Brother.

Brother John had been a professor in a College at Courtrey[102] in Flanders & had 70 boys under him. He says the Indian boys are as quick to learn knowledge & trades as any of his former pupils. He has great satisfaction seeing the younger men all speak English. The Indians called John Lereux Three in One. He once explained the mystery of the Trinity & it was very curious to them so they called him Three in One. Lereux never spoke of his past life & never remained long in one place.

(Diary page 162)

The Indians brought many ancient relics for me. Chief Old Swan gave me his skin leggings trimmed with Indian hair, & I bought from him quiver for bow & arrows, cow skin. From Bad Boy I got a quiver full of arrows & bow—made of skin. From others, medicine rattles, wooden cups, buffalo stones, bags made of unborn weasels, & c.

When the school pupils tell the stories of the Bible to their parents & the old men, they all laugh & think them very strange. All except the Flood. This was also handed down in their legends.

Father Doucet says a spot is marked at the Blackfoot Crossing where a great fight was fought by the Blackfoot against the Crows. They drove them away. The Blackfoot were at that time allied with the Crees against the Crows. An aged Blackfoot, Running Wolf, member of this tribe, told him this. It was perhaps 100 or 150 years ago.

(Diary page 163)

Brereton told me, on the side of the Red Deer valley near Berry Creek, on the top of a butte, there is a large rock, crudely shaped like a head, large mouth from ear to ear and eyes, hollow in the rock where the Crees placed offerings.[103] It was their custom & is still, I believe, to make journeys to this spot about July.

Amongst the ancient relics I have got is a fine specimen of the fossil shell entril, sections of which are found by the Indians & treasured as talismans or charms. They called them I-nís-kim, the buffalo stone. The owner is regarded as very fortunate.

(Diary page 164) There's a legend about the first buffalo which was found, see Grinnell's *Blackfoot Lodge Tales,* p. 126.[104] Running Wolf told me it was their custom to set one up on their lodge & in the morning the direction it pointed they would go after the buffalo & find lots & lots of buffalo. I have sections of this sort of shell which the Indians gave me & which they had carried in their fire bags as charms.

Mrs. Black, the wife of the clerk at Piegan Reserve, has a fossil resembling a fish or lizard. It also breaks into sections & forms the I nís kim (they are ammonites or sections of baculites). All these things were regarded as supernatural & had some great power. Just as the Crees used to worship the bones of a mammoth partly submerged in the ground—see Hind, *Red River, Saskatchewan & Assiniboine Expeditions.*[105]

I had heard of a buffalo robe with Indian history & life painted on it which the Blackfoot had presented to Col. Macleod. I asked Mrs. Macleod what had become of it. She said she gave it to Hon. R. W. Scott in Ottawa. I wrote to Col. Fred White & he replied that Mrs. Scott told him it was ruined by rats & insects & was destroyed some years ago. It had been originally a parfleche case.

(Diary page 165)
[Clockwise from top: the quivers of war—when in war, when riding, when walking long distance]

It is what the Indians were, & what a noble life they had, roaming the plains after the game & living in their lodges of buffalo skins rich in the robes of this animal, and how superbly they fit into the surrounding landscape that interests so many of us.

15TH The wife of Head Chief Butcher is a fine old woman, stout & healthy—her father was a chief called White Buffalo in the Middle. She has a brother called White Buffalo _____.

I walked over to see my old friend Running Wolf. He lives in the same beautiful valley of the Bow where his father, Iron Shirt, camped before him *(Diary page 166)* when he was hunting in the north. The river takes several curves through cut banks—a plain on one side, then a stretch of prairie, & rising above this the Porcupine Hills & the so named Fort Steel. He gave me a present of a precious relic bag which belonged to his father, Iron Shirt. It is worked with porcupine quills & beads—an ancient spearhead, made by the Indians when they first found iron, and 2 buffalo stones. Though he is nearly eighty or over, his mind is perfectly clear. He had just returned from the hunt & had his catch of two eagles & gave his eagle song.

I questioned the old man again about the early chiefs of his nation. He says The Boy and Sun Bull were the chiefs over all the Blackfoot. Sun Bull was his grandfather. His early name was Running Wolf.

Sār co mā pe (boy)

In the evening a long conversation with Father Doucet. He says, & it is true, that the early history of the Blackfoot nation is involved in the dim mist. They were in the north, as he before told me, & again repeated that the Crees called Greater Slave Lake the Lake of the Strangers after the Blackfoot whom they named strangers.[106] On the other hand, when he first came amongst the tribe, he was told that an old Piegan woman who kept the traditions of her people came from the south country, up north. Also that Sisuiake's father had gone with his band far south to a tribe who spoke the same language. They called them the people who talked Blackfoot. They remained there some time there was no frost—all sunshine—lots of fruit & buffalo & they found black people as slaves. The Indian who told Father Doucet this was an old Blackfoot. He had escaped with the few who got away from their enemies on the journey back. Some of them remained with that tribe.

15TH

(Diary page 167)

Speaking to him of the origin of the three tribes, he was told by Indians that their common ancestor, so the legend goes, had three sons—Pi kŭni, Kai' nah and Sik si kau. The youngest was his favourite & whenever they met in the hunt & at sports he was always the best & bravest. These sons were the fathers of the different tribes. Doucet says the Blackfoot, though fewer in numbers, were always the leaders. He has seen Bloods come, often 40 at a time, to be initiated into their societies & mysteries.[107] They kept better, too, the traditions & records of the race. Coming from the north, the Piegans evidently took the lead for they stretched farthest south, then the Bloods, & the Blackfoot. On their march they found the Crows, or part of that tribe, occupying the country they now possess, and fought them at High River, three miles from the mouth where it empties into the Bow River (Dunbow).[108] They defeated them here & again had a big battle about a mile below the Blackfoot Crossing. The Crows had dug huge pits, some about 15 ft. wide.[109] The Blackfoot had a few flintlock guns, though most of them used the arrows, & after two or three fights drove the Crows out of the country, & they retreated to the Missouri. At the time the Crees were in alliance with the Blackfoot.

(Diary pages 168–169)

Doucet & [Lereux] camped here amongst the Blackfoot. Lereux, when he saw these huge circular pits with stones where fires had been built, thought it was ruins of the Mexicans or Spaniards—but an Indian told them it was where he once had fought the Crows.

Again going back to the chiefs—he says Natos, The Sun, was a powerful Blackfoot chief who died about 40 years ago, and Rain Chief of the Bloods, a great man, died 25 years ago, and thinks Iron Shirt, Running Wolf, Big Swan of the Piegans were _____ with the Southern Piegans tho' they sometimes traded at Rocky Mountain House. Crow Eagle & Eagle Tail were more to the north, then they went south, too.

It is impossible to sum up the power of these chiefs—the Indians remember only a little of the past and when an Indian dies his name is not mentioned— or sung. Crowfoot was morally Head Chief of the three tribes. All claimed _____ as their chief. Back of him, they speak of as their great leaders—

(Diary page 170)

Western Journey 1909 / 123

names renowned amongst their tribes—Many Swans, Three Suns, Chief Bird—these two held a similar position—Kyaiyii, The Boy, who was the first great chief they remember. Other prominent chiefs were The Sun (Blackfoot)—Rain Chief of the Bloods—Sun Bull and Iron Shirt of the Piegans. They hand down a great name but have forgotten the story of their lives. There lived on the Blackfoot Reserve an old man who kept the records of the race fresh in his mind, Running Wolf (the male wolf). He was always pointed out as the man who knew these things.

_____ offered by the enemy.

(Diary pages 171–172)

It was a custom for the Indians to give names to different parts of a river. The name Old Man comes from place where the old men played—referring to a part of the river. The Indians used to get a certain wood for their bows & arrows, of the bank of the Bow, above Cochrane—& so named the river Bow River—thus the Eng. name Swift Current referred to a certain part.

16TH The Indians brought many ancient relics and I bought a fine _____ skin coat, from Wolf Coat. It is a Sarcee coat & Piegan leggings. From Bad Boy I got many old wooden bowls, & c. An Indian brought a kinnikinic[110] _____— very old—belonged to a Blood chief.

The Blackfoot legend of the Creation:

The legend of the Creation as told by Doucet, many times by old Indians of the North Blackfoot, differs somewhat from the one given by Grinel. Mr. Grinel has given many of their legends & goes deeply into the mysteries of the various societies, customs, religions & social organizations.

Napi—all was water—so he sent a beaver to find the bottom of the big waters but it could not. He then sent a muskrat—it was gone a long time and brought up a small bit of earth. He made the land out of that. It got larger and larger and mountains came. He made a woman out of the clay, tried three times but every time something was wrong, nose crooked, eyes crooked, or something wrong. It took 4 days. He tried the fourth time (no. 4 is a sacred number with the old time Indians) and the woman was made well.[111] She was his woman—but was always talking against him. Napi said it would be good that their children would live always. No, she said, they will die—but he said, they will come to life again—no, she said, they will be gone forever. He said, we will always have berries—no, they will fall away. The first woman was always talking against and cranky, and so they have always been. They separated. The woman made a corral—at Porcupine Hills—still called the pound of the woman—Akăpiskan. Napi and his pound of men were poor. They could not prepare hides or make moccasins, so he told them he would look up the woman. He went to her camp and asked for the chief woman. She came but he did not give his right name but called himself Red Skin and said they were poor but if they would marry they could kill buffalo & the women could make the robes & skins. So they agreed and the men came up, and every man took a wife. The chief woman was not yet married. She knew Napi had lied so she said, You are the chief man and I am the chief woman, let us marry, but he made sport of it and the woman said, I will never marry you, but will choose one of the men who has not yet got a woman. You will always be single. Napi was very powerful—he got angry and broke his corral &

(Diary page 173)

upset everything. The woman turned him into a lone pine tree and his spirit went some other place. Napi means old. The Indians regard children as foolish & old people as perfect, so it also suggests something perfect.[112]

About the year 1865 the Blackfoot were wintering in the timber country where the buffalo had gathered from the plains. The bands were apart. A large party of about 8 or 900 Cree and Assiniboine warriors at night crept on the camp of the Blackfoot Chief—The Sun, Nathos[113]—a powerful chief. They were all asleep at the time and it was a cold winter night. They shot very low in order to wound the sleeping Blackfoot. Nathos was very old—he called his few men. He took his rifle and like a flash they were on guard. Father Lacombe and John Lereux were in camp (in the lodge of Calf Child as he relates on his robe). Lacombe shouted to the Crees—do not fight us, go away, and the Cree name they had given him—but the noise drowned his voice. Nathos was wounded & though he was a brave chief, could not stand to fight. The Blackfoot retreated to some of the far lodges, & when Lacombe went out the Crees rushed in to kill the women & children. He tried to muster himself here but again the voice was lost in the din of the fight. An Assiniboine _____ his prayer book and next moment was shot dead by a Blackfoot bullet. After a time the priest made himself heard, & the Crees retreated for they were attached to Father Lacombe and had they known he was in camp, would never have attacked. Blackfoot from Crowfoot's camp were heard coming and this quickened the retreat of the Crees.

The Crees had made several attacks through the night and Lacombe was struck on the chest by a spent bullet & escaped uninjured. The Blackfoot thought him a great medicine man who could resist bullets. The Crees had taken his prayer book & other things but, when they knew of the owner, returned them. Assistance from the other Blackfoot came early in the morning, but the enemy had retreated.

Chief Red Crow of the Bloods had all his herd of horses stolen at night. It was one named Head Elk by the Mandan Indians or the nomads of the Plains.

Sweet Grass was shot accidentally by his brother-in-law by a revolver he had got & which he was examining. He _____ about _____ & excl., my brother you have shot me by accident. The men went nearly crazy with grief, for Sweet Grass was loved by all.

Calf Child one of the most intelligent & manly of the Blackfoot. Running Rabbit a good old fellow—but wavering.

Old Running Wolf had returned from the eagle hunt with two of the great birds.[114] He knelt beside them & crossed his arms over his breast to show how he loved the hunt. He took from an old bag decorated with coloured porcupine quills, buffalo stones & placed a row in front of the birds and sang his eagle song. He has a noble old head. I hope to paint him next summer for Edmonton. His youngest son, Good Rider, is a handsome fellow & must be as

(Diary page 174)

(Diary page 175)

This was the only occasion in which Lacombe was in an Indian fight.

(Diary page 176)

(Diary page 177)

the old man was in youth. R. W. has sons, Took the Gun, _____, Iron Shirt & Good Rider, a son dead—daughter in Montana.

Read works of de Smet, Jesuit who was the first to come amongst the Blackfoot. He was a Belgian and there is a statue to his memory in his country. He went into the Rocky Mountains.

Ten years ago, Hodgson told me, the Sarcees had a light boat. They were crossing the ice and drifted south, their kindred remaining in the north.

The Blackfoot Crossing (Du yoh pah' wah ku).

A wah heh'—take courage.

In their sign language the Crees are known by drawing the hand across the throat—unlike other tribes, they used to cut the throats of those killed in battle. Bloods got their name from one who was fond of drinking blood. He

(Diary page 178)

was out hunting & was seen to drink _____ blood & the tribe got the name—in sign language draw the fingers across the mouth in referring to the Bloods.[115]

The Piegans, rub the right side of the face with the hand.

Flat heads, touch top of head.

Snakes, the movement of a snake with hand.

Crowfoot was not properly Head Chief of the three tribes, but he was wise & had more influence than the other tribes & so they gave way to him. Three Suns was very powerful. Many Swans powerful & influence; even more authority than Crowfoot. The Gros Ventres were allied to the Blackfoot but one of them killed a Piegan & this broke the tie & they were driven away.

17TH I question Chief Running Wolf about the Piegan Bands.[116]

Lone Fighters, of which he is chief, are now North Piegans. They were formerly known as Fat Roasters in his father's day, _____ was the chief

(Diary page 179)

Iron Shirt. He used to hunt up north but crossed to Montana to take treaty with the Munroe government.[117] Running Wolf came north two years after Col. Macleod & the police entered the country, in 1876.[118]

Seldom Lonesome, most of these are northern Piegans though some are in Montana. Big Swan is chief of the band.

Dried Meat, this band is in the north & south. Little Plume is chief.

White Breasts, most of them in the south, a few up north. They got their name from a woman having a white breast.

See report of 1901 on North Sioux.

Big Top Knots—northern Piegans.

Back Fat—in the north & south.

No Parfleche—in the north.

In the south are the Black Pitched Moccasins; Black Fat Roasters; Small

(Diary page 180)

Robes; Worm People; Don't Laugh; All Chiefs; Skunks named after a chief who had that name.

A band of Bloods, Buffalo Dung, got their name in this way. Mik a pi, Red Old Man, an Indian, went to another lodge & took his woman away. This enraged the Indian & Red Old Man told the woman to take a buffalo chip & put it in her bosom before she returned to her man—and if he got mad to touch the chip & ask it to protect her. She went back & her husband got his knife to cut her. She saw the knife and touched the chip and asked it to guard her—and his anger left and they made friends, and the man found the buffalo chip in her bosom and asked her how it got there. She answered, when out to get buffalo chips it must have slipped in, but he said, no, it was Red Old Man who told you.[119]

The Blood bands are—Black Elks, Many Lodge Poles, North Bloods, Woods Bloods, Long Tail Lodge Poles, Lone Fighters, Black Blood, Hair Shirts, Many Children, Short Bows, Skunks, Many Horns.[120] *(Diary page 181)*

(The Gambler, called John Tanner, lives at Silver Creek—825 acres. The remainder of the reserve was surrendered & he & his family live there alone. It is on E. side of another river—5 miles from Binscarth.)[121]

Father De Smet, S.J., is a Flemish Jesuit from Terremond in Flanders where a statue is erected in his memory, met various tribes—in _____ the Blackfoot, Snakes, Kootenays & others.[122] He was commissioned by the United States Govt. to treat with these Indians & induce them to make peace. They met and agreed, and for a time peace lasted. He went amongst our Blackfoot & Crees. Hugh Munroe & Running Wolf knew him well. He was called Beaver Teeth.

Hugh Munroe's lst name was Rising Wolf & his 2nd name Wolf Talk. *(Diary page 182)*

George Bird Grinnell was called Marten Hat.

De Smet, Father Pierre-Jean, S.J., 1801–1873. *Life & Letters & Travels* (8.00) 4 vols. cloth 15.00. W. L. Blake, 123 Church Street, Toronto.

De Smet was the first priest to visit the Blackfoot. A son of la Verendrye had been amongst them.[123] Lacombe followed de Smet. Lereux had been there & sent word to his church to send a priest—they were suffering with the smallpox, the dead all lying about, so Lacombe volunteered. He was a young man then & rode down to them. Father Scullen followed. He was younger than Lacombe. These two travelled from the tribes & the settlements. Doucet was the first to be fixed with the Blackfoot & the _____ Bishop Legal* started the mission to the Piegans with Brother Birchman, building the church & belfry to the old retreat. He also started the mission to the Bloods.

*Now at St. Albert, Alberta.

Father Doucet says Crowfoot was cunning as a fox & crafty & that Commissioner Dewdney was like a child in his hands. When his adopted son Poundmaker was fighting he was pleased & felt it keenly when he was afterwards imprisoned. The Blackfoot were kept in full knowledge of what was going on during the whole conflict. Doucet came across some lodges of Crees amongst the bushes by the river. Denny also censures Dewdney, in his *Riders of the Plains*, for urging the authorities to get the Blackfoot to fight the Crees.[124] Doucet held that he had no knowledge of the Indians & their mode of thought. *(Diary page 183)*

Notes to Western Journey 1909

1. This would be a reference to Edmund Morris's family's summer home on Morton Island (now called Home Island), Lake Joseph, Muskoka.

2. The Ontario government commissioned a total of fifty Indian portraits and Morris executed twenty-five during each summer in 1907 and 1908.

3. The Toronto Art Museum, established in 1909, became the Art Gallery of Toronto and is now the Art Gallery of Ontario. The "old Court House" would be the court house for the judicial district of York, at 57 Adelaide St East; it ceased to operate in 1899 but the building still stands (Crossman 1978, p. 45).

4. The Canadian Art Club was formed in 1907 by a group of young artists with the primary aim of setting up annual exhibitions of their work. Along with Edmund Morris, members included Horatio Walker (1858–1938), Curtis Williamson (1867–1944), Homer Watson (1855–1936), William E. Atkinson (1862–1926), J. Archibald Browne (1864–1925), Franklin Brownell (1856–1946), William Brymner (1855–1925), Maurice Cullen (1886–1924), and James Wilson Morrice (1865–1924). The club disbanded in 1915; Morris joined several members on sketching trips.

5. The headquarters of the Imperial Bank were at 51 King St West, Toronto; in 1961 it combined with the Bank of Commerce to become the Canadian Imperial Bank of Commerce.

6. E. D. Martin, of Martin, Boyle, and Wynne Company, a wholesale drugs company, was president of the Winnipeg Board of Trade in 1910 (courtesy Provincial Archives of Manitoba).

7. Thomas Inglis, an architect and civil engineer, held private drawing classes in Winnipeg (courtesy Provincial Archives of Manitoba).

8. Colin Inkster (1843–1934) was sheriff of the Eastern Judicial District of Manitoba, 1876–1928; technically speaking his father, John Inkster, was not a Selkirk settler since he came to Manitoba as an employee of the Hudson's Bay Company, although he only worked for the Company for a short time (courtesy Provincial Archives of Manitoba).

9. Walter Scott (1867–1938) was premier of Saskatchewan, 1905–19; the Saskatchewan government commissioned fifteen portraits of band chiefs living in the Saskatchewan area, and Morris painted these during the summers of 1909 and 1910.

10. Alexander Phimister Proctor (1862–1950), an American sculptor, was a close friend of Morris and an avid big-game hunter. Among Proctor's sculptures are Theodore Roosevelt on horseback in Washington, the lions around the McKinley Monument in Buffalo, New York, seven mustangs at the University of Texas, and the buffalo either side of the stairway in the entrance of the Manitoba Legislature.

11. This is one of the very few complaints that Morris makes in his diaries about the conditions he experiences as he travels; he mentions being bothered by horseflies (p. 111), and a disagreeable drive in snow, with a piercing wind (p. 31). He set up his camp and easel in the field.

12. Alexander Cameron Rutherford, first premier of Alberta, 1905–10. Morris drew the five portraits for the Alberta government in the summer of 1910.

13. Inspector Francis J. Dickens of the NWMP was a son of the English author Charles Dickens; he was appointed inspector in the NWMP in 1874 and was in charge of Fort Pitt, Saskatchewan, with twenty-two men at the time of the North West Rebellion. The Plains Cree chief Big Bear surrounded the fort with three hundred or so Cree warriors and demanded its surrender; Big Bear then offered to allow the

NWMP officers to escape if they would leave all arms and supplies behind. When Dickens refused to accept this offer, Big Bear attacked the fort, but Dickens succeeded in driving off the Cree. Dickens then ordered that all arms, ammunition, and supplies be destroyed and, with his unit, retreated to Battleford, Saskatchewan. This decision was controversial: to some, Dickens seemed to be showing cowardice; to others, he was heroic in saving his men and in protecting their arms and supplies from capture. (See Mulvaney 1885, pp. 115–26.)

14. W. J. MacLean, a chief factor of the Hudson's Bay Company, was taken captive by Big Bear when he went to Big Bear's camp to parley during the siege of Fort Pitt in 1885. Big Bear persuaded MacLean to yield to the overwhelming advantage the Indians had in strength of number, and MacLean wrote a note requesting his wife and family, and several other settlers shut up within the fort barracks, to surrender to the Cree and follow him to the Cree camp. Everyone but the NWMP members did so, and until 17 June 1886 they shared the hardships of shifting camp with the Cree. (See Mulvaney 1885, pp. 122–25; Haydon 1971, p. 140; Gowanlock and Delaney 1885.)

15. Mrs Amelia M. Paget (1909) gives a view of Cree and Saulteaux customs.

16. High Eagle, Pitauspitau, and John Drunken Chief, Awatsiniamarkau, were brothers, sons of the deceased head chief John Three Bulls, and nephews of head chief Crowfoot, also deceased. Morris's portrait of High Eagle was for the Government of Alberta (0367–300–65).

17. The term "gens" was used in referring to a group of persons who were actually or theoretically consanguine, in the male or female line. Morris probably drew his information from Grinnell (1962, pp. 208–9), who listed the "gens" of the Blackfoot Confederacy tribes.

18. Heavy Shield was possibly a younger brother of Old Sun (Dempsey 1979, p.15).

19. Frank Tried to Fly but Could Not, Blackfoot, was deceased at the time of Morris's visit to the South Camp; during his life, this Indian had dreams about swimming and flying, and he died in trying to fly.

20. The Crow lived south of Alberta and were pushed farther south by the southward migration of the Blackfoot in what is now the USA.

21. The portrait faces p. 112 in the book by Paget (1909).

22. The four buffalo robes were part of Edmund Morris's bequest to the Royal Ontario Museum. The stories painted by the Indians on these four robes were of war history and, as Ewers mentions (1945, pp. 22–23), the illustrations on Blackfoot buffalo robes are "more properly termed picture writing than art," these figures being "generally more notable for their information than for their aesthetic quality;" he illustrates (1945, pp. 22–24) and explains the meanings of some common symbols used by the Blackfoot in painting such war robes.

23. Bull Head was head chief of the Sarcee, not the Sioux.

24. Morris's portrait of Spring Chief, Ninauksiskum, Blackfoot minor chief, is Government of Alberta 0367–300–66.

25. Wolf Collar (1853–1928), Makoyo ki na si, Blackfoot, a nephew of Running Wolf, was also known as the Barrel Maker; he was a well-known medicine man and visionary, and also a hunter and warrior; in 1906 he joined the Anglican church and was baptized Silas Wolf Collar. Through dreams he was guided to several other skills including those of barrel-making, photography, blacksmithery, and sculpting; moreover, in a dream he was told to write the Blackfoot language in syllabics, after which he assisted Canon Stocken in the development of a syllabary. (See Brasser 1977, pp. 38–41.) Edmund Morris's portrait of Wolf Collar was for the Government of Alberta (0367–300–62).

26. D. L. Brerton is listed as a farmer in Gleichen in an issue of *Henderson's Directories* (courtesy Alberta Provincial Archives).

27. This may be a buffalo-tail brush that is among the artifacts that Morris bequeathed to the Royal Ontario Museum (ROM HK 295).

28. I. G. Baker and Company operated a large log store at Fort Benton, Montana, near the source of the Missouri River. Baker lived in St Louis, Missouri, and directed business from there; Charles and William Conrad, his partners, worked in the Fort Benton store. The company owned Missouri River steamboats, herded horses and cattle, and transported goods including mail deliveries on land by ox trains in summer and by dog sled in winter. They had contracts to provide supplies for the NWMP, operated a store in Fort Macleod (see Morris 1971, p. 255), and set up tents for selling supplies and trading at the site of the signing of Treaty Seven at Blackfoot Crossing (see Denny 1905, p. 46). See also Hughes (1914, pp. 168–71) for mention of a visit by Lacombe to the Fort Benton store in 1869.

29. Fort Brisebois was established in 1875 at the junction of the Bow and Elbow rivers by Inspector G. A. Brisebois and a detachment of NWMP, in order to stop American whisky traders from selling alcohol to the Indians of southern Alberta; Colonel Macleod renamed it "Calgarry" after his birthplace in Scotland; the second "r" was dropped over the course of years (see Haydon 1971, p. 46).

30. Crowfoot was sympathetic to the rebels, and received into his camp and fed for months many Cree families; he was much displeased when attempts were made to send the Crees away. However, he had visited Winnipeg during the previous year and seen the size of the police force so decided to remain at peace (see Dempsey 1979, p. 17).

31. Joseph Kipp (1849–1913), half Mandan Indian and half European, was a trader based in Montana; he worked for I. G. Baker between 1870 and 1881, and then established himself on the Blackfoot Reserve in Montana. He maintained a number of trading posts in Montana and built forts Standoff and Kipp in Alberta. (See West 1960, p. 41.)

32. The buffalo robe relating the life of Calf Child is believed to be ROM HK 460.

33. Peter Erasmus, the son of a Danish settler and a Swampy Cree woman, made his headquarters at Smoke Lake. He translated the St John's Gospel into Cree for the Roman Catholics and assisted the Reverends Robert Rundle and James Evans, both Methodist missionaries, in their preparation of a dictionary and a syllabary of Cree. Erasmus was interpreter for the Indians during the signing of the treaty at Fort Carlton and Fort Pitt in 1876 (see Morris 1971, pp. 185, 196) and was a guide for the Palliser Expedition. He was influential in convincing the Cree chief James Seenum not to participate in the North West Rebellion. For further information, see Erasmus (1976).

34. The Indians often named physical features in the landscape after parts of the body or familiar objects.

35. The Flathead Indians speak a Salish language and live in Montana. Their territory was divided in half by the Continental Divide, with the Flathead considering their range to be on the western side. They gathered berries and roots, hunted deer and elk, and fished. They also made excursions to the east and may have encountered the Blackfoot on such expeditions.

36. The Blackfoot Hills, near Lloydminster, are on the border between Saskatchewan and Alberta.

37. The Cypress Hills, spanning the border between Alberta and Saskatchewan, were a constant battleground for tribal conflicts.

38. The Nez Percés, a Sahaptian people, dwelt in the early days of European settlement on a plateau region between the mountain ranges in Oregon, Washington, and Idaho. Haines (1972, p. 14) states, "Although the Nez Percés are usually considered a tribe...they had no definite tribal organization until this was urged

upon them by the white men. Up to that time they were a group of people with a common language and a common culture who lived in. . .small independent communities in the same region." The name Nez Percés (Pierced Noses) was given to these people by French-Canadian trappers in the early 1800s. Haines (1972, pp. 14–15) discusses two possible explanations for this name: the first "that the French-Canadians saw a few women in Nez Perce villages who wore nose ornaments of [dentalium] shell. Such ornaments were among people of the lower Columbia [River], and these women probably came from there. The second explanation is based on the sign language of the Plains Indians. One of their signs for the Nez Perce was made by passing the extended index finger of the right hand from right to left close to the nose. The French-Canadians [may have] assumed that this sign meant a pierced nose. Some of the Indians explain that the sign means a person who would not flinch from an arrow shot right by his nose, hence a brave man."

39. James Seenum, Pakan, Cree, chief of the Whitefish Lake band, signed the Treaty at Fort Pitt in 1876 (see Morris 1971, pp. 191, 358). He was converted to Christianity and was a close friend of the Indian missionary Henry Bird Steinhauer, and the European missionary John McDougall. He controlled the vengeful actions of his band during the North West Rebellion, deciding that Indians should adjust to their new life as farmers and live peacefully with the European settlers in the Fort Edmonton area (see MacEwan 1971, pp. 37–44).

40. The Reverend Thomas Woolsey, a Methodist (Wesleyan) minister, arrived in the west in 1885 to assist the Reverends Robert Rundle and James Evans in mission work among the Assiniboine and Blackfoot, giving frequent services at various visiting stations on the reserves (see Hodge 1969, p. 300); Woolsey was in charge of the Fort Edmonton mission. The Reverend Robert Rundle, a Methodist missionary, went to work among the Assiniboine and Blackfoot in 1840. The Reverend James Evans, appointed superintendent of missionary work by the Council for the English and Canadian Wesleyan Society, moved west in 1840 to Norway House, with his assistant Henry Steinhauer, to teach among the Cree. Evans founded several missions, mastered the Cree language, and, with the assistance of Rundle and Peter Erasmus, wrote a dictionary of Cree, and devised a syllabary of the language, which he published on his homemade press. (See Hodge 1969, p. 299.)

41. Captain John Palliser (1807–87) was appointed by the British government to explore the area between latitudes 49° and 50° north, and longitudes 100° and 115° west. With members of his expedition he travelled from the Red River to the Pacific Coast between 1857 and 1860, concentrating on the Prairies. The apex of the journey reached 52° north and the area explored became known as the Palliser Triangle. He reported woodlands suitable for settlement to the north, but advised the British government not to lend aid to the construction of a railway between Canada and the Red River settlement since the prairies were arid and unsuitable for agriculture, and the community would never become wealthy enough to repay the construction costs of such a railway. After a previous expedition in North America (1847–48), he wrote a book on his adventures (Palliser 1853). For further information, see Spry (1968), Archer (1980, pp. 46–48).

42. The Reverend John McDougall, (Wesleyan) Methodist, son of the Reverend George McDougall, took over the missionary work of his father upon the latter's death and became well known, working over a wide area of the west. He interpreted for the Stoney Indians in Treaty Seven discussions (see Morris 1971, p. 256). Morris marked an "X" in the margin beside this sentence, perhaps indenting to fill in later the correct relationship that this sister of the Steinhauer brothers had to John McDougall; she was McDougall's wife.

43. Robert and Egerton Steinhauer were the eldest of ten children of the Ojibwa

Methodist missionary Henry Bird Steinhauer (ca 1820–84) of Rama, Ontario. The missionary father had been adopted by an American (not German) merchant, H. B. Steinhauer, who paid for his education; their father worked with the Methodist church, first at Rainy Lake, and then at Norway House, where he assisted the Reverend James Evans in the development of a system of syllabics for the Cree language. In the 1850s he went farther west, where he set up a mission among the Cree at Whitefish Lake on Pakan's Reserve in present-day Alberta; he stimulated interest in agriculture and set up a school, marking the beginning of a successful association with that community that lasted for thirty years. For further information, see MacEwan (1971, pp. 19–27).

44. George Henry Wheatley, federal Indian Affairs agent for the Blackfoot Reserve, 1897–1900 (courtesy Public Archives of Canada), was farm instructor on the reserve at the time of Scraping Hide's attack (see Anderson 1973, p. 56). According to Anderson, Scraping Hide resented in general the intrusion of Europeans on the reserve, but it was against another Indian, Rabbit Carrier, that he bore the grudge. When he did not find Wheatley at home, he went to Rabbit Carrier's shack; the latter, suspecting his intent, refused to admit him. At this point, Scraping Hide sought out Frank Skynner as the victim.

45. According to RCMP records, Frank Skynner, federal government rations officer on the Blackfoot Reserve, was killed by Scraping Hide in April 1895.

46. Probably a reference to Henry Yarwood Baldwin who was appointed assistant surgeon in the NWMP in 1885 (courtesy RCMP).

47. There are no doubt several versions to the story of Scraping Hide, Ay ye wa'na. The grave may not have been Crowfoot's but rather that of Scraping Hide's son.

48. The Beaupre family operated a store at Gleichen, Manitoba, and the father acted as postmaster for the period of ca 1886 to ca 1914; they were also ranchers, as listed in *Henderson's Directories* (courtesy Alberta Provincial Archives).

49. Morris named his campsite on the prairies after the former Blackfoot chief Kyaiyii, Bear Robe; Running Rabbit had given Morris this name on their first meeting.

50. Edmund Morris portrayed Water Chief, Okena, Blackfoot minor chief, for the Government of Alberta (0367–300–63).

51. The painting of the wife of Water Chief has not yet been located. Morris portrayed very few Indian women.

52. The buffalo robe recording events in Running Rabbit's life was part of Edmund Morris's bequest to the Royal Ontario Museum, ROM 913x1.3.

53. Lieutenant Governor David Laird negotiated Treaty Seven.

54. Sir Cecil Edward Denny (1850–1928) joined the North West Mounted Police in 1874 and became an inspector; he resigned from the force in 1887 and later recorded the history of the force from its formation through the North West Rebellion (see Denny 1905).

55. Public Archives of Canada records indicate that A. E. Jones was stockman on the Blackfoot Reserve in 1905.

56. Jack Bergess, Morris's cook on this journey.

57. The St John's Mission was organized by the Anglican church.

58. These would have been the greater prairie chicken, *Tympanuchus cupido* (see Godfrey 1966, p. 133).

59. The buffalo suddenly disappeared in the winter of 1878/79. While much of the blame was put on the introduction of repeater rifles, the natural migrations of the buffalo north from Montana ceased when the American government burned the grass along the border between Canada and the United States, in order to keep the herds to the south for American Indians but also to force the Sioux chief Sitting Bull to return from Canada.

60. This is one of the few mentions Morris makes of preparing sketches for portraits. Many Indian subjects were reluctant to be portrayed and wanted the session to be over as quickly as possible (for example, Iron Shield, p. 22). A photograph taken by Morris shows Calf Child examining a portrait of himself on an easel in the field, presumably just completed (p. 105).

61. Twin Butte, Alberta.

62. The medicine men Weasel Heart and All Thought He Was Holy are possibly legendary characters. Edmund Morris referred to the two as "the first medicine man" and "the other" or "the 2nd" when he first wrote this paragraph, and then crossed out these words and replaced them with the appropriate proper names.

63. Epidemics of smallpox often decimated the Indian population after they came in contact with the Europeans. Examples of its effect follow: in 1781, the Peigans attacked a village of Shoshoni Indians on the Red Deer River, only to find the few members of the village who had not died from smallpox had fled southwards, and two days later the Peigans themselves were struck by the disease (see Ewers 1961, pp. 28–29); the disease reached the Mandan Indians in 1837, leaving one hundred and fifty out of a population of sixteen hundred (see Powers 1973, p. 14); in 1837, some six thousand Blood and Blackfoot Indians, or about two-thirds of the entire Blackfoot nation, died in the 19th century and the junction of the St Mary and Belly rivers was named "the Graveyard" because the mortality rate there rose so high (see Ewers 1961, pp. 65–66); in his history of the NWMP in the west, Denny states (1905, p. 10), "In the years 1870–71, a frightful epidemic of smallpox swept more than a third of the Indians belonging to the plains tribes. In some cases what had been powerful tribes dwindled down to only a few hundred souls. The Sarcees, who previous to the epidemic numbered several thousands, on the arrival of the police [in 1873] could only show three or four hundred."

64. William Black was clerk at the federal Indian Affairs agency for the Peigan Reserve near Brocket, ca 1903–9 (courtesy Public Archives of Canada).

65. The full title of this book is *Where the Buffalo Roamed: The Story of Western Canada Told for the Young;* it was written by E. L. Marsh (Toronto: W. Briggs, 1908). Canadian artist Paul Kane (1811–71) travelled extensively in western Canada and the northwestern United States painting scenes from the lives of Indians he encountered, and wrote an account of his travels (see Harper 1971). Many of his paintings are in the Royal Ontario Museum.

66. George Catlin (1796–1872), American ethnologist and artist, travelled among the Indians in the United States between 1832 and 1839, painting numerous portraits of Indians and scenes of Indian life; he recorded and published his observations of Indian customs (see Catlin 1841).

67. George de Forest Brush (1855–1941), American artist, travelled in the southern United States and in Mexico, painting scenes of Indian life.

68. Jean-Léon Gérôme (1824–1903), French painter and sculptor, was famous for classical historical paintings. Morris, too, studied under Gérôme while in France.

69. Edgar Dewdney (1835–1916), civil engineer and administrator, was appointed Indian commissioner in the federal government in 1879; he retained this post when appointed lieutenant governor of the North West Territories, 1881–88; in 1888 he was named minister of the interior in the federal government. He had come to British Columbia from England in 1859 and had practised as a surveyor.

70. T. C. Wade was one of the Canadian lawyers appointed as a member of the arbitration board set up by Canada and the United States to clarify the boundary between British Columbia and Alaska along the Panhandle, at the time of the 1898 Klondike Gold Rush.

71. Captain Denny of the NWMP states in his book of memoirs (1905, pp. 202–3)

that he received a telegram about this matter in May 1885: "A few Crees, some thirty in number, skulking around Cypress. Would the Blackfoot like to clean them out. Could this be done quietly?" Denny refused to take action on this request, commenting in his book, "Not only was there plenty of work required to keep the Indians quiet on their reserves, but you also had to combat orders issued with an utter ignorance of Indian ways. The result of such an action as that advised above would have taken all the able-bodied Indians out of Treaty No. 7, and have started a nice little war to get them back again."

72. Hugh Munroe, called Rising Wolf or Wolf Talk, Mahkwoipwoahts or Makwi Ipwoatsin, spent many years among the Peigans as a representative of the Hudson's Bay Company and learned to speak Blackfoot and Cree; his Peigan wife, the Fox Woman, Ap' ah ki, was a daughter of Peigan head chief Lone Walker (Schultz 1907, pp. 175–87). The incident of Munroe and his family being surrounded by a war party of Assiniboine is related by Schultz (1907, p. 185).

73. James Henry Morris, son of James Morris after whom Morrisburg was named, was first cousin once removed of Edmund Morris.

74. Trois Rivières, P. Q.

75. Rocky Mountain House, Alberta, Hudson's Bay Company trading post.

76. The expedition in 1804 led by Captain Meriwether Lewis and William Clark was authorized by the American government to explore territory between the Mississippi and the Pacific coast (see Lewis and Clark 1904–5).

77. Munroe remained in the service of the Hudson's Bay Company for a number of years, and then lived the rest of his life working mostly as a free trapper wandering between the Canadian prairies and the Yellowstone River. He never returned to Montreal.

78. Dr Richard Bright (1789–1858) of London, England, first diagnosed nephritis, which became known as Bright's disease.

79. Senator Matthew Henry Cochrane; Edmund Morris's sister Ann Eva was married to Senator Cochrane's son James Arthur Cochrane.

80. The Mormons are members of the religious sect called the Church of Jesus Christ of the Latter-Day Saints, founded in 1830 by Joseph Smith in New York.

81. Edmund Morris's sister Margaret Cline Morris married Andrew Malloch.

82. Jerry Potts (ca 1840–96) grew up among the Indians and traders. He was much valued by the NWMP for his service as guide and interpreter because of his vast knowledge of the prairies and his understanding of the Indians. In 1874 he guided Colonel Macleod's command to the site of the first NWMP post. During the North West Rebellion, he assisted the police in keeping the peace among the Blood and Peigan tribes. (Courtesy RCMP, and see Haydon 1971, p. 187.)

83. John West, an Anglican minister sent by the Church Missionary Society of England in 1820 to serve as chaplain to the Hudson's Bay Company establishment at Upper Fort Garry.

84. The village of Victoria, Alberta, located on the North Saskatchewan River, was renamed Pakan in honour of the Wood Cree chief and to avoid confusion with other places in Canada named Victoria.

85. These would be the ministers of the Ontario provincial parliament.

86. Sir James Pline Whitney, premier of Ontario, 1905–14.

87. The popular name "Quaker" referred to a member of the Society of Friends.

88. Pocahontas (1595–1617), the daughter of chief Powhatan of the Powhatan tribe, part of an Algonkian confederacy in Virginia, arranged a supply of food and protection for the colonists in Jamestown, Virginia. Captain John Smith (1580–1631) was one of the leading figures in the colony.

89. Albert Henry George Grey (1851–1917), fourth Earl Grey, governor general of

Canada from 1904 to 1911, presided over the creation of the provinces of Saskatchewan and Alberta in 1905.

90. Li Hung-chang, Chinese statesman and diplomat (see p. 56, n. 34).

91. This buffalo robe, decorated by chiefs Running Wolf, Big Swan, Butcher, and Bull Plume, was part of Edmund Morris's bequest to the Royal Ontario Museum (ROM HK 461). The exhibit was held in the spring of 1909, 29 March–17 April, and was accompanied by a catalogue written by Edmund Morris (Morris 1909), a copy of which is in the ROM collection; included in the display were fifty-five portraits he had drawn and a wide selection of artifacts he had collected.

92. Between 1895 and 1901 Father Albert Lacombe founded St Paul de Métis, which was a Métis colony, and St Mary's Mission; construction of a school for the Métis children began but the building was burned down. The biography referred to is by Katherine Hughes (1914).

93. "Bungee" meant "give me a handout" or "give me a present" (courtesy B. Johnson, Department of Ethnology, ROM). The Saulteaux, or Plains Ojibwa, are called in their own language "Bungee" (Kehoe 1981, p. 289).

94. See Strange (1893). Reference is to Major General Thomas Bland Strange, of Scottish descent, who moved west upon retirement from a career in the Royal Artillery in 1881; he was chief factor in the organization of the Military Colonization Company, with a ranch 35 miles southeast of Calgary. He led a column of troops in 1885 in pursuit of Big Bear (see Mulvaney 1885, pp. 394–95, 397–98). The rancher son whom Morris met is Harry Bland Strange (courtesy Alberta Provincial Archives).

95. On the spread of tuberculosis in the west, Archer (1980, p. 144) states, "The susceptibility of Indians and Metis and the lack of treatment centres had led to an epidemic spread of the disease among the Indians and in some isolated areas by 1905. The reputation of the North West Territories as a health resort for consumptives may have been a reason for the large number of tuberculosis deaths reported."

96. Trachoma, or granular conjunctivitis, produces granular lids and leads to blindness if untreated; it is very contagious in the early stages.

97. The Kootenay, a tribe of Indians of the plateau between the Rocky Mountains and the Selkirk Mountains, in northern Idaho and southern British Columbia, were divided into two groups. Those of the Upper Kootenay River frequently crossed the mountains onto the prairies to hunt buffalo. In the early part of the 18th century, they lived on the eastern side of the Rockies as well, but were driven westwards by the Blackfoot. In their dress, customs, and religion they resembled the Plains Indians far more than they did the tribes of British Columbia. The group on the Lower Kootenay River, however, seldom joined the buffalo hunt and lived principally on fish. (See Jenness 1977, pp. 358–59.)

98. The Ninth Voltigeurs de Québec, under Colonel Guillaume A. Amyot, arrived in Calgary in April 1885, and served in Alberta as garrison troops at Calgary, Fort Macleod, Crowfoot, Gleichen, and Langdon until July 1885 (courtesy Alberta Provincial Archives).

99. Before 1920, all irrigation projects—a total of fifteen—in western Canada were undertaken by private companies; the first such project was by the Alberta Railway and Irrigation Company in 1883. From 1920 until 1942, the province of Alberta had jurisdiction over all such works within its boundaries.

100. The story related by Grinnell in the chapter "Two War Trails" (1962, pp. 82–90) is told from the Blackfoot viewpoint, as part of the tales of the heroic warrior, a Blood Indian called Low Horn, Ekus kini. The Cree chief Kominakus, Round, with a large party of Cree, encountered Ekus kini and a small war party of six Sarcee. Ekus kini succeeded in killing fifteen Cree, including Kominakus, singlehandedly before he himself was killed and his body cut into pieces.

101. George Allen of Moss Park, Toronto, received the artifacts collected by Paul Kane on his 1846–48 journey in the west. Major Raymond Willis, a descendant of George Allen, presented the collection to the Royal Ontario Museum in 1946, and it is now housed in the ROM Department of Ethnology. The Luxton Museum at Banff, Alberta, is now part of the Glenbow Museum's operation; the Glenbow Museum in Calgary houses a small number of the artifacts collected by Canon Stocken (courtesy Glenbow Museum).

102. Probably Courtrai, in the region of Flanders, Belgium.

103. Berry Creek, in Alberta, runs south into the Red Deer River, at the northern tip of what today is Dinosaur Provincial Park.

104. As Grinnell explains (1962, pp. 125–26), the buffalo stone (Inis kim) was usually a small cephalopod—an ammonite or a section of a baculite—but sometimes merely an oddly shaped piece of flint, giving the possessor the power to call buffalo. It was said that an Inis kim wrapped up and left undisturbed for a long time would have two young ones.

105. See Bibliography (Hind 1860) for the full title. Henry Youle Hind and S. J. Dawson were commissioned by the Canadian government to investigate the Northwest, Hind reporting on the possibilities of agricultural settlement on the Prairies. Like Palliser, Hind became interested in the Indian customs and artifacts he observed and included details on them in his report. For more information on Hind's career, see Morton (1980).

106. Greater Slave Lake should read Great Slave Lake; however, it was Lesser Slave Lake (then also known as Little Slave Lake) that the Cree called Lake of the Strangers (courtesy Hugh Dempsey, Glenbow Museum).

107. Such societies existed essentially to enforce law and order within the tribe at large. Grinnell (1962, pp. 220–25) lists the religious societies of the Peigans that existed or had once existed and details various rights of membership.

108. The town of High River is located on the Highwood River about 32 km (20 miles) from where it empties into the Bow River.

109. See sketches by Edmund Morris (pp. 157–58).

110. Kinikinic wood is silky dogwood (*Cornus obliqua*), a member of the Cornus family. The word kinne-kinick (he mixes) was an Ojibwa term referring to the cranberry leaf or willow bark, ingredients which were mixed with tobacco and smoked. (See Maclean 1896, pp. 277–78.)

111. Storm (1972, p. 181) mentions that number four was sacred.

112. The Blackfoot legend of creation related by Grinnell (1962, pp. 137–44) is very different. No mention is made of a flood or of the muskrat; Napi moulded not only a woman but also a child out of clay; he did not attempt the moulding four times, but did wait four mornings as the clay shapes developed. When the woman was developed, she threw a stone in the water saying, "If it floats, we will always live; if it sinks, people must die. . . ." The rest of the legend told by Doucet, as transcribed by Morris, goes beyond any corresponding details in Grinnell.

113. More usually spelled Natos.

114. Grinnell (1962, pp. 236–40) describes eagle-hunting techniques, giving examples of the setting up of a bait in a deep pit, singing of eagle songs, and other steps in the ritual, and comments as follows: "The Indian standard of value was eagle-tail feathers. . . .The capture of these birds appears to have had about it something of a sacred nature, and. . .was invariably preceded by earnest prayers to the Deity for help and for success. There are still living many men who have caught eagles in the ancient method."

115. Powers (1973, p. 28) explains the origin of the tribal name "Blood" differently: ". . .probably came from the Cree designation of the tribe's custom of painting their

hands and bodies with a red clay for certain ceremonies."

116. It would seem that Morris got the band names from a list in Grinnell under an illustration of a Peigan camp of about 1850–55 (1962, p. 225), with the lodges of the band chiefs in an outer circle and those of law-enforcing society bands in an inner circle. Grinnell included quite a few more bands not mentioned by Morris.

117. Reference is to the United States government of James Monroe, 1816–23; in the treaty signed by the Blackfoot nation with this government, the Indians surrendered the major part of Montana in return for exclusive hunting grounds, annuity payments, and other benefits (see Dempsey 1979, p. 12).

118. The NWMP was formed in 1873 and the first contingent spent the winter of 1873 at Upper Fort Garry; the second contingent was sent west in 1874 and established Fort Macleod (Macleod 1978).

119. Grinnell devotes a chapter (1962, pp. 61–69) to another legend of Red Old Man, Mik a pi, and identifies him as a Peigan, not as a Blood.

120. It appears that Morris copied this list of bands from Grinnell as well (1962, p. 209); Grinnell included the transcription of the Blood names, and Morris has omitted one name for which there was no English translation given—Ah-knik-sim-iks.

121. The Gambler referred to here is a Sioux of the Tanner family. Their reserve, near Binscarth, Manitoba, is on the Assiniboine River. It was established under the Manitoba Treaty, Treaty Two, in 1872; the original area was 7770 hectares (19 200 acres) but all but 348 hectares (860 acres), according to federal government records, were surrendered. Morris may have inserted this note for reference to his earlier mention of the Gambler (p. 80 [margin note]).

122. Father Pierre-Jean de Smet (1801–73), S.J., was born in Belgium and emigrated to North America in 1821; he trained as a Jesuit priest at White Marsh, a Jesuit estate near Baltimore, and was ordained in 1827. De Smet travelled widely in the United States and Canada; he was famed for missionary zeal, coupled with a pleasant personality. For further information, see Chittenden and Richardson (1905).

123. Pierre Gaultier (1685–1749), Sieur de la Verendrye, explored with his sons Lake Winnipeg, the Saskatchewan River, the upper Mississippi River, and farther west.

124. Morris is probably referring to Denny's quoting of a telegram he received from Dewdney's office (see p. 133, n. 71.)

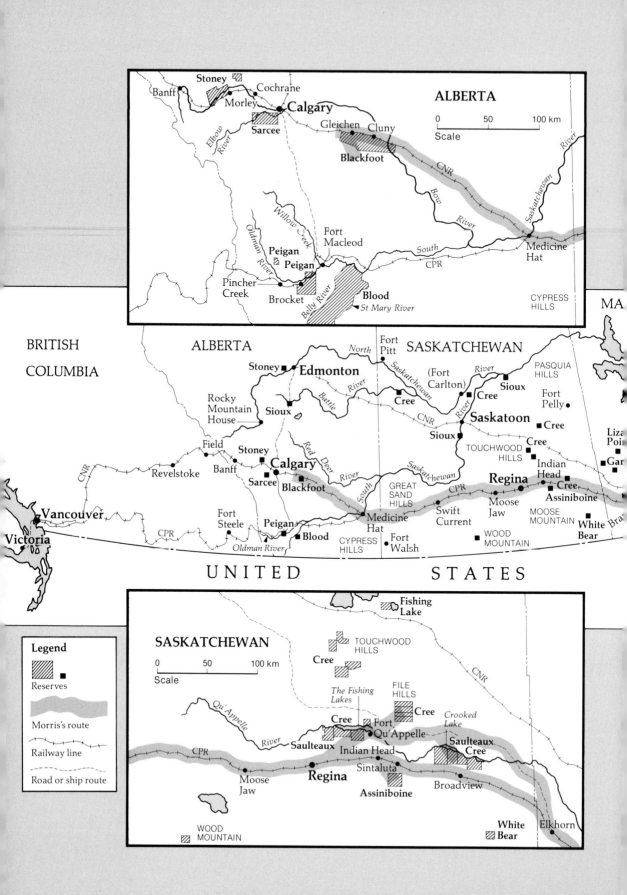

Western Journey 1910

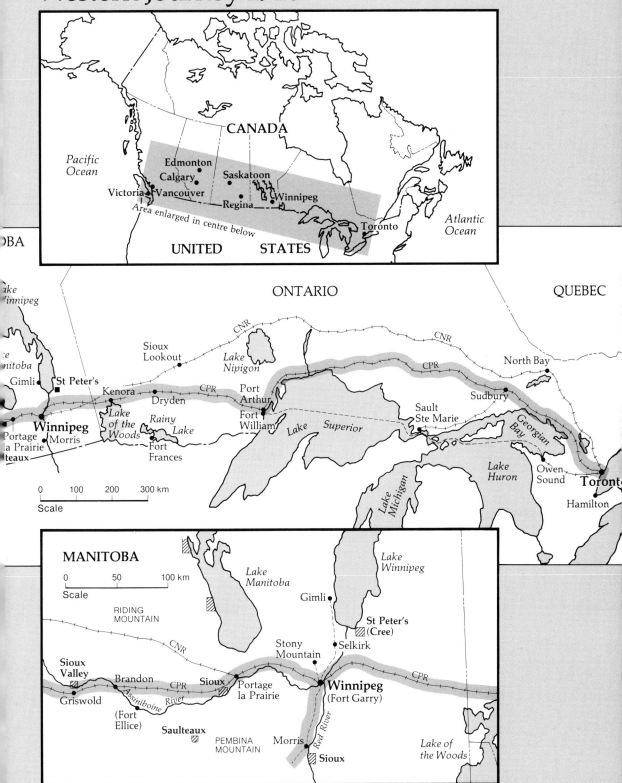

CANADA

Pacific Ocean

- Edmonton
- Calgary
- Saskatoon
- Victoria
- Vancouver
- Regina
- Winnipeg

Area enlarged in centre below

UNITED   STATES

Toronto

Atlantic Ocean

ONTARIO   QUEBEC

Lake Winnipeg

Gimli ■ St Peter's

Sioux Lookout

Lake Nipigon

CNR   CNR

North Bay

CPR

Kenora   Dryden   CPR   Port Arthur

Winnipeg

Lake of the Woods   *Rainy Lake*   Fort William   *Lake Superior*

Sault Ste Marie

Sudbury

Georgian Bay

Portage a Prairie   Morris

Fort Frances

Owen Sound   **Toronto**

Lake Huron

Hamilton

Lake Michigan

0   100   200   300 km
Scale

MANITOBA

0   50   100 km
Scale

RIDING MOUNTAIN

Lake Manitoba

Lake Winnipeg

Gimli

St Peter's (Cree)

CNR

Stony Mountain

Selkirk

Sioux Valley

Brandon   CPR   **Sioux**   Portage la Prairie

Griswold   *Assiniboine River*

Winnipeg (Fort Garry)   CPR

(Fort Ellice)

Saulteaux

PEMBINA MOUNTAIN   Morris

Red River

Sioux

Lake of the Woods

*Went south to
see Morris
Municipality &
town named
after my father.
Drove out to
Rosenhoff, a
Mennonite set-
tlement in the
Municipality,
picturesque vil-
lage with trees—
& old Russian

Left Toronto on CPR, 9 am, 16 July. Spent a fortnight in Winnipeg. J. H. MacDonald gives order for landscape of Qu'Appelle Valley[1] & a portrait of a Sioux.* On 16th July arrive at Balcarres. Following day drive out to File Hills to stay with my friend Inspector Graham.[3]

I drive out to the Indian encampment about six miles away.

This is a circular camp. Many coloured lodges—the sun and the Thunder-bird on most of them.

I make medicine with the old chief Star Blanket. He will not consent to sit unless I agree to let them have a dance. He imagines I have great power—his mind is confused—asked if money dies—says he used to get $25 annually as chief but it is now cancelled. I told him Graham settles all these matters & as he remained obstinate, I drove off.[4]

Paint Pimotat out in the sun. He is a younger brother of Star Blanket—a handsome man of 47.[5]

21
clocks—the
houses with
cross pendulums
& c. The other
village is
Rosenort—all
the country is
free for farming.[2]

Drive out to Star Blanket's camp—his reserve is a beautiful one, studded with ponds & lakes edged with rushes & various grasses—& innumerable ducks. In the distance you see the Pheasant Hills & two other ridges.

Old Tying Knot was with the chief—we talked a long time.[6] I brought the chief tobacco & presents & he was in good humour. He wanted to know if anyone would trick him. I told him no. Again he asked for the dance. I promised to speak to Graham & Scott to see if _____ _____ all the Indians might have a dance on their respective reserves but would make no promises.[7] He could not understand why I made portraits. I told him to recall the men who used to paint stories on buffalo robes & this made it clear. He agreed to come tomorrow. We talked of Poundmaker. They tell me his father's name was Skunk Skin.[8] He held no position of authority in the tribe & Poundmaker from his influence with the Indians arose to be chief. They say he may have brought about peace between the Blackfoot & Crees, but that it had been impending for some time. Tying Knot, when I mentioned the

*These two old
men got very
excited telling of
Sweet Grass, one
of the great men,
Tying Knot
accompanying
his talk by signs.

name of Sweet Grass, sat up & told of his brave deed.* Said he was a very short man.

Once he with his following encountered the Blackfoot. He had them make a circular trench & cover themselves, but Sweet Grass came out & fired into the enemy, all the bullets passing on all sides of him—they overcame the Blackfoot. Again, he was out one day & saw a strange figure carefully looking down the river. He rode up to him & said he would shoot him. The Blackfoot, for he was one, rolled down the hill, Sweet Grass shooting the whole time, but did not kill him. The enemy then all rushed out & Sweet Grass following, joined him. He rode on in advance & rushed in to the very heart of the enemy, they separating as he advanced. He killed none of them & bullets passed on all sides of him.

Tying Knot was in his lodge when he died. It was not long after the treaty. He had got a new revolver. He rode in & encamped. Soon there was a report & Sweet Grass, thinking someone was trying his revolver, asked his brother-in-law to see if it was there. He got it & examined it. There were three

The Walker, Pimotat, Cree. Pastel on paper, 1908. Dimensions 63 × 49.5 cm. Edmund Morris Collection. ROM HK 2442.

Indian tipis, Manitoba. Oil on panel, ca 1911. Dimensions 10.8 × 15.5 cm. Edmund Morris Collection 1981-211. Courtesy Provincial Archives of Manitoba.

(Diary page 187) cartridges spent showing, & he thought that was all. He pulled back the trigger not looking at _____ opposite & meant to let it back lightly but it snapped, & the bullets entered the side of Sweet Grass's cheek & went through his head back of his ear. The people all rushed to the lodge. He said, I have killed our brother, & tried to shoot himself.

The old chief & Tying Knot's wife came out as I drove off & danced & sang. Mr. J. H. MacDonald of Winnipeg showed me two old HBC books.

York Factory, Chief Factor & Governor of the said Factory, Hudson's Bay, North America, for the Governor & Company of Adventurers of England trading into said Bay.

The accounts of the said Governor containing his transactions of trade & c. from Aug. 1784 to Aug. the 5th, 1785.

Beaver being the chief commodity or trade fur we therefore make it the standard whereby we value all furs & commodities dealt for in trade.[9]

The Comparatives:[10]

(Diary page 188)

			Beaver
parchment moose	1	as	2
drest "	1	"	1½
old bears	1	"	3
cub "	1	"	1
quiguahatches	1	"	2
wolves	1	"	2
old cased cats	1	"	2
split "	1	"	1
cub "	1	"	1
foxes black	1	"	4
" grizzled	1	"	3
" red	1	"	1
" brown	2	"	1
" white	2	"	1
wenusks	2	"	1
otter prime	1	"	2
" ordinary	1	"	1
" damaged	2	"	1
" wejacks	2	"	1
buck deer	1	"	1
doe "	2	"	1
martens prime	2	"	1
" ordinary	3	"	1
jackashes	3	"	1
musquashes	6	"	1
rabbit skins	8	"	1
castoreum lb.	2	"	1
goose feathers lb.	10	"	1
" quills	2000	"	1
swan skins	6	"	1

(Diary page 189)

Trading goods received as for invoice from on board the Sea Horse, Capt. John Richards, amongst other things:[11]

> 1634 gallons of English brandy.
> Brazil tobacco 4601 lb.
> roll   "   403 lb.
> leaf   "   632 lb.

Trading goods received from on board the Sea Horse not mentioned in invoice: Brandy, English gal. 400.

Leakage & waste of Brandy, English: 284 gallons, which is deducted from general the charge.

All recorded by John Ballanden.

These books were found in No. 4 House on the Assiniboine River in 1893.[12] The later one, 1835, records having observed Halley's comet.[13]

Alex Brass, the interpreter, questioned his aunt, an Indian woman, why the Indians are so reluctant to have their portraits made. She says it is superstition, & that in the early days the medicine men, if they had a grudge against another Indian, would make a figure representing him on bark. Then he would place his bad medicines on it & evil would come to the man. *(Diary page 190)*

Chief Star Blanket came to have his portrait painted—his son Red Dog & a brother with him. To satisfy the old Indian he & I dined during rests.

Tying Knot, a head man of the Crees & in his day one of the warriors, came to be painted. I had painted him two years ago for the Ontario Govt. & we are friends. 27TH

Tying Knot talked much of the old fighting days. He was one of the war party led by Kan na nas kis against the Blackfoot. They came upon them on a hill in a coulee—or trench—between the present city of Edmonton and the Rockies. This gives the braves courage. Kom in a kus, one of the party, rushed out from amongst them, up the hill & grabbed hold of one of the guns which was pointed at him. In doing it one of his fingers entered the muzzle. It was blown off & the bullet entered his eye. Kom in a kus used to be with Sweet Grass's followers. He is the Indian who had the dream & located the Blackfoot.[14] *(Diary page 191)*

Another time, Tying Knot was with the Blackfoot on a war party. An old man, a Cree chief, had said he would lead them. He was told if he would make them victors, he was to select a young virgin—and if the Crees were winners, he was to wed her. They started off—& the old Cree made the virgin sleep alone in a lodge ahead of the camp—but she disappeared. Tying Knot thought nothing of it till he had the _____ & heard the reason. Then he said that his brother-in-law had acted in a strange way the night before, _____ _____ property & leaving the lodge—he had carried her off. *(Diary page 192)*

The Blackfoot had come across a number of Cree girls drawing water & had killed all of them excepting one. An old man of the tribe much thought of had two of his girls killed & his grief & restlessness moved the Crees to

Western Journey 1910 / 143

revenge. They started off—Tying Knot was not quite a man yet (he is now 78) but he was with the party. They travelled on showshoes & near Buffalo Lake they came across the Blackfoot. Moonias was the leader of the Crees.[15] There was a priest among the Blackfoot who called out to them to go away. The party was divided about him, some wanting to kill him, others saying no. This was Father Lacombe, but they did not know it was him. They killed many Blackfoot & found lots of crosses & bibles which they heaped in a pile & burnt.[16]

(Diary page 193)

The last day Chief Star Blanket came with his youngest wife, for he had five—three of them died, and a little boy, his last child, about $1\frac{1}{2}$ years. The last day he sat for his portrait, he & his wife & grandson had camped in the woods nearby making a lodge out of branches & covered with cloth with a fire burning in front.

(Diary page 194)   Extract of letter from Hon. A. Morris to his son William, dated, The Island, Muskoka, 1 Aug. 1888:

> "I would rather give it (the island) my father's name when he was made a chief—I can't recall it but the translation was the 'Rising Sun'."[17]

Père Lacombe published two dictionaries, one of Cree, the other of Chippewa. I have the former, it is in my study in the bookcase. The dialects are _____ alike. In his trusty book he spells it—Shakeishkeik.
    Extract of letter from Gov. Morris to his cousin James H. Morris dated from Fort Garry, 10 Oct. 1873:

> "I announced myself to them (the Saulteaux) as the son of Ihn ki kei chick, i.e., the Man Who Stands Up before the Sky."

(Diary page 195)   It is the same nation as we had at Perth, the ancient Chippewas.[18] Star Blanket's father, Wa pii moose too sus, signed the Treaty at Fort Qu'Appelle negotiated by my father in 1874.[19] His name White Calf.

A number of Indians, Saulteaux, came up from Pasqua's reserve, one of them a man Mrs. Graham wanted me to _____ _____ & paint[20] so I took advantage of his presence & got them to camp over till next week. His name is the Gambler—a finer type of the Indian.[21]

Tying Knot or the Man Who Ties the Knot, Kah to kope chamakasis, Cree chief. Pastel on paper, 1908. Dimensions 62.5 × 50 cm. Edmund Morris Collection. ROM HK 2434.

Photograph of the only image of horn in the Edmund Morris Collection at the ROM. Carved, with remaining patches of red ochre round eyes and on chest that may testify to its use as a ritual object. In the catalogue accompanying his 1909 exhibition, Morris included a description of an artifact probably the same as the one illustrated here: "Image made of Moose horn, found by a French settler buried under the ground in a box made without nails on the Yellow Quill Trail, Manitoba, 1878. The medicine men held that these images gave them control over the souls of others." Length 17.5 cm. Bequest of Edmund Morris. ROM HK 956.

After this I left File Hills. The day before, Graham & I drove along the Fort Pelly trail to the ranch.[22]

Stop at Balcarres & take train in morning for Broadview via Elk Horn.[23]

Stop overnight at Broadview & drive out next morning to the Reserve. In

Broadview I met Joe Bird who is _____ to the Govt. _____ & his disciple, Sandy McMillan. I walk to the old medicine man's camp, Sitting White Eagle, & arrange for sittings.

He came with an old friend from back of Fort Pelly, Saddi & O'Soup[24]—& sits for the painting. He related some of his experiences.

A head man of the Saulteaux led a war party of the tribe & the Crees against the Piegans. His name was Little Knife. Beyond the Sweet Grass Hills he told his men they would soon see the enemy. They were on top of a hill & looking down the valley, saw two Indians approaching on one side of the stream. Soon the others appeared on the other side & the alarm was given when the whole camp of Piegans came out & gave chase. They got to a coulee & kept on firing at the enemy, keeping them at bay all day. The Piegans encamped all around them so they could not get out. They consulted with Sitting White Eagle and he told them to do as he said. The fire still lingered _____ _____. It was moonlight, & he rose with his blanket about him and walked in a straight line through the Piegan camp, the others following in his footsteps, & not one Piegan saw them. When they were out of distance of the camp he told them to run for their lives. They fled to the Sweet Grass Hills where they could hide from the enemy. He stayed with a wounded Saulteaux till he died, then joined the others there.

Again he was out alone, _____. He found it less dangerous to hit the trail alone. He went to the Gros Ventres after horses. As he neared the camp he heard the singing of a dance & slipped around the throng. He tried to induce one of the young women to go off with him but she would not leave, so he thought he might get known & walked off to the camp. He saw two horses, tied up, & as he was untying them a scout came up. He _____ the herds & _____ into the lodge—there were Gros Ventres asleep—& when he saw the scout had passed on he cut the ropes & rode off with the horses. He afterwards met these Gros Ventres & they reacquired the horses. It was after peace was declared, & when he told them how he had got them, they thought him very brave.

Another time he rode into an enemy camp & got a girl to elope with him. After the first night he wanted to get rid of her. She had brought two horses, & he told her if she went back to camp he would come again. He gave her his horses & took the two & never set eyes on her again.

Not long ago he saw some of the Sioux whom he said he had often made dust fly at.

He named me Kei zis so ka pow, Standing Sun. He tells me the name the Saulteaux gave my grandfather means Man Standing Against the Sky.

(Diary pages 197–198)

They had camped a little beyond Cypress Hills and made a fire—around the coulee. Started on foot on the war path—a party of 13.

Across the border.

Five of 10 Crees were killed in the coulee, then found John _____ sitting on a butte. His skin was burnt with bullets & his coat rent to pieces.

He is much sought after as a medicine man, even the white people sometimes calling him out. He bought his knowledge of roots from an old Saulteaux.

Again the medicine man comes. I ask him about the image made of elk horn found on the Yellow Quill trail which I have in my collection, making a drawing of it. He said it may have occurred in two ways. Either the medicine man who used it became too infirm to practise his art & having no one (Diary page 200) capable of succeeding him, he would bury it—or else it was bad medicine used against an enemy or one against whom he had a grudge, & when this man died or was killed, by reason of this image, the medicine man would bury it.

He tells me Grandfather's name Sha ke ke z ick meant The Man Standing Against the Sky. T

He tells me the war clothes were carried & only donned when going into battle. They consisted of, in _____ head dress, of eagles, either this head dress, [drawing] or, [drawing] and from the neck, this streams, hung from behind, swinging about made it a different mark—[drawing] or a buffalo head dress, [drawing] & around the upper arms, buffalo tails [drawing]. On the outside of the arm, paint _____ which _____ red, all over, & they loosened their hair loose, except when taken unawares.

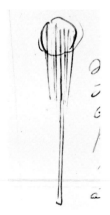

After they are done with the scalps they would not bury it but dress it up in cloth and put away in some place. Kept them for about a month—sometimes placed at the grave until the snow falls on the ground—then they put it by for good.

Sitting White Eagle—

Returning from the war, if successful the war party blackened their faces with coal & lead greased. Then if seen, a war cry would go up from camp & all would rush out. Then a dance followed, the women donning the war clothes.

Sitting White Eagle says it is true that the Saulteaux used to eat the Sioux killed in battle. He himself has done it—says they cut the flesh in narrow strips & let it slip down—says it is very rich.[25]

In taking the scalp, they would scrape it & make it dry & tan it, then make a hoop with a stick.

Nepahpenais comes to sit for his portrait. The first fight he was in was when he was 14. He was with the large camp after the buffalo & they were attacked by the Sioux. The next, at 18, he joined a war party of Red Lake Saulteaux. He was in 7 battles altogether. He tells me when they took a scalp in the battle sometimes there was a rush to get it, two or three swooping down with their knives. His hand was once cut in this way by the other's knife. While the fight was going on the first who made a coup would hold up the scalp before the enemy, calling out his name. This is one—the 2nd would do likewise.

He said the Saulteaux or Chippewas who came against the Sioux in 1866 & fought them near Fort Garry were from Red Lake across the border.[26]

When first engaged by HBC he used to go from Fort Pelly overland to Swan River—then York boats to York Factory, furs.

He was the guide at Fort Qu'Appelle[27] & the _____ MacDonald, & would journey to Wood Mountain where men were stationed, to get the furs of buffalo, & would bring them back—sometimes 8 teams of dogs. Again he would take teams of steers with the Red River carts from there. They would be shipped by flat boats to Winnipeg. Every summer he would journey to Fort Pelly to take the furs to York Factory, in the winter time resting at Wood Mountain.

For 7 years travelled with HBC, at _____ 30, then 6 years Chief of Saulteaux. His father was Matchi Kesick, The Day Going Away, who lived about Fort Francis,[28] then to Fort Garry & _____. He got a woman—a Saulteaux—called Min neway way ya seek, Something That Sounds Fine on the Wind.

He has had but one wife, who is with him today, Ne kan na peke, That Gets Away Before.

From White Fall—Robinson's carrying place—going to York Factory—he would carry three rum casks, 28 gallons, English meas.—25 yds. short of a mile—on a portage, one after another, from water to water.

Saddi the half breed says Spotted Eagle was the war chief of Sitting Bull who killed Custer's company. Sitting Bull did not fight but directed them. Custer was leading his men through a canyon. As they came to a narrow point the Indian scouts who had seen them reported & the whole body swept down upon them.*

*Mrs. Aspdin _____ does not confirm this.

Night Bird, Nepahpenais, Saulteaux chief. Pastel on paper, 1910. Dimensions 63.9 × 50.1 cm. Government of Saskatchewan Collection.

Photograph of Night Bird. Edmund Morris Collection 56. Courtesy Provincial Archives of Manitoba.

Sitting Bull, when he crossed the border, was asked by some of the Sioux to join with them to fight again. He refused & was killed by one of the scouts.

(Diary page 205)

Broadview is a good place for landscape painting—large stretches of prairie—with foreground of the buffalo or silver willow & poplar trees—clear open spaces & ponds fringed with rushes covered with duck.

The drive to Walter Ochopowace's is a good route & at his place a fine lodge & millpond.

Walter comes to be painted and later his father-in-law, Shee Sheep, a nickname he got when a baby, meaning Little Duck. His other name is Thunder Bear.[29]

He is the old type of Indian—well set up, thick through the chest & a fine bearing. His horses had strayed & he walked the 18 miles from his lodge rather than disappoint me. He brought a fur band or cap, large pipe & other things.

(Diary page 206)

Walter first asked his wife to marry him, then the parents, & when that was granted, he got the oldest man in the camp to tell it to the people & he asked the Great Spirit to guard them.

14   I drove out to Walter's camp—his eldest brother was there & Jack.[30] Made a drawing of Manitou, the designs of the Great Spirit & the Thunderbirds handed down from father to son.

15TH   Leave Broadview for Sintaluta. Stop overnight & drive out to reserve of the Assiniboines. Next morning, 16th Aug., Mr. W. S. Grant, agent, seemed as hearty as before. I got Adam, an Indian, to drive me to see Big Darkness & the Chief Carry the Kettle. I paint portraits of both of these & The Runner, brother of the chief.

On July 21st, drive 7 miles to Mr. J. C. Halford's farm in the Red Fox Valley outside the reserve. He had been farm instructor with the Assiniboines—first entered the scene at 18 when he assigned there from Fort Walsh.[31]

(Diary page 207)

About 300 of these Indians, Chief Long Lodge, & Chief Jack, The Man Who Took the Coat—a police escort went with them & the long trail of travois, some carts, horses, dogs & c. They were taken to Fort Qu'Appelle & from there on to Indian Head Hills, the present reserve. Indian Head got its name from the Assiniboines. Smallpox had swept over them. They crept out of their lodges into the sun & so died—the others fleeing from the dread disease. White men found the skulls & named the settlement Indian Head. Sintaluta is from the Assiniboine—tail (fox) red.

In the fall of 1882 the Assiniboine all went off to Cypress Hills after the buffalo & were brought back to the reserve.

Halford was instructor with the Crooked Lake Indians in 1884—that year they were starving. The Commissioner cut off all rations except for feeble & incapables.[32] Aemi Penepikink & others broke into the store & took supplies. They then installed themselves in a log hut, armed to the teeth. The Police were sent for. Capt. Huchins entered the lodge & an Indian levelled his gun at his head. A son of Nepalipen threw it back. The police could do nothing.

Walter Ochopowace, Cree hereditary chief.
Pastel on paper, 1910. Dimensions 63.9 × 50.1
cm. Government of Saskatchewan Collection.

Carry the Kettle, Chagakin, Assiniboine
chief. Pastel on paper, 1910. Dimensions
63.9 × 50.1 cm. Government of Saskatchewan Collection.

Col. Macdonald, the agent, a friendly man, spent the night with them talking & they finally gave themselves up.[33]

The Runner—whose portrait I paint—on Aug. 8, Saturday, 1885, shot down Eagle Child at 6:30 pm. He died slowly, _____ at 10 pm. He had been too familiar with the Runner's wife. His brother, the Chief, handed him over to the agent & the police.

Some Assinboine names—on the register 1910, Treaty no. 4.

Band of Carry the Kettle:
The Man Who Took the Coat—Che wic a noc ah co; Carry the Kettle—Chag a kin—chief; Stands on Stone—Eash gun nasha; Big Darkness—O paz a tonga; He Who Tells—Oge esa; Sun Daughter—Ah we win chilla; Yellow Tent—Wes e can; Walks by Water—Mene sarkne; Can Fly—Ke appie; The Star—Win charg pay; Man Afraid of His Blanket—Ta shina
co unc pa by; Medicine Grower—Wah kan ka in gah; Walks Like a White Man—Wah such many; Red Eagle—Wai aga shaw; Red Lodge—Ti pi shaw; Grew Together—Kehi yah gah; Little Woman—Wen du cena; Crooked Legs—Hook sha sha; Eagle Man—Womde wais chastis; Walker—O too many; Runner—Een gana; Wild—Wo go en hen; Rattlesnake—Oe sicha; The First White Man—To gah pay wash sicha.

Day Dawn—Umpa co; Cut Nose—Wes he hen; The Moon—A ha ta bris.

Of Piepot's Band:
Iron Shield, Red Star, Four Fires, Raised from the Ground, Red Thunder, The Devil, Dead Body, Rock Chief, Buried in the Ground, Thunder Bear, Lightning Legs, Rattle Snake Woman, Big Sky, White Sky, Wolf Voice, Coming in Sight of a Hill.

To the north—near Wetaskiwin—are the Peace Hills, which commemorate the peace between the Blackfoot—the Crees. Mr. Grant was the first agent with the Assinboine of Sintaluta. In 1897, Mr. Aspdin took his place & he went to the Cree at Hobbema, again returning when Aspdin died.

Big Darkness, Opazatonga, comes again to sit for his portrait. I question him about their famous warriors of the early days. He named Yellow Clay a great chief & warrior who fled in a battle with the Bloods. This is the one described by Gil Butler—he was left handed but was known to them as Yellow Clay. He also named the Arrow, Knife Keeper, Standing in Water, and Little Mountain as great warriors—and men often recalled in the camp.

Here is a story which Big Darkness heard from the old men & women when he was a boy & which he believes to be true. An Assiniboine, called Arrow, was one of a war party against the Blackfoot. They fell in with a large
band of them & found that they were greatly outnumbered, so turned & fled. Arrow got far behind & his pursuers were gaining on him. He called on his feet—feet try hard; but his feet said—no, you always give food to your head (after eating it was a custom of the Indians to rub their hands on their heads),

The Runner, Een gana, Assiniboine. Pastel on paper, 1910. Dimensions 63.9 × 50.1 cm. Government of Saskatchewan Collection.

Piapot, Assiniboine band chief. Pastel on paper, 1910. Dimensions 63.9 × 50.1 cm. Government of Saskatchewan Collection.

ask him to help you. All right, said Arrow Head, the Blackfoot will take my hair for pride but the dogs will get you. He then threw himself down on the ground. Feet then took fright & began jumping about, so he rose and his feet carried him so quickly, he soon outran his enemies. After that he used always to give food to his feet by rubbing his hand on them after a meal. This practice is still sometimes in use by the Assiniboines.

Again he told of an Assiniboine who made a coat out of the top of a buffalo skin lodge. Seeing it flap in the wind, he shaped the sleeves like a bird's wings, and moving them as he had seen the birds, found that he could fly. Every evening he used to travel far & watch the movements of their enemies. Once the Assiniboine had encamped on the side of a hill—as usual he took his flight, but the Blackfoot were camped not far off & some of them who had seen him hid in the bushes till he soared near them & then shot him with their arrows.

(Diary page 212) About the 25th I go to Regina to hand over five of the portraits to the Govt. Hon. Mr. Scott & his ministers come to the King's Hotel to see them & are much pleased with the result (the Deputy Minister & the Minister of Education).[34] I find that the Governor, Mr. Forget, had been trying to influence the ministers against my work but he is a French Canadian & I do not forget the French Canadians throwing sticks & stones at Sarah Bernhardt, the great French actress, when she went to Quebec.[35] Here I meet D. C. Scott, the poet, & his wife. He had been to the coast & is on a tour of inspection of the reserves, now going to Duck Lake & File Hills.

I find old Peter Hourie here. He is failing fast. His wife died a year ago. I give him a calabash pipe with long stem—much pleased.[36] He described the Thunderbird, says the design I have from the tent of Walter Ochopowace, grandson of Loud Voice, he remembers well on the lodge of the old chief Loud Voice. It represents the first Thunderbird. His feet stand firmly on the Earth to protect his friend, as much as to say, no one will harm him while I am here. The Eagle & the Thunderbird are closely connected with Indian legends. The small birds on the side are to protect the human being. Peter *(Diary page 213)* Erasmus tells me the human heads represent men he had slain in battle sacrificed to the Thunderbird.

I meet a man here, Ernest Dixon, who had been working at the agency at Sintaluta, & he agrees to come & look after camp for me. The 1st Sept. we go to Qu'Appelle. All the teams are engaged & the ships so crowded we cannot get across to the Fort till next day.

Drive to Fort Qu'Appelle. Old Archie McDonald is away, his son John is there.[37] I camp on the north side of the lake about a mile or 1 1/2 from the town to paint a landscape of the valley for J. H. McDonald—already they have begun grading & the little town will soon be changed.

The old Saulteaux chief Muscopetung heard I was here & came with a number of others to see me.[38] He brought with him the parchment treaty. He said all had been broken, but I afterwards learnt that he agreed with the majority to sell a portion of their reserve. To my mind this surrendering of the lands is a grave mistake for the Indians.

I go to the mission at Lebret to see Father Hougonnard and surprised to find 9TH
D. C. Scott, Wm. M. Graham & their wives. I stop overnight. Hougonnard
tells me he came to assist Father de Corbet at the mission in 1874.[39] A (Diary page 214)
fortnight later my father & the other commissioners arrived to negotiate the
treaty with the Indians.[40] They had an escort of 100 Mounted Police, &
camped the first night by the lake in the valley near the mission, & called on
the priests, who returned the visit.[41] They then moved on to the plains—near
the old crossing—not far from the present town. I located the spot & take a
photo.

It was in 1877 that Hougonnard had the meeting with Sitting Bull, who
with his band had come to the Fishing Lakes as the buffalo were scarce.
Hougonnard tells me the word Sun Dance is not known in the Cree
language. It comes from the west.

Go with Scott & Graham to the Sioux Reserve—Standing Buffalo's. Arrange 10TH
with mission—Good Will to get sittings—& buy a pair of moccasins.

Good Will comes to be painted. 11TH
12TH
I make a sketch of the treaty ground. 13

Go to Regina. Peter Hourie is unable to see me. He is thought to be dying. I 15TH
meet Holtaine & McKay of Prince Albert, who tells me the Sioux of Prince
Albert & Moose Woods near Saskatoon settled there in this way. One of the
early chiefs of the Sioux, Standing Buffalo, had been out on the plains after (Diary page 215)
the buffalo when the Minnesota massacre took place, but hearing of it &
fearing that he also would be punished, he crossed to Canada & camped at
Fort Ellice. Mr. McKay's father was in charge then—later he was removed to
Fort Pitt where Mr. Campbell had been and Standing Buffalo said he would
prefer to move north & trade with him. They afterward settled at Prince
Albert & near Saskatoon—& were augmented by others who crossed, having
taken part in the massacre.

Go on to Gleichen—drive to the Sand Hills to Calf Bull's camp—this is old
Running Wolf's home. Encamp—Ernest Hutton Dixon is with me. Paint Calf
Bull—buy a porcupine fire bag from him. Dixon is ill, troubled with indiges-
tion or his heart, & after a week he has to go to Calgary to the doctor.

Get a necklace made of wampum—made by the Crow Indians. 3 of the
beads for 5¢, 5 for 10¢.

Mike Running Wolf is here.[42] Will go with Proctor with democrat, 2 horses,
& 2 riding horses, 6$ day.[43]

Mike Running Wolf rides down & has supper with me. He has to ride to his
camp through the dark, passing the ghosts' coulees in the sand dunes and as (Diary page 216)
he departs I hear him chanting loud to keep away the spirits.

Pretty Young Man, son of Iron Shield, drives me along the cut bank—
overlooking the river & the valley. The river bed winds & curves, a great
valley—plains on either side fringed with trees & again with trees edging the

river—& here the _____ Blackfoot Crossing. The banks of sand are very high. This plain in the valley used to be covered with lodges as far as the eye could see.

Crowfoot's last camp when he died is about a mile from the mission on the _____ prairie not far from the edge of the east bank. The large circle of stones with the small circle of stones for the fireplace & an inscription which I painted on a stone marks the spot. About a mile farther on are the pile of stones & inscript I had placed to mark Poundmaker's grave. Near to it arise a pile of graves in wooden coffins, above ground.

(Diary page 217) The Indians are coming in from their haying[44]—many small lodges near to new ferry.

3RD OCT. I go to the old earthworks thrown up by the Crow Indians when the Blackfoot came from the north. This was their last stand. It is situated on a plain—near the end of the great plain of the Blackfoot Crossing—where the cut banks converge. The ground at the hole falls away, & a tree extends to the rim—in _____ & to one side plain, on the other not far off the high cut banks, which were fine outlooks—in front in the distance—again trees. The trench is of horeshoe shape—must have been 6 feet deep by 4. There are 10 large pits 15 ft. in diameter & four feet deep. I had an Indian dig one of these

(Diary page 218) out. A fire had been built in the centre. These fires built to illuminate so that the enemy could not creep on them unawares. We unearthed many bones. I found a rock which they had used for grinding the arrows. Père Doucet says there were many of them around the pits. The Archaeological Society would be wise to use a plough & scraper on this field, as there are doubtless many relics of this great fight but the earthworks & pits should be preserved in their original form. I piled stones & marked on one, the last stand of the Crows when the Blackfoot took the country.

(Diary pages 220–221)

Ancient Crow
Earthworks

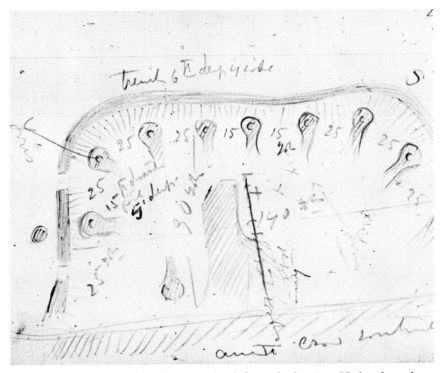

Ancient Crow
Earthworks

Old Chief Running Rabbit has come back from the haying. He has been long too ill to do anything & has given up. I called at his lodge & found him greatly changed. He will soon join his fathers. I am told the surrender of land told on him very much.[45] He, Iron Shirt & Weasel Calf opposed it strongly but Yellow Horse & others carried it against their will. He says little but broods on it.

(Diary page 218 continued)

For camp—2 cups flour, 2 water, little syrup, 1 egg, little baking powder. Still & leave overnight. Next day add dried _____ powder, stir & put in frying pan.

(Diary page 219)

Calf Bull, one of four brothers, the other boys—Many Bears d., Three Eagles & Bear Hat. Some years before the police came, the Blackfoot fell in with the Crees. They had a hand-to-hand fight. Calf Bull faced a large fat Cree who came at him knife in hand & they met, each guarding off the knife of the other. Still holding knife in hand, Calf Bull slipped his left hand to a revolver he had concealed & shot him. Many Bears got his arm shot.

(Diary page 222)

Calf Bull crossed the border & worked as a scout for the Amer. army.

He found 2 men frozen & carried them to his lodge & placed them away from the fire, then took them to Macleod. He is _____ & then he went to Col. Macleod to go to some of _____ _____ _____. (A. E. Jones, S. Camp.[46])

Wolf Collar sits today. I ask him about Running Wolf—to remember—he was his father's brother. He says anything he told Doucet would be correct.

OCT. 5TH

Chief Spring Chief is back & calls. I gave him a meal.

Western Journey 1910 / 157

Weasel Calf _____ killed by 2 Indians. Scouts (Indian) after them.

(Diary page 223) The Sand Hills are fine in colour, willows & rose bushes still in leaf, also buffalo willow—other trees brown.

Sam Red Old Man & Mike Running Wolf interpreted.

On 7th I got old Wolf Carrier to give the translation of the robe—his own history.[47] I had left it to have recorded the history of Sapo Maxika, but the _____ John Drunken Chief, after promising to do it, would not.[48] Chief Yellow Horse who is present says—a man can only record his own history according to the custom.

1. 3 Blackfoot in a coulee around which they had placed rocks. Pretty Young Man was the leader. They had gone to the Crow country to steal horses.[49] Wolf Carrier was still a boy but had gone with them.

2. The Blackfoot went to the Cypress Hills to steal horses from the Assiniboines.

(Diary page 224) Before they reached the camp they came on a large gather of Assiniboines, Gros Ventres & Crows—at a Sun Dance. They turned on the Blackfoot & killed 6 of them—then let the others escape. Big Beaver was leader of that war party of the Blackfoot—it happened about 47 years ago.

3. ⌐ Wolf Carrier had been an Indian scout, these record the

4. ⌐ number of times he sighted the enemy.

5. Two sons of an old Blackfoot had been killed & to revenge this a large war party of Bloods & Blackfoot numbering over 100. They followed the Bow River down—& on to the camp of the Assiniboines & Crees. They came on the camp & hid in the bushes till morning. It was winter. They attacked but were outnumbered & 50 of the braves were killed, the rest retreated.

6. Flat Heads had stolen Blackfoot horses. They went after them—& took horses. They were followed & a fight took place.

7. A Cree he killed, & a horse he took from a Flat Head.

(Diary page 225) 8. While sleeping—the Flat Heads came upon them—2 killed. They took a powder horn.

9. He crept on the Flat Head camp & killed 2 men, 2 women & 4 kids. It was in the daytime.

10. He crossed the mountains & found some Indians—at night captured a horse.

11. 40 Blackfoot went against the Crows, to steal horses. Weasel Tail was the leader. Near the Missouri the Crows outnumbered them & drove them out of a coulee—killing a number of them—a head man & Wolf Flat Head amongst them.

12. Buffalo robes taken from the Crow Indians. His hands are represented.

13. They are again after the Crees. Wolf Carrier got wounded—an arrow went through his cheek & another through his foot.

14. Eagle Chief led a party of Blackfoot against the Crows. They fought from a coulee.

15. A Flat Head lodge. He took a gun & 2 buckskin horses & 2 sorrel horses. *(Diary page 226)*

16. Took a Flat Head horse & mounted it.

17. Cree scalps of women. He killed them because they were ugly.

18. A chief of Crees called "Wood". Fought him & took his gun—he says the Cree cried, so he did not kill him.

19. He got 9 horses from the Flat Heads—the same time.

20. Killed a Cree woman & took 4 _____.

21. Crow robes he stole.

22. Again to the Crows & at night, tried to take horses. The Crows hid & fought them & drove them away.

23. A horse stolen from Flat Heads.

24. Blackfoot against the Crows. He & another scout out ahead—came on a large camp. The other scout got killed.

25. Took 2 Flat Head horses.

26. Took horse of Crow Indian. He is on it, then off.

27. Crow pipes.

Great excitement in the camp. The Indians come at night & tell me Mike Running Wolf & another young buck _____ threatened to kill chief Weasel Calf & chief Spring Chief. They went to the house of the former & called for him to come out & fired. 6TH
(Diary page 227)

Spring Chief is near my camp, he came over next day, said he had no arms & could not sleep—none of the Indians sleep—are all over, scouring the country—& have moved their lodges in a bunch.

Iron Shirt catches the young devils & gives them up to the police. They are tried & on the charge of drinking, given 2 months. The man who sold them liquor also arrested. Wolf Collar has more authority than Spring Chief. 8TH

_____ _____ _____ _____ my father's guide. He afterwards became interpreter for the police at Regina, the Headquarters.

Hon. Jas. McKay who owned Silver Heights, & had a herd of buffalo there, had the Govt. contract for carrying mail from Fort Garry to Battleford via Fort Ellis.[50] He sent his dog teams & carts. He brought 300 lb. His _____ with half breed also brought about 800 lb. & my father used to say he had a very weighty estimate. *(Diary page 228)*

I engage chief Spring Chief & Wolf Collar to come with teams & plough & we examine the ground in the old fort or earthworks of the Crows—where the final fight with the Blackfoot was—about 8 inches to 1 ft. into the ground. We ploughed where they had built fires & about them. I got pieces of the pottery, buffalo bones & antelope horns. In other places, human bones & broken shell earrings. We dug out one of the pits till we came to the fireplace. I found one of the stones they had used as guides for the arrows, also stones used for grinding or beating buffalo meat.[51] Wolf Collar is a nephew of the old leader Running Wolf, who told him of the Crow fortification. He had said the centre hollow was where they kept their horses. 10TH OCT.
(Diary page 229)

Many Suns no. 2 comes often to see me. He shows me the way he tortured himself in the sun dance about 20 years ago—the tips of both little fingers cut off—at start of the nail. The scars through the pectoral muscles & again through the back—where a buffalo skin was attached to be torn away.

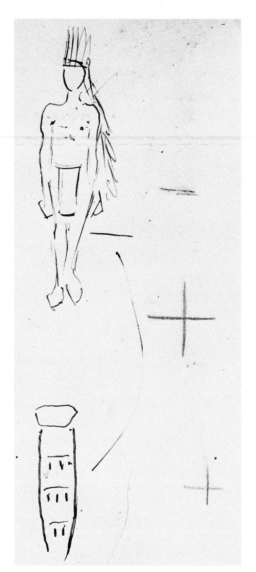

Notes to Western Journey 1910

1. John Archibald McDonald (1865–1929), son of Archibald McDonald, was a member of the Saskatchewan legislature from 1908 to 1914.

2. Morris, Manitoba is a community south of Winnipeg named after Alexander Morris, Edmund's father. Rosenhoff is a hamlet located about halfway between Morris and Rosenort, on the Morris River, and appears at least as late as 1977 on a topographical map (courtesy Provincial Archives of Manitoba).

3. Indian agency inspector William Morris Graham.

4. Star Blanket, Cree chief and medicine man, was the son of White Calf, one of the Indians who signed Treaty Four at Fort Qu'Appelle. Star Blanket was portrayed by Morris a few days later and the pastel is in the collection of the Norman Mackenzie Art Gallery, University of Regina.

5. Pimotat (ca 1871–?), the Walker, of Algonkian and Cree blood, the younger brother of Star Blanket, lived on the File Hills Reserve in Saskatchewan; he was known for kindness and an even-tempered disposition (courtesy Saskatchewan Archives Board). Morris portrayed Pimotat in 1908 (ROM HK 2442).

6. The Man Who Ties the Knot or Tying Knot (ca 1832–ca 1923), Kah to kope chamakasis, of Algonkian and Cree blood, chief of the Little Black Bear band on the File Hills Reserve, was a famed warrior of great physical strength and stature and was also well known as a storyteller (courtesy Saskatchewan Archives Board). Morris portrayed him twice, in 1908 (ROM HK 2434) and in 1910 (Government of Saskatchewan Collection).

7. Duncan Campbell Scott (1862–1947) was a poet and a public servant who held many positions including those of federal government superintendent of Indian Affairs and lieutenant governor of Manitoba and the North West Territories. He was a good friend of Edmund Morris and wrote a eulogy to Morris at the time of the latter's death; an excerpt is included in the Introduction.

8. Skunk Skin died when his two sons, Poundmaker and Yellow Blanket, were young, leaving them with very little (see Sluman 1967, pp. 6–7).

9. The beaver skin was the standard by which all other furs were valued. Short wooden sticks, and then coins bearing a portrait of a beaver, were issued.

10. Edmund Morris has transcribed a series of excerpts from one Hudson's Bay Company York Factory account book; there are a number of omissions and differences between Morris's transcription and the original accounts text. The account book is stored in the Hudson's Bay Archives, Provincial Archives of Manitoba, and the original texts read as follows:

York Factory, America Anno Domi^{ie} 1785 By Mr Humphrey Marten Chief Factor and Governor of the said Factory in Hudsons Bay, North America for the Governor and Company of Adventurers of England Trading into the said Bay. The Accounts of the said Governor containing his Transactions of Trade from the 1st August 1784 to Augst the 1st 1785.

(HBCA, PAM, B.239/d/75 fo. 1b)

Beaver being the Chief Commodity we Trade for, We therefore make it the Standard whereby we value all Furs & Commodities dealt for in Trade.

The Comparative:

			Beaver
Parchment Moose skins	1	as	2
Drest do	1	"	1½
Old Bears	1	"	3
Cub do	1	"	1
Quiguahatches	1	"	2
Wolves	1	"	2
Old cased Cats	1	"	2
Split do	1	"	1
Cub do	1	"	1
Foxes black	1	"	4
Grizzled	1	"	3
Red	1	"	1
Brown	1	"	1
White	2	"	1
Wenusks	2	"	1
Wejacks	2	"	1
Buck deer skins	1	"	1
Doe deer do	2	"	1
Badgers	2	"	1
Martins prime	2	"	1
Do ordinary	3	"	1
Jackashes	3	"	1
Musquashes	6	"	1
Rabbit skins	8	"	1
Castorum lb.	2	"	1
Goose feathers lb.	10	"	1
Do quills	2000	"	1
Swan skins	6	"	1
Otters prime	1	"	2
" ordinary	1	"	1

(HBCA, PAM, B.239/d/75 fo. 8)

Trading Goods received as pr Invoice from on board the Sea Horse, Captain John Richards Commr

. . .

Brandy English Galls	1634

. . .

Tobacco Brazil lb	4601
Roll	403
Leaf	632

. . .

Trading Goods received not mentioned in the Invoice,

. . .

Brandy English-Galls	400.

. . .

Leakage and Waste of Brandy English 284 Gallons, which is deducted from the General charge.

. . .

All recorded by John Ballenden.

(extracts from HBCA, PAM, B.239/d/75 fos. 3d–5, 40)

The record that Morris cites of an observation of Halley's Comet is in a second book, a Hudson's Bay Company journal, in the 10 October 1835 entry (HBCA, PAM, B.239/a/149 fo. 8d).

The modern equivalents of various items included in the list of furs are as follows: parchment moose—untanned moosehide; drest moose—tanned moosehide; quiguahatch—wolverine; cased cat—lynx skin removed without slitting; split cat—slit lynx skin; wenusk—groundhog; wejack—fisher; jackash—mink; musquash—muskrat. Castoreum is the oil produced by the beaver near the base of its tail and it was obtained in the past for use in medicine and perfumery.

11. The Sea Horse made voyages across the Atlantic in the 19th century.

12. Number Four House was a warehouse in Winnipeg where the Hudson's Bay Company records were stored; in 1920, the head office of the company in London, England, requested that the records be gathered and sent to London; they were transferred back to Canada in 1974 and are now stored in the Provincial Archives of Manitoba (courtesy Hudson's Bay Company Archives, Winnipeg).

13. Halley's comet, which returns every seventy-six to seventy-nine years and is visible as it nears the sun, was observed in 1834 and 1910, and is next to be seen from Earth in 1986.

14. The story of Kominakus and his fame as a warrior is related by Paget (1909, pp. 145–52).

15. Moonias (the name means a novice or green horn and was used by the Indians as a derogatory term for a European) was a Cree war leader in Saskatchewan; Morris's portrait of him is at the Glenbow Museum (60.14) and is dated 1905. A note on the back of the portrait states that it once belonged to Duncan Campbell Scott, superintendent of Indian Affairs. A note signed "G. H. Gooderham" on the portrait states that it was one of Morris's first western portraits—this could be John Hamilton Gooderham, Indian agent on the Peigan and then the Blackfoot reserves (courtesy Public Archives of Canada).

16. The battle between the Cree and the Blackfoot, under Moonias and Crowfoot, respectively, took place in October 1866 near Battle River, some miles east of Hobbema, Alberta; Morris recorded the story (p. 106) as illustrated on Calf Child's buffalo robe; see also, Hughes (1914, pp. 115–23) for further details about the incident.

17. The name given to Morris's grandfather is Ojibwa.

18. The Saulteaux tribe are a branch of the Ojibwa (called Chippewa in the United States); the Indians in the area of Perth, Ontario, would also have been a branch of Ojibwa.

19. See Morris (1971, pp. 331, 334).

20. The wife of William Morris Graham.

21. This portrait of the Gambler, Saulteaux, from the Pasqua Reserve, is now in the Government of Saskatchewan Collection. This Gambler is the man who negotiated with Alexander Morris during the Qu'Appelle Treaty; he is distinct from the Gambler on the reserve near Binscarth, Manitoba.

22. Fort Pelly, Saskatchewan, was designated as the headquarters of the E division of the NWMP in 1874–75 (see Haydon 1971, p. 44, n.).

23. Elkhorn, Saskatchewan.

24. The Saddi O'Soup Reserve is near Norquay, Saskatchewan, north of Fort Pelly.

25. It is probable that cannibalism was practised among all peoples at some point in their history during periods of famine or during wars.

26. A probable reference to Upper or Lower Red Lake, Minnesota.

27. A Hudson's Bay Company post was set up at Fort Qu'Appelle in 1854 and was closed down in 1912 (see Cowie 1913, p. 361).

28. Fort Frances, Ontario.

29. Morris's portrait of Thunder Bear, Peeaysaw Musqua, Saulteaux chief, is in the Government of Saskatchewan Collection.

30. Jack, the Man Who Took the Coat.

31. Fort Walsh, in the Cypress Hills of southern Saskatchewan, was built rapidly in 1875 as a NWMP outpost that would provide protection for officers against the winter weather; however, the structure of the fort was condemned in 1882 and demolished in 1883 (see Haydon 1971, pp. 46, 90, 114).

32. This would be Edgar Dewdney, who was commissioner of Indian Affairs at the time.

33. Colonel MacDonald was the agent at Crooked Lake. Morris's handwriting is extremely difficult to read on these pages of the Diary. Denny (1905, pp. 177–78) describes the unrest among the Cree camped at Crooked Lake just before the North West Rebellion—a number who had gathered there to hold a medicine dance broke into the agency storehouse on the reserve and stole a large quantity of provisions.

34. Walter Scott was premier of Saskatchewan, 1905–17; the deputy minister of education in the Scott government was Duncan C. McColl, and the minister of education, J. A. Calder. King's Hotel remained a leading hotel in Regina for many years; it was refurbished and renamed in early 1972, and then torn down in 1978 (courtesy Saskatchewan Archives Board).

35. Amédée Emmanuel Forget (1847–1923) was lieutenant governor of the Northwest Territories, 1896–1905, and of Saskatchewan, 1901–10. Sarah Bernhardt (1845–1923) was an internationally famous French actress.

36. The calabash pipe was a large smoking pipe made from the neck of the bottle gourd, *Lagenaria cujete*.

37. Archibald McDonald (1835–1915), the last chief factor of the Hudson's Bay Company, in the Saskatchewan District (for further information, see Stanley 1953).

38. The Muscopetung Reserve, located west of Fort Qu'Appelle, was named for the chief Muscopetung.

39. Father Jules Decorby (not de Corbet) was first resident priest at the Saint-Florent Mission of Qu'Appelle at Lebret, just east of Qu'Appelle, between 1868 and 1880; from Lebret he was transferred to the mission of Fort Ellice, from 1880 to 1895. He worked and lived with both Indians and Métis, and learned three Indian languages. (Courtesy Diocese of Prince Albert, Saskatchewan.)

40. The other commissioners at the Fort Qu'Appelle Treaty were David Laird, and William Joseph Christie, the latter being retired from his position as Hudson's Bay Company factor at the time (see Morris 1971, p. 78).

41. Much of the arranging and signing of Treaty Four took place at an encampment set up on the shore of Lake Qu'Appelle; the site is now marked by a stone cairn (Morris 1971, pp. 80, 330).

42. A young Blackfoot, this Running Wolf is not to be confused with either the Peigan chief or the Blackfoot historian of the same name.

43. Two horses pulled the "democrat" carriage; the two others galloping beside it were for the passengers to ride on at their place of destination.

44. By 1900, haying was one of the main sources of income for the Blackfoot (see Dempsey 1979, p. 17).

45. Dempsey describes the surrender of land (1979, p. 18): "a major change in the life of the Blackfoot occurred in 1910, when they were encouraged to sell part of their reserve. The first sale consisted of lands for putting in an irrigation canal through the reserve and later in 1910 for a railway line to Carseland. By this time hundreds of settlers were pouring into the west, the best lands were taken up by the homesteaders, and people began looking at the vast acres of unused lands on various reserves.

Because the Indian population had been decreasing through disease and poor health conditions, many believed the Indians should sell their excess land to settlers."

46. A. E. Jones was a stockman at the South Camp of the Blackfoot Reserve (courtesy Public Archives of Canada).

47. The buffalo robe that was illustrated by Wolf Carrier, showing events in his life, is ROM HK 457.

48. Sapo Maxika is the Blackfoot name for Crowfoot; the John Drunken Chief mentioned here is the nephew of Crowfoot.

49. The advent of the horse among the Plains Indians revolutionized their culture and economy. Hundreds of new words associated with riding and outfitting the horse were added to tribal language. Entire camps could be moved quickly and easily and hunters could chase the buffalo at its own speed. Because of the usefulness of the horse, it became a status symbol and a man's esteem rose with the number of horses he owned. Thus, horse stealing played a prominent part in the life of the Plains warrior. (See Powers 1973, pp. 14, 90.)

50. The honourable James McKay (?-1879), of Indian and European blood, was the eldest son of James McKay, who worked for many years for the Hudson's Bay Company; the son held several administrative positions in Manitoba, including president of the provincial executive council, in 1871, and member of the provincial legislative council from its creation in 1871 (see Morgan 1874, p. 483; courtesy Provincial Archives of Manitoba) to its abolition in 1876. He was provincial minister of agriculture, 1874–78. He participated in the negotiations of treaties One and Two, the Stone Fort and Manitoba Post treaties, in 1871 (see Morris 1971, pp. 25, 31).

51. In the preparation of pemmican.

Bibliography and Additional Reading

Included below are full details of the bibliographic references in the notes and also some additional reading.

Adams, Alexander B.
    1975   *Sitting Bull: An Epic of the Plains*. 2nd English ed. London: New English Library.

Anderson, Frank W.
    1973   *Sheriffs and Outlaws of Western Canada*. Calgary: Frontier Publishing.

Archer, John H.
    1980   *Saskatchewan: A History*. Saskatoon, Sask.: Western Producer Prairie Books.

Boultbee, W. M.
    1908   "Edmund Morris, Painter." *The Canadian Magazine,* vol. 30 (June), pp. 121–127.

Brasser, Ted
    1977   "Wolf Collar: The Shaman as Artist". In *Stones, Bones and Skin: Ritual and Shamanic Art*. Reprint of *Artscanada,* Dec. 1973–Jan. 1974. Toronto: The Society for Art Publications, pp. 38–41.

Cat. of Hist. Paintings
    1933   *Catalogue of Historical Paintings in the Legislative Building, Regina, Saskatchewan*. Regina: Ronald S. Garrett, King's Printer.

Catlin, G.
    1841   *The Manners, Customs and Condition of the North American Indians*. 2 vols. London: published by the author.

Chittenden, Hiram Martin, and Alfred Tallbot Richardson, eds.
    1969   *Life, Letters and Travels of Father Pierre-Jean de Smet, S.J., 1801–1873: Missionary Labors and Adventures among the Wild Tribes of the North American Indians. . . .* Reprint of 1905 ed. 4 vols. New York: Kraus Reprint Co.

Cowie, Isaac
    1913   *The Company of Adventurers*. Toronto: William Briggs.

Crossman, K.
    1978   The Early Courthouses of Ontario. Vol. 1, ms. report 295. Ottawa: Parks Canada.

Dempsey, Hugh A.
    1972   *Crowfoot, Chief of the Blackfeet*. Edmonton: Hurtig Publishers.
    1978   *Charcoal's World*. Saskatoon: Western Producer.
    1979   *Indian Tribes of Alberta*. Calgary: Glenbow Museum.
    1980   *Red Crow: Warrior Chief*. Saskatoon: Western Producer.

Denny, C. E.
    1905   *The Riders of the Plains: A Reminiscence of the Early and Exciting Days of the North West*. Calgary: The Herald Co.

Dic. of Can. Biog.
    1982   *Dictionary of Canadian Biography*. Vol. 11. General editor Francess G. Halpenny. Toronto: University of Toronto Press.

Erasmus, Peter
    1976   *Buffalo Days and Nights*. As told to Henry Thomson. Calgary: Glenbow-Alberta Institute.

Ewers, John Canfield
    1945   *Blackfeet Crafts*. Indian Handcrafts 9. Lawrence, Kansas: United States Office of Indian Affairs.
    1961   *The Blackfeet: Raiders on the Northwestern Plains*. Reprint of 1958 ed. Norman, Oklahoma: University of Oklahoma Press.

Godfrey, W. Earl
    1966   *The Birds of Canada*. Bulletin 203. Ottawa: National Museums of Canada.

Gowanlock, Theresa, and Theresa Delaney
    1885   *Two Months in the Camp of Big Bear: The Life and Adventures of Theresa Gowanlock and Theresa Delaney*. Parkdale: Times Office.

Grinnell, George Bird
    1962   *Blackfoot Lodge Tales: The Story of a Prairie People*. Reprint of 1892 ed. Lincoln, Nebraska: University of Nebraska Press.

Haines, Francis
    1972   *The Nez Perces: Tribesmen of the Columbia Plateau*. 2nd printing. Norman, Oklahoma: University of Oklahoma Press.

Harper, J. Russell
    1971   *Paul Kane's Frontier, Including Wanderings of an Artist among the Indians of North America*. Toronto: University of Toronto Press.

Haydon, A. L.
    1971   *The Riders of the Plains: A Record of the Royal North-West Mounted Police of Canada 1873–1910*. Reprint of 1910 ed. Edmonton: Hurtig Publishers.

Hind, Henry Youle
    1860   *Narrative of the Canadian Red River Exploring Expedition of 1857 and of the Assiniboine and Saskatchewan Exploring Expedition of 1858 by Henry Youle Hind....* 2 vols. London: Longman, Green, Longman, and Roberts.

Hodge, F. W., ed.
    1907,   *Handbook of American Indians North of Mexico*. Bulletin 30, parts 1 and 2.
    1910   Washington: Smithsonian Institution, Bureau of American Ethnology.
    1969   *Handbook of Indians of Canada*. Reprint of 1913 ed. New York: Kraus Reprint Co.

Hughes, Katherine
    1914   *Father Lacombe: The Black-Robe Voyageur*. 4th impression. Toronto: William Briggs.

Hummel, A. W., ed.
    1943   *Eminent Chinese of the Ch'ing Period (1644–1912)*. Vol. l. Washington: United States Government Printing Office.

Jefferys, Charles William
    1942– *The Picture Gallery of Canadian History: Illustrations Drawn and Collected by*
    1950   *C. W. Jefferys...Assisted by T. W. McLean....* 3 vols. Toronto: Ryerson Press.

Jenness, Diamond
    1977   *The Indians of Canada*. 7th ed. Toronto: University of Toronto Press.

Kehoe, Alice Beck
    1981   *North American Indians: A Comprehensive Account*. Englewood Cliffs, New Jersey: Prentice Hall.

Lewis, Meriwether, and William Clark
    1904– *Original Journals of the Lewis and Clark Expedition 1804–1806*. 8 vols. Edited
    1905   by Reuben Gold Thwaits. New York: Dodd, Mead.

Lowie, Robert H.
    1963   *Indians of the Plains*. 2nd ed. Garden City, New York: The American Museum of Natural History.
MacEwan, J. W. Grant
    1971   *Portraits from the Plains*. Toronto: McGraw-Hill.
    1973   *Sitting Bull: The Years in Canada*. Edmonton: Hurtig Publishers.
Maclean, the Rev. John
    1896   *Canadian Savage Folk: The Native Tribes of Canada*. Toronto: William Briggs.
Macleod, R. C.
    1978   *The North West Mounted Police, 1873–1919*. Historical Booklet 31. Ottawa: Canadian Historical Association.
McKee, Sandra Lynn
    1973   *Gabriel Dumont: Indian Fighter*. Frontier Book 14. Aldergrove, B.C.: Frontier Publishing.
McGill, Jean
    1979   "The Indian portraits of Edmund Morris," *The Beaver*, Summer 1979, pp. 34–41.
    1984   *Edmund Morris: Frontier Artist*. Toronto: Dundurn Press.
Morgan, Henry J., ed.
    1874   *The Canadian Parliamentary Companion*. 9th ed. Montreal: Printed by John Lovell.
Morris, Alexander
    1971   *The Treaties of Canada with the Indians of Manitoba and the North-West Territories. . . .* Reprint of 1880 facsimile ed. Toronto: Coles Publishing.
Morris, Edmund
    1909   *Canadian Art Club Exhibition of Indian Portraits with Notes on the Tribes by Edmund Morris, together with Loan Collections of Objects of Indian Art and Curios. . . .* Toronto: Canadian Art Club.
Morton, Desmond, and Reginald H. Roy, eds.
    1972   *Telegrams of the North West Campaign, 1885*. Toronto: Champlain Society.
Morton, W. L.
    1980   *Henry Youle Hind, 1823–1908*. Toronto: University of Toronto Press.
Mulvaney, Charles Pelham
    1885   *The History of the North-West Rebellion of 1885. . . .* Toronto: A. H. Hovey.
Paget, Amelia M.
    1909   *The People of the Plains*. Edited by Duncan Campbell Scott. Toronto: W. Briggs.
Palliser, J.
    1853   *Solitary Rambles and Adventures of a Hunter in the Prairies*. London: J. Murray.
Powers, William K.
    1973   *Indians of the Northern Plains*. New York: G. P. Putnam's Sons.
Ralph, Julian
    1892   *On Canada's Frontier: Sketches of History, Sport, and Adventure, and of the Indians, Missionaries, Fur Traders, and Newer Settlers of Western Canada*. New York: Harper.
Schultz, James Willard
    1907   *My Life as an Indian: The Story of a Red Woman and a White Man in the Lodges of the Blackfeet*. Boston and New York: Houghton Mifflin.
    1962   *Blackfeet and Buffalo: Memories of Life among the Indians*. Edited by Keith C. Seele. Norman, Oklahoma: University of Oklahoma Press.

Simmins, Geoffrey, and Michael Parke-Taylor,
   1984   *Edmund Morris "Kyaiyii" 1871–1913*. Regina: Norman Mackenzie Art Gallery, University of Regina.
Sluman, Norma
   1967   *Poundmaker*. Toronto: McGraw-Hill Ryerson.
Spry, Irene M., ed.
   1968   *The Papers of the Palliser Expedition, 1857–1860*. Toronto: Champlain Society.
Stanley, George F. G.
   1953   "Archibald McDonald: The Fur Trade Party." *The Beaver,* September 1953, pp. 36–39.
Stocken, Canon H. W. G.
   1976   *Among the Blackfoot and Sarcee*. Calgary: Glenbow-Alberta Institute.
Storm, Hyemeyohsts
   1972   *Seven Arrows*. New York: Harper & Row.
Strange, Thomas Bland
   1893   *Gunner Jingo's Jubilee*. London: J. Macqueen.
Walker, Sir Byron Edmund
   1909   *A History of Banking in Canada*. Reprint of 1899 ed., with supplement. Toronto.
West, Helen B.
   1960   "Blackfoot Country," *Montana,* vol. 10, no. 4 (October), pp. 34–44.

Index

made of horn of, 147; tooth of, 113
Elliot, John Gilbert (-Murray-Kynyn-
mound), Fourth Earl of Minto, 18,
118
Erasmus, Peter (Danish/Swampy
Cree), 104, 107, 110, 112, 116
Ermine Skin, 78, 119
Evans, the Reverend John, 107

Far Away Voice, a (Piiskini, Blackfoot),
22
Farming, Indian: drying corn, 76; hay-
ing, 20, 101, 156, 157; instruction in,
73; irrigation, 120; planting tobacco,
35 (margin note); on ranches, 20, 101
Fire bags, 67, 80 (margin note), 155
Fire in Ontario parliament buildings,
116–17
Fleetham, Thomas James, 52
Forget, Amédée Emmanuel, 154
Forts: à la Corne, 76; Benton, 34, 101;
Calgary (Brisebois), 46, 101; Carlton,
14, 67, 76; Edmonton, 28, 31, 78, 116;
Ellice, 70, 73, 155, 159; Frances, 148;
Garry, 12, 14, 26, 144, 148, 159;
Macleod, 36; Pelly, 146, 148; Pitt, 14,
28, 36, 49, 80, 89, 104, 155;
Qu'Appelle, 14, 66, 70, 73, 144, 148,
150, 154; Steele, 122; Walsh, 70, 150
Fox Woman (Peigan), 115, 121
Fur trade: post for, 101. *See also* Trade
of Hudson's Bay Company with Indi-
ans

Gambler, the (Ometaway, Saulteaux),
80 (margin note), 127
Gambler, the (Saulteaux), 144
Genereux family (of Saskatoon), 76
Geographical names, origins of: Blackfoot Crossing, 112; Bow River, 112,
124; Calgary, 101; Gleichen, 88;
Indian Head, 70, 101; Sintaluta, 150;
Slave Lake, 45, 123; Swift Current,
112
Gérôme, Jean-Léon, 114
Gifts given by Morris to Indians, 16, 26,
34, 112, 154
Gifts received by Morris from Indians,
50, 121, 122, 150; buffalo-tail brush,
101; fire bag, 67; headdress, 67;
horse's head decoration, 68; medicine bags, 107; medicine rattle, 50;

peace pipes, 16, 22, 50, 52; shirt, 34
Gooderham, John Hamilton, 14
Good Will (Sioux), 155
Government, federal: allocation of
reserves, 18, 72 (margin note), 120,
154; construction of bridge over Bow
River, 20; payments to Indians, 52,
67, 114, 140; rations to Indians, 20,
24, 26, 150; relationship with Indi-
ans, 18, 26, 66, 114, 119, 154. *See also*
Agents; Treaties
Governments, provincial, 116; premiers
of, 88, 116, 154
Graham, James F., 72
Graham, William Morris, 73–74, 76,
140, 146; colony for schoolboys of,
73, 155
Grant, Willam Samuel, 70, 72, 150, 152
Grey, Albert Henry George, Fourth
Earl, 118
Grinnell, George Bird, 32; *Blackfoot
Lodge Tales,* 89, 120, 122, 124 (margin
note)

Halford, I. C., 150
Headdress, Indian, 67, 147
Healey, Joe (Potaina, Blood/European),
34
Heavy Shield (Blackfoot), 90, 107
Hieroglyphs, Indian, 16, 18, 147, 158
High Eagle (Pitauspitau, Blackfoot), 22,
24, 102; on Crowfoot, 90; diagram of
Blackfoot groups by, 89–90; por-
trayed, 89
Hodgson, George, 28, 30–31, 126
Hoke, Antoine (Dakota Sioux), 49, 66,
88; portrayed, 80 (margin note)
Horses: arrival of on the plains, 32;
beadwork head decoration for, 68;
given away, 73; import tax on, 70;
stealing of, 32, 46, 67, 78, 80, 104,
116, 125, 146, 158
Hourie, Peter (Saulteaux/English): as
interpreter, 14, 67, 68, 70, 155
Hudson's Bay Company, 12, 14, 28, 32,
52, 78, 148; accounts of, cited, 142–
43; factors of, 32, 49, 67, 74, 89, 101.
See also Trade of Hudson's Bay Company with Indians
Hugonnard, Father Joseph, OMI, 73–
74, 155
Hunter, Chief (Stoney), 52